Financing Trade and International Supply Chains

For Dad and Mom, with love, admiration, and gratitude: it would take another book to thank you both for everything, and I know what would happen if this dedication were too long and detailed! Love you both.

To Alain, Jennifer, and Lauren: Jenn, Lauren, your Dad was by far the cooler of the Malaket Brothers!! Love you, too.

In memory of Uncle Walter "Pascha" Helmreich, until the next injera and kitfo …

For Agnieszka, with love: if ever there was a partnership of international reach and character … kocham cie, Gusia! All this to finally (!!) explain the mystery of the four houses!!

Financing Trade and International Supply Chains

Commerce Across Borders, Finance Across Frontiers

ALEXANDER R. MALAKET

Routledge
Taylor & Francis Group

LONDON AND NEW YORK

First published in paperback 2024

First published 2014 by Gower Publishing

Published 2016 by Routledge
4 Park Square, Milton Park, Abingdon, Oxon OX14 4RN

and by Routledge
605 Third Avenue, New York, NY 10158

Routledge is an imprint of the Taylor & Francis Group, an informa business

Gower Applied Business Research
Our programme provides leaders, practitioners, scholars and researchers with thought provoking, cutting edge books that combine conceptual insights, interdisciplinary rigour and practical relevance in key areas of business and management.

British Library Cataloguing in Publication Data.
A catalogue record for this book is available from the British Library.

The Library of Congress has cataloged the printed edition as follows:
Malaket, Alexander R.
  Financing trade and international supply chains: commerce across borders, finance across frontiers / by Alexander R. Malaket.
    pages cm
  Includes bibliographical references and index.
  ISBN 978-1-4094-5460-1 (hardback: alk. paper)—ISBN 978-1-4094-5461-8 (ebook)—ISBN 978-1-4724-0366-7 (epub)
  1. International trade—Finance. 2. Export credit. 3. Business logistics. I. Title.

  HG3753.M27 2014
  332'.042—dc23
                                                            2013027899

ISBN: 978-1-4094-5460-1 (hbk)
ISBN: 978-1-03-283741-3 (pbk)
ISBN: 978-1-315-58243-6 (ebk)

DOI: 10.4324/9781315582436

Contents

List of Figures

About the Author

Alexander R. Malaket, BA, CITP, is the President of Canadian consultancy OPUS Advisory Services International Inc., and Managing Director of Trade Finance Associates Pte Ltd., Singapore. He possesses over 25 years of professional experience in investment, financial services and senior-level consulting. After working for several years with a Canadian trade bank, he joined the New York-based corporate banking/trade finance practice of a billion-dollar global consultancy and technology firm.

Alexander established OPUS Advisory in 2001 and has since focused on engagements in international trade, investment, international development and trade and supply chain finance, providing advisory services to top-tier financial institutions, government and private sector clients and international institutions around the world. Additionally, he has developed and delivered training programs and seminars on various topics in markets across the globe.

Internationally recognized as a specialist in trade finance, Alexander is frequently invited to speak or chair panels at leading industry conferences and events. He is a regular contributor to various industry publications, including London-based *Trade Finance Magazine* (Euromoney), *Global Trade Review* (Exporta), *Trade & Forfaiting Review*, *financial-i*, as well as Bahrain-based *Cash & Trade Magazine* and London-based *Trade & Export Finance*.

Alexander is a long-time member of FITT (The Forum for International Trade Training) in Ottawa, the Toronto Region Board of Trade and World Trade Centre and a member of the World Trade Centre Winnipeg, where he serves on the Executive Committee of the inaugural Board of Directors. He is a member of the SWIFT/ICC Industry Education Group related to the Bank Payment Obligation, and a member of the Executive Committee of the Banking Commission at the International Chamber of Commerce in Paris.

Alexander is a graduate of the University of Toronto (Honours Economics and Political Science) and holds the Designation of Certified International Trade Professional.

Foreword

I wish I had a copy of this publication 29 years ago when I commenced my career as it would have provided both an excellent overview and a more in-depth treatment of the trade finance world I was entering.

Having traversed the globe (working with various financial institutions/banks including HSBC, ABN AMRO, Emirates NBD and The Bank of New York Mellon in India covering the Indian sub-continent, in Hong Kong covering North Asia, Singapore for South Asia, Dubai for Middle East/Africa and Sao Paulo/Miami for Latin America/Caribbean and North America), I have never come across such a straightforward, simple, clear and effective publication – equally suitable to serve the needs of new entrants to the trade finance arena or to those like me who claim expertise in this subject matter.

In short, it is a "must read" for those who want to learn as well as those who want to refresh their perspective on trade and supply chain finance, or to obtain an update on "what's new" in the industry. The book is equally relevant to bankers, trade financiers and other specialists in the business, as it is to finance and treasury executives, even entrepreneurs and small business owners needing to understand the business of financing international trade.

Financing Trade and International Supply Chains is an easy read, with clarity of explanation and flow, which keeps one interested while comprehensively covering the trade finance arena.

Alexander's experience and expertise have been clearly depicted in the examples and comparisons used to bring key concepts to life, while keeping the world in view. This is truly an excellent portrayal of trade finance – making a complicated subject very logical. My sincere thanks to Alexander for putting this book together and making the trade finance world easy to grasp.

Maninder Bhandari, Founder, Partner and Managing Director,
The Encore Group, and The Derby Group, Dubai, U.A.E., April, 2013

Acknowledgments

The writing of this book finds its personal roots in Addis Ababa, Ethiopia, at the start of a life immersed in "things international," and its professional roots in Toronto, Canada, at the start of a trade finance career in 1991. The early years with a Canadian bank provided important foundational knowledge, and a combination of lessons learnt – many positive and constructive, some far less so – that I still draw upon in consulting and training activities today. To my colleagues from those initial years – particularly those who were prepared to innovate and to apply thoughtful energy to the business of trade finance, thank you.

The shift from banking to consulting, as a member of the Corporate Banking and Trade Finance team at American Management Systems (now part of CGI) in New York, provided the opportunity to work with highly committed, top-flight consultants and world-class clients on a range of engagements. The positive impact of my time at AMS – and immersion in the strong and unique culture of the company – has had lasting positive impact, and created numerous valued, enduring relationships. Thank you AMS and fellow AMSers.

Since establishing OPUS Advisory Services International in 2001, consultancy and training activities have covered the full scope of trade banking and trade finance, from strategy to product, operations to technology and beyond, extending to advisory engagements with non-bank trade finance organizations, international institutions, export credit agencies, government clients and other such organizations. Our assignments have required client interactions ranging from front-line, operational specialists to board-level executives, policy experts to senior civil service and political leaders: a range of experience that underpins the approach and content of this book.

Broader engagement in international business, trade and investment assignments, including trade-related international development activity, has provided important context and an appreciation for the positive impact of finance – and for the challenges arising from a lack of adequate liquidity in support of international commerce.

Thank you to our valued clients and to the many colleagues and associates we have been privileged to work with over the years, all of whom have contributed very directly to shaping my understanding of trade finance and to the development of this book. Long-standing contributions to leading industry publications along with regular participation as a speaker and panel chair at trade finance conferences around the world have provided invaluable access to industry leaders, to explore important trends and developments shaping the business of trade finance. Those interactions, invariably interesting and informative, have contributed to a broad view of the business of financing international trade.

A word of acknowledgment and appreciation to Caroline Tompkins, President and CEO of FITT in Ottawa, and to the team at FITT, a unique organization committed to the development and delivery of international trade training materials and programs, and to the enhancement of trade competencies in Canada and internationally.

My sincere appreciation to Jonathan Norman and the team at Gower Publishing in Farnham, UK, whose invitation to author this book was very welcome, and whose support and guidance has made the process enjoyable, while assuring the creation of a text that will, we hope, do credit to the world of trade finance.

The following individuals, each highly respected and accomplished in our industry, kindly agreed to provide their impressions and comments on an advanced draft of the manuscript, and have contributed to a greatly improved final product.

Many thanks to:

- Mr. Maninder Bhandari, Founder, Partner and Managing Director, The Encore Group and The Derby Group, Dubai, UAE.

- Mr. Johan Bergamin, Director, Trade and Commodity Finance, ING Bank, Amsterdam, The Netherlands

- Mr. Eduardo Klurfan, Chief Representative and Country Head, Cuba, Bank of Nova Scotia, Havana, Cuba

- Mr. Simon G.D. Walker, Regional General Manager, Europe, Qatar National Bank, London, UK

Special thanks for particularly comprehensive reviews and comments to:

- Mr. Jonathan Bell, Editor in Chief, Trade and Export Finance, London, UK

- Mr. Avin Mehra, Vice President and Investment Advisor, Member of the Executive Council, CIBC Wood Gundy, Toronto, Canada

- Mr. Stephen S. Poloz, Governor of the Bank of Canada and past President and Chief Executive Officer, Export Development Canada, Ottawa, Canada

- Mr. Markus Wohlgeschaffen, Managing Director, Global Head of Trade Finance and Services, Global Transaction Banking, at Unicredit Bank AG, Munich, Germany

Financing Trade and International Supply Chains has been written with the objective of providing a practical overview and introduction to trade and supply chain finance. The intent was to provide sufficient detail and depth to be of value to practitioners as well as to treasury and finance executives in companies of all sizes. The feedback and comments from industry experts ensures that this objective has been achieved; however, any errors or omissions remain entirely my responsibility.

It is my hope that this book serves to support the conduct of vital international trade by reducing some of the mystery and complexity associated with international trade finance, even among seasoned bankers and finance experts. In addition, I hope that the approach and treatment of the subject will help to inspire interest in international business and trade finance among the next generation of business leaders and entrepreneurs across the globe.

Alexander R. Malaket, CITP
President, OPUS Advisory Services International Inc., Canada
Managing Director, Trade Finance Associates Pte. Ltd., Singapore
Canada, May, 2013

Testimonials

This is an essential source of reference for anyone involved in international trade and using or seeking to use short-term financing. Alexander Malaket not only provides a thorough and logical insight into how trade and supply chain finance can work for companies today, but also does this through an easy and interesting read. This is a book long overdue, and Malaket has nailed it for users and practitioners alike.

Jonathan Bell, Editor in Chief, Trade and Export Finance, London, UK

The environment around international trade and trade finance has changed considerably in the years I have known Alexander Malaket. While banks have dedicated departments to meet the many requirements related to trade and supply chain finance, they also need to rely on external specialists, of which Alexander is one of the most knowledgeable representatives. This book is another evidence of his ability to stay on top of all the major market developments. It is valuable for both newcomers as well as experienced staff working in the arena of international trading. For newcomers it shows the many rules and customs that come with international trading and gives advice; for those who are more experienced it gives information on the latest developments in regard to international supply chains. In my opinion, this book benefits all those working in this field, as well as those who look for more information on the topics involved in this playing field.

Johan Bergamin, Director, Trade and Commodity Finance,
ING Bank, Amsterdam, The Netherlands

I wish I had a copy of this publication 29 years ago when I commenced my career as it would have provided both an excellent overview and a more in-depth treatment of the trade finance world ...

Maninder Bhandari, Founder, Partner and Managing Director,
The Encore Group and The Derby Group, Dubai, UAE

... very informative, full of useful information and a great read for anyone involved in international trade or trade finance, at any level or angle. A remarkable and very contemporary approach to issues that are currently very hot in international commerce.

Eduardo Klurfan, Chief Representative and Country Head, Cuba,
Bank of Nova Scotia, Havana, Cuba

Malaket offers an insightful compendium of facts, figures, practices and case studies that show the reader how the world's trade finance architecture actually works. His portrayal is thematic, and grounded in theory, but he somehow manages to bring that theory to life. He also captures the evolutionary nature of the system - the fact that we are watching a movie, not examining a snapshot, comes through loud and clear. This book will be required reading for beginners and veterans alike.

Stephen S. Poloz, Governor of the Bank of Canada and
past President and CEO of Export Development Canada

A very comprehensive description of all relevant aspects all stakeholders in financing trade and international supply chains have certainly waited for.

Markus Wohlgeschaffen, Managing Director, Global Head of
Trade Finance and Services, Global Transaction Banking,
Unicredit Bank AG, Munich, Germany

1

International Trade: Where Does Financing Fit In?

International trade has been a driver of growth, economic prosperity and development since the dawn of business and commercial activity. The system around international commerce is far from ideal, and no objective observer would claim that trade, even when it is linked to international development, is conducted equitably, or that its mechanisms work well in all respects.

There are legitimate and important efforts to enhance the model under which global commerce is facilitated, supported and conducted, and even with that, it must be acknowledged that trade between nations has evolved well enough to allow for an enriching flow of goods and services across the globe. With that flow, comes economic value, growth, prosperity and improved standards of living for people across the world.

Trade is viewed as an effective tool in international development, and fair trade activities, meant to improve the distribution of revenue to producers in developing economies, is gaining traction. Trade has also been seen as an effective means of engaging nations to participate in the international community, and as an indirect means of mitigating or reducing threats to international peace and security.

In short, while there is undoubtedly room for significant improvement, trade is an important contributor to growth and development: so much so that robust trade was seen as one of only a few paths to recovery following the global financial and economic crisis that erupted in 2007. The solution to the imperfections around international trade and investment – from wealth distribution to carbon footprint issues and beyond – is to improve the system, its processes and some of the less than constructive underlying political dynamics.

The solution is not, as some have been suggesting, to retreat from international engagement. The damaging effects of protectionism and isolationism are well known, as are the benefits of trade that generate value for the parties and the nations involved, now less on a purely bilateral basis and increasingly, in the context of complex global supply chains and far-reaching networks of relationships.

Politics and ideology aside, and considering developments strictly in terms of the evolution of the international system in which trade operates, it is notable that the influence of emerging and developing economies is increasing significantly. There are active efforts to support the development of a next-generation model of globalization – perhaps a "kinder, gentler globalization" that recognizes the limitations of zero-sum models in international affairs, appreciates the long-term risk of inflated commodity prices and the need to raise the water level so that all ships can benefit.

The international system – including the system of international trade and investment – requires a way forward that is grounded in a more nuanced and finessed understanding of international affairs, including business, trade and investment.

There are promising indications of a continued and more positive evolution of the global system, including those elements related to trade and international business. Examples include:

- The EU-funded "Hub & Spokes" Program aimed at aiding developing economies in enhancing their capacity and capability to better negotiate trade agreements;

- The concerted global effort to assure adequate flows of trade finance through the G-20 and the World Bank's International Finance Corporation (IFC) at the peak of the global financial crisis;

- The increasing awareness around fair trade, including an observable increase in consumer attention in this area;

- The development of the Equator Principles to guide the activities of export credit agencies (ECAs)in trade and project finance;

- The creation of institutions such as the Financial Stability Board, specifically mandated with a protection and oversight role relative to the global financial system;

- The recent, nearly global, focus on supporting the success of small businesses in international markets, on the basis of the importance of this segment to national economies;

- Continued focus on corporate social responsibility, including in international activities.

In business, the successful pursuit of opportunities in international markets, including the pursuit of import, export and investment activity, serves multiple purposes, such as increasing revenues and profitability, diversification of risk and facilitation of growth. International business and international trade, undertaken with care, is commercially very attractive and can be very lucrative for businesses of all sizes, from small or mid-sized entrepreneurial start-ups to large corporations.

In short, trade is extremely important, and creates a great deal of value. Trade benefits nations, enriches businesses and improves or enriches the lives of families all over the world.

The vast majority of world trade today is supported by some form of financing, which combines traditional and long-established instruments and mechanisms, as well as newer solutions or combinations of solutions, an understanding of which is important to any entrepreneur or executive with a mandate that covers international trade activities.

It is widely acknowledged among practitioners that 80–90 percent of global trade flows are supported by some form of trade or supply chain finance (SCF), according to various industry sources. Financing is important in all markets across the world and valuable to businesses of all sizes, from small businesses to large multinationals.

As a business owner, manager or executive, you may do everything absolutely right, but if you fail to understand – and manage – the financial dimensions of your international activities, your venture is likely to fail, and may even put your domestic operations at risk.

The good news is, although financing in the context of international trade (commonly called "trade finance") is poorly understood, even by experienced bankers and financiers, it can be understood both at a strategic level, and in very practical, transactional terms, by entrepreneurs as well as non-financial business executives.

International Trade

International trade touches every country on the globe in some way. The average growth of trade flows has exceeded the growth of global productivity (as measured by Gross Domestic Product GDP) over most of the last four or five decades, until the global economic crisis of 2008, and has once again begun to overtake productivity growth rates as we come out of this ongoing crisis.

The fundamental importance of international commerce was brought sharply into focus by the global financial and economic crisis, in that trade has been – and continues to be – seen as the single most effective engine of recovery and growth, by political, business and academic leaders throughout the world.

Even as national self-interest prompted protectionist responses by some jurisdictions at the peak of the crisis, the overwhelming consensus was that robust and sustained trade was essential to recovery.

Selected Sector	Exports (USD billions)
Manufactures	US $11,511
Machinery & Transport Equipment	$5,753
Commercial Services	4,170
Fuels & Mining Products	4,008
Other Commercial Services	2,240
Chemicals	1,997
TOTAL Merchandise Trade	17,816

Figure 1.1   World exports 2011 – excerpt
Source: World Trade Organization, ITS 2012

The Geneva-based World Trade Organization (WTO) reported that total merchandise exports alone were worth close to US $18 trillion in 2011 as shown in Figure 1.1.

Success in international markets brings attractive revenues and returns, and may even lead to favourable changes in domestic business operations.

Analysis has shown that companies that succeed internationally often become significantly more efficient and competitive in their domestic operations as well.

International practices, lessons learned from trade and investment activities and the infusion of perspectives from international staff all contribute to enhancing domestic operations.

Growth rates and attractive profit margins, together with the opportunity to diversify markets, combine to argue strongly in favour of pursuing business in international markets.

The pursuit and conduct of business internationally involves a wider range of risk types, and a higher degree of risk overall, however, the potential returns and/or the opportunity to enhance competitiveness tends to counter-balance those risks, many of which can be effectively offset.

The additional risks and challenges encountered in the pursuit of international business opportunities can be wide-ranging, and should be understood by entrepreneurs and senior executives in large companies alike. They include:

- Country, political, economic and commercial risk in international markets;

- Longer and more expensive sales cycles, from feasibility assessments to multiple visits to the market during business development;

- Limited information about buyers or suppliers (counterparties) in international markets;

- Lack of credit history or credit data on potential partners, in markets where credit reporting is rudimentary or non-existent;

- Differing practices in financial reporting, ranging from differing accounting guidelines, to the absence of sound reporting practices, including access to audited financials;

- The conduct of business in and across a variety of legal jurisdictions, with the attendant cost, risk and complexity;

- Challenges and complexities related to cross-cultural interaction and engagement;

- Increased complexity related to transport and logistics;

- Increased risk of fraud;

- Risk of significant delay of payment or delivery of goods, or outright non-payment or non-delivery;

- Risk related to foreign exchange and currency volatility, and in some jurisdictions, difficulties in accessing foreign currency to pay for trade;

- Risk of default or outright failure of a bank in an international market.

International trade can generate great value and very attractive returns, but ought not to be pursued without careful consideration of, and planning for, the additional risks and complexities.

The benefits of engaging in international business, including trade and investment, can include significantly higher margins on sales, the ability to sell certain ancillary products that are not attractive to local consumers and may be desirable elsewhere, the opportunity to generate additional profitability through foreign exchange advantages, and the potential to reduce marginal costs of production by producing larger volumes destined for international markets. Investment in foreign markets can assist businesses in accessing technology or know-how, lower-cost labor pools and access to global supply chains and trading relationships that may not be in proximity to the home market.

The Trade and Investment Dynamic

Trade, historically, was a discrete activity, clearly distinguishable from investment. It was common for business and academic discussions to consider whether investment follows trade or trade follows investment.

Importers were engaged in importing, exporters focused on selling their products and services in international markets. Cross-border investment, likewise, was a separate area of activity.

More recently, supply chain and international sourcing activities have evolved in a manner which sees exporters frequently sourcing inputs to production from international markets. Investment activity, likewise, has become closely connected to international trade, no longer as clearly distinct from trade as once was the case.

The need for flexible financing solutions to meet the requirements of businesses engaged in import, export and international sourcing activities of all types, are more pronounced in this post-crisis environment. Banks, financial services organizations and others involved in trade and supply chain finance are increasingly aware of the interrelationship between import, export and investment activity, and are well-positioned to assist clients in these areas.

Trade and Supply Chain Finance

In addition to facilitating payment, and providing financing solutions for business partners, trade and supply chain finance can play a central role in effectively mitigating the risks related to international commerce. Trade finance is about much more than payment or financing, though clearly, the financing and liquidity element is particularly key in international transactions, where transaction timeframes can be long.

Figure 1.2 illustrates how settlement can take a significant amount of time, impacting cashflow and working capital. Financing options that assist in accessing liquidity, such as various trade and supply chain finance solutions, can be very valuable to businesses of all sizes, and that value is further enhanced when effective risk mitigation solutions are also included. The risk mitigation aspect is often a determining factor, without which a deal – or even a trading relationship – would probably not exist.

Pan European level	Average payment duration in days			
	2008	2009	2010	2011
Consumers	40	41	39	40
Business	56	57	55	56
Public sector	65	67	63	65

Figure 1.2   Average payment duration in days, Pan-European view
Source: Intrum Justitia, European Payment Index 2012

Payment timeframes and delays related to public sector transactions in Europe vary significantly from country to country. The issue was deemed sufficiently important to lead to the "Late Payment Directive," which limits payment by public sector entities to 60 days – a significant reduction for some jurisdictions that averaged 120 days or longer, with delays averaging an additional 67 days, according to 2010 estimates from the European Economic and Social Committee.

The majority of global trade – estimates from various sources suggest 80 to 90 percent of trade – is supported and enabled in some way by trade and supply chain finance. Put another way, most business partnerships, and certainly, most cross-border or international supply chains, require some form of trade finance in order to function successfully. Large, cash-rich companies may benefit from financing solutions offered to their less established suppliers; small businesses across the globe are in need of financing and liquidity, particularly if they seek opportunity in international markets.

Financial intermediaries such as banks and others providing trade finance play a critical role in improving the risk profile of a transaction, in transferring risk between parties (and countries) and in establishing, in certain cases, a balanced protection of the interests of buyers and sellers, as will be explored in greater detail in subsequent chapters.

Figure 1.3 illustrates that a significant percentage of respondents to the 2012 European Payments Index survey identify international transactions as sources

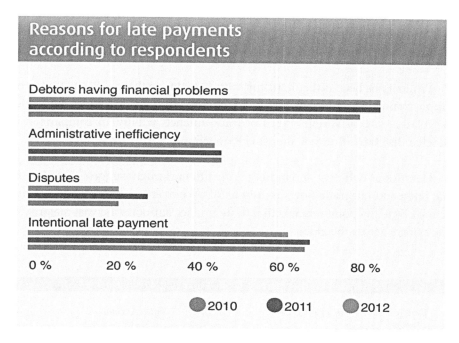

Figure 1.3   European payment index – reasons for late payment
Source: Intrum Justitia, European Payment Index 2012

of late payment. International transactions can have material implications for cashflow and working capital, particularly in credit-constrained markets, and especially for cash-starved small businesses.

The role of short-term credit and trade finance has been acknowledged as critical to the expansion of trade in the last century or longer, and has been described by a leading international institution as "providing fluidity and security" to the movement of goods and services. [Trade] finance, notes this same institution, is the "true life-line" of international trade.

The global economic crisis has demonstrated that financing is fundamentally necessary to the conduct of international trade. At the peak of the crisis, when liquidity in the market evaporated and certain types of trade finance became practically unavailable, the world saw a constriction of certain trade flows of about 40 percent in very short order.

The long-established practices, tools and techniques of trade finance combine to help businesses of all types, to manage many of the risks inherent in international commerce, and, very effectively work to address the financing requirements of buyers and sellers seeking to do business across borders.

While it has been difficult, historically, to estimate the size of the trade and supply chain finance market, Figure 1.4, adapted from an IMF paper, illustrates the relative size of various types of trade finance activity, in comparison to merchandise trade flows of almost US $16 trillion globally in 2008.

Definitions will vary, and industry practitioners might suggest, anecdotally, that open account trade flows represent 70–80 percent of global trade activity. In any event, the point remains that trade finance supports the vast majority of trade flows across the globe.

Estimated Market Share – Trade Financing Arrangements				
Cash in Advance 19-22% $3-3.5 Trillion *Exporter may have leverage or provide a unique product*	**Bank Trade Finance** 35-40% $5.5-6.4 Trillion *Includes 'traditional' trade finance such as letters of credit (~ 10%), collections (~2%)*	**Open Account** 38-45% $7.2 Trillion *Increasingly common, generally less expensive and less complicated than traditional bank trade finance, requires risk mitigation*		
		ECA Guaranteed $1.25-1.5 Trillion	**Arm's Length Non-Guaranteed**	**Intra-Firm** *Significant volume among multinationals and their affiliates, globally 2008 estimate $31 Trillion in trade flows or 10% of global GDP, partially financed*
Global Merchandise Trade, 2008 $15.9 Trillion (IMF Estimate)				

Figure 1.4   Estimated market share of trade financing arrangements
Source: IMF Working Paper, January 2011 (Adapted), OPUS Advisory Analysis

Trade and supply chain finance is about more than financing. Trade and supply chain finance, at its simplest or most complex, is about some combination of four things:

- The facilitation of secure and timely payment across borders;

- The provision of financing for buyers, sellers, banks and other members of the value chain around international trade transactions;

- The mitigation of a variety of risks in the context of international trade;

- The provision of information about a transaction and about related financial flows.

Several of the foregoing issues are also increasingly the focus of domestic transactions, and the supply chain finance model can apply to both local and cross-border business. Information flow, both transactional and financial, is an area of increasing focus and emphasis, as various solution providers seek ways to distinguish their offerings from competitors – a fact that can prove valuable to businesses of all sizes, and could become a factor in the selection of trade and supply chain finance providers.

The optimal combination of these four factors will vary on the basis of the nature of the relationship between buyer and seller, the markets involved and perhaps the goods being traded. The combination of these four elements of trade and supply chain finance will also determine which of the numerous risks and challenges of international commerce, listed earlier, can be mitigated in the context of a particular transaction.

The products, practices and mechanisms related to international trade and supply chain finance have, for hundreds of years if not longer, assured that exporters are paid, and importers receive the goods that they sought to purchase. Despite this history, trade finance is a specialized and generally unfamiliar type of finance; consequently, a brief discussion of basic concepts is worthwhile.

Trade finance is an expression generally reserved for what practitioners define as "short-term" financing of trade transactions, typically involving durations (terms or tenors) of up to 18 or 24 months, though some will limit this category to 360 days or less. Transactions that involve financing over longer periods, up to seven years or so, are often referred to as medium-term trade finance, or in some cases, "structured trade finance," and those with longer exposures, perhaps 15 or 20 years or longer, commonly involve large-scale capital projects, and are referred to as project finance. Timeframes will vary, and the use of the expression "structured", for some, refers more to the presence of risk mitigation and more complex financing, than purely to the duration of a deal, but the distinctions are worth noting despite some inconsistency in definition.

The notion of supply chain finance is relatively new to this business. Certain industry specialists maintain that supply chain finance is little more than a marketing-driven repackaging of existing products and solutions, in a bid by banks to remain relevant to the financing of international trade flows. Others see a clear and discernible new dimension to trade finance under the broader umbrella of supply chain finance.

Trade and Supply Chain Finance facilitates timely and secure payment across borders, provides financing, enables the effective management of risk, and supports information flow between partners in a transaction. The emphasis on each of these elements will vary with each relationship and/or transaction, as noted earlier.

For our purposes, the discussion is interesting to the extent that supply chain finance represents an evolution of the value proposition around the financing of international commerce, and to the degree that it facilitates greater access to liquidity and financing across international or global supply chains. We believe supply chain finance is relevant in both respects, and that its role in the financing of trade flows has practical commercial implications for entrepreneurs, company managers and treasury and finance executives in the largest multinationals.

While industry definitions related to supply chain finance and its relationship (subset or superset) to trade finance are still under development, our approach at this moment will be to refer to both trade and supply chain finance, to distinguish "traditional" solutions from the newer solutions being presented to the market under the banner of supply chain finance.

The fundamentals – such as the four elements of trade and supply chain finance identified earlier (payment, financing, risk mitigation and information) – will apply equally to trade finance as they will to supply chain finance.

Similarly, the commercial challenges related to the conduct of business across borders are common to both.

It is useful to consider however, that traditional trade finance instruments and mechanisms generally apply between a buyer and a seller (with, perhaps, a broker or agent acting in between), whereas supply chain finance takes a broader view of a network of relationships (the supply chain to which a given buyer and seller might belong) across borders – even a network of many supply chains to which a buyer (importer) or seller (exporter) might belong.

Where some providers use the expression "supply chain finance" to refer to a single banking product, our approach is to refer to a suite of products and solutions aimed at responding to a comprehensive set of requirements from buyers, sellers and the potentially dozens, even hundreds, of business partners invited to participate in a supply chain finance program.

Trade finance exhibits a combination of longevity and robustness, together with degrees of innovation and evolution. While the Documentary Credit has been in existence as a core instrument of trade finance for hundreds of years at least, the broader world of trade finance exhibits an ability to adapt to the needs of individual business of all sizes, or to the requirements of trading nations.

> It is valuable to understand the positions, requirements and key expectations of the parties involved in a trade transaction and in a trade or supply chain relationship.
>
> Appreciating the position of a business partner, service provider or counterparty helps to better position your interests, and to tailor your financing options or solutions to maximum effect.

While there are undeniably areas of trade finance that seem to cling to antiquated practices, and have demonstrated a lack of desire to innovate, it is equally true that the system overall has been remarkably adaptive and successful in contributing to the flow of trade.

The value of trade finance is seen through the contributions and activities of certain highly effective organizations, including world-class export credit agencies and top-tier boutique firms specialized entirely on trade finance. Likewise, the way in which international institutions have mobilized to apply trade finance to the challenges of international development demonstrates the fundamental soundness and the wide-ranging impact of trade and supply chain finance.

A Few Basics to Set the Stage

Financing is fundamental to the growth and success of businesses at various stages of development. It is particularly vital to the sustainable conduct of business by small and medium-sized enterprises (SMEs) – especially in the context of international transactions, where risks are amplified and settlement cycles are longer than in domestic business. Micro-businesses, in developing economies, are in even greater need of liquidity and cashflow – and therefore in the great majority of cases, require some form of financing.

Textbook scenarios suggest that the needs of businesses, generally defined, change as a company grows. SMEs seek cash, mid-corporates generally require working capital and financing, while larger corporates, generally more cash rich, might be more focused on risk mitigation solutions.

Small business owners and managers across the globe consistently identify financing – specifically, difficulty in securing affordable financing if any at all – as one of the most significant obstacles to growth and success.

Financing and its related elements in the context of international commerce can be valuable to every party in a trade relationship or transaction, and we will explore in detail the ways in which trade and supply chain finance can be fundamental to success for businesses trading internationally.

The business of finance, including treasury and financial management, involves the balancing of several objectives:

- Collecting receivables in as timely a manner (i.e., as quickly) as feasible, while managing customer relationships, which can involve extending credit to certain suppliers;

- Settling payables while extending payment timeframes as much as possible (i.e., paying as late as feasible), while maintaining focus on client supplier relationships;

- Arranging financing in some form, through debt or equity, to cover shortfalls or assure funding for specific business objectives;

- Investing excess funds to ensure that company resources generate maximum value.

These same considerations apply in the context of trade and supply chain finance.

Most commonly, exporters will seek to be paid as promptly as possible, importers will seek to delay payment where feasible and banks will aim to devise products and solutions to assist in meeting both objectives. Buyers and sellers alike may seek financing, and most will look to ensure the protection of their commercial interests through effective risk mitigation.

Trade and supply chain finance specialists refer to these objectives in terms of extension of DPO or Days Payables Outstanding for buyers and shortening of DSO or Days Sales Outstanding for sellers. Some companies also focus on DIO, or Days Inventory Outstanding, including the optimization of their inventory levels as a consideration in the structuring of trade finance solutions.

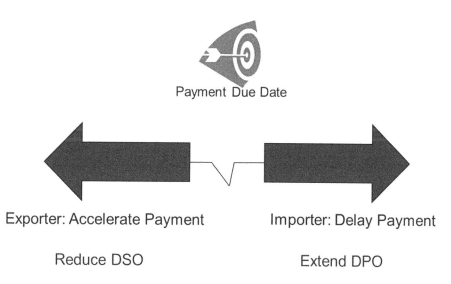

Payment Due Date

Exporter: Accelerate Payment   Importer: Delay Payment

Reduce DSO   Extend DPO

Figure 1.5   Objectives of exporter and importer
Source: OPUS Advisory

Selected Parties and Their Interests

Parties to a trade transaction are individuals, small businesses, large companies and service providers engaged in, or helping to facilitate an import/export transaction, or a longer-term trading relationship involving multiple shipments.

Parties will have varying, sometimes divergent, interests in the context of a transaction or trading relationship (the exporter wants to be paid quickly; the importer may wish to delay payment as long as possible, as shown in Figure 1.5 above). Trade and supply chain finance providers – themselves parties to a transaction – can be very effective in assisting importers, exporters and others in meeting a wide variety of business requirements, and in responding to the interests of multiple parties, concurrently.

TRADING PARTNERS: IMPORTER/BUYER, EXPORTER/SELLER

The importer in a trade transaction is primarily focused on securing cost-effective and trusted sources of supply. Importers seek international suppliers to obtain goods, or inputs to production, which will allow for lucrative margins on resale.

Importers seek to ensure that they receive the goods that have been contracted for, in the agreed timeframe and at the agreed price. At the same time, importers will seek, legitimately, to delay payment as long as feasible in order to ensure adequate liquidity over the life of a transaction or over the lifecycle of a trading relationship, while managing their supplier relationships.

An exporting company seeks to ensure that payment is received in the agreed timeframe, in consideration of goods and/or services provided to a buyer in an international market. Exporters look to international markets to pursue business with more attractive margins, and will, naturally, seek to collect funds – accelerate payment – as promptly as possible. This objective is amplified in importance, given the longer settlement timeframes in international business, and can become more important to an exporter when dealing in a volatile or risky market.

In addition to seeking to ensure timely conclusion of a trade transaction – an exchange of goods or services for payment – companies engaged in international trade will seek to protect against the risks that threaten their respective interests. Additionally, businesses will often require some form of financing in order to be able to conclude a transaction.

The exporter may require financing to be able to produce the goods to be sold, or specifically to finance the transport of the goods to final destination. This is often referred to as pre-shipment finance, An importer, on the other hand, might need financing, to pay for the goods purchased prior to their eventual sale and the generation of related profits. This option is referred to as post-shipment finance.

Good faith and the desire to build a lasting and trusted trading relationship are fundamental to the efficient functioning of the business of international commerce, but the reality is that leverage by one party over the other can create real challenges – and risk – for the other trading partner, and the risk of fraud is amplified in international dealings.

It is notable that financing is once again a competitive factor in international trade, under current, liquidity-constrained conditions. Specifically, exporters competing for business can again differentiate on the basis of their ability to package attractive commercial terms – including financing – along with their product. There was a time, prior to the global financial crisis, where financing and liquidity were easily accessible and did little to assist an exporter in closing on a new deal or relationship, however, current conditions are such that the ability to put together an attractive financing package can be an important competitive advantage for exporters.

Similarly, in the context of global supply chains, large importers can enhance the overall health, robustness and sustainability of their supply chain, including so-called "strategic suppliers," by facilitating access to financing for suppliers, based on the borrowing capability of the importer/buyer.

The maturity of a trading relationship is an important consideration in the selection of trade and supply chain finance solutions, as is the experience of each trading partner in international markets.

New, unproven relationships where one or both parties are novices in international commerce present the most significant risk, either of outright fraud, or of failure to deliver or pay as contracted. Generally, as relationships develop and trust is established, trade and supply chain finance solutions shift from an emphasis on risk mitigation to other areas, such as acceleration of payment, or access to more financing. In the event that the trading relationship is solid and trusted, but the political or other risk factors in either or both markets remain high, mitigation must of course remain central to trade finance options used by the trading partners.

Even in the ideal scenarios however, conditions can change quickly: a particular resource, commodity or product is suddenly unavailable, causing an upward spike in pricing, leading the supplier or exporter to seek a way out of current contracts that may be at significantly lower prices. Such situations occur regularly and trading partners must ensure their respective interests are well protected, even for such unforeseen shifts in trading dynamics.

Trade and supply chain finance practices, transactions and instruments can offer solutions to meet those core business objectives. It is worth noting that the practices and solutions around supply chain finance in particular, are often very relevant and applicable in purely domestic transactions, as well as being valuable in the context of international trade. Leading trade financiers have sought ways to extend the proposition around supply chain finance to meet the needs of clients in the context of both local and international commercial activity.

BROKERS OR MIDDLEMEN

These entities, often one-person operations, source goods, components or production inputs through their contacts, and arrange for delivery of such shipments to the ultimate buyers. Brokers earn revenue by charging a commission to buyers, and can, through certain mechanisms in trade finance, effectively secure the goods required without having to rely on their own credit or borrowing capacity, or financial resources. Such mechanisms, properly used, also allow the broker to manage the transaction while concealing the identity of the ultimate supplier from the buyer, in order to avoid being bypassed.

BANKERS AND TRADE/SUPPLY CHAIN FINANCE PROVIDERS

There are numerous sources of trade and supply chain finance in the world. The majority of trade finance – some estimates suggest over 80 percent – across the globe is provided by banks, and of that market share, the large majority is the domain of top-tier, international and global banks.

There are however, small boutique providers of trade finance, typically aiming at the SME sector, that have carved a lucrative niche in a highly competitive business. Likewise, there are public sector entities, public/private organizations and international agencies that provide trade and supply chain finance, or facilitate access to financing through various forms of insurance and guarantee programs, in addition to pure financing.

Trade finance is a specialized and potentially complex type of financing. Effective communication and well-managed relationships with trade bankers and other trade financiers can prove invaluable to businesses of all sizes and levels of expertise, in navigating the uncertainties of international markets.

Banks are driven to create value and attractive returns for shareholders, and compete in a global arena, subject to significant levels of regulation. Trade and supply chain finance specialists within banks are challenged to compete for (limited) bank capital and lending capacity, as well as risk appetite, against other businesses within the bank, which may generate far higher returns for what is believed to be lower risk.

Bankers with primarily domestic experience possess a limited, often poor understanding of trade and supply chain finance, but in most financial institutions, they exercise a great deal of influence, if not outright control of the activities of trade finance units. Central credit committees often called upon to approve or increase credit facilities at the country level or at the level of banks located in international markets, are very often dominated by domestic bankers with little appreciation for the nature of trade and supply chain finance.

Some would go so far as to suggest that many international bankers possess a limited understanding of trade and supply chain finance, and that this esoteric knowledge must be more broadly disseminated across financial institutions. This is important to business executives and entrepreneurs, in that it suggests the need for great care and a well-informed choice, in selecting a provider of trade finance solutions.

Trade bankers then, seek to strike a balance between conducting business that is relatively safe or effectively risk mitigated, and undertaking more lucrative business that may be riskier in fact, or in perception.

Major financial institutions in the United States, Europe and elsewhere are pushed to lend more to SMEs and to ensure access to necessary levels of trade finance in order to assure recovery and growth through trade; yet, for very legitimate reasons, those same banks face unprecedented levels of regulatory pressure and demands.

Internal competition for capital, political pressure to lend and the pressures of oversight and regulation combine to shape the way banks approach financing in general – and trade finance in particular – at this moment in history.

These realities have direct and practical implications for the way in which entrepreneurs, managers and corporate executives interact with their bankers. An appreciation for the objectives and challenges of bankers can help in securing financing in a timely fashion, even on price-competitive terms.

Bankers will value transparency, and will respond well to financing requests that are carefully thought out, appropriately documented and convincingly risk mitigated. In international business and trade, the foreign jurisdiction involved, the other bank engaged and its profile, as well as the duration of the loan, or term of exposure, will all influence a bank's assessment and influence its decision on a particular loan or financing request.

A transaction between a Canadian exporter and a long-standing German buyer involving maple syrup, with financing extended over 60 days, will look very different to a banker or the bank's credit committee, than a deal between an importer using a middleman to source price-volatile commodities through an unfamiliar supplier in an unstable, politically risky international market, with a local financial institution of questionable reputation or weak financials.

Non-bank providers such as boutique financing firms also provide trade and supply chain finance solutions. While the volume of funding is significantly smaller, such specialist firms often offer useful alternatives for SMEs. Some have also created niche expertise in selected industry sectors within their client base, and develop a market position associated with such specialties, again providing an alternative to bank trade finance.

For lenders, the key objective is to generate revenue and returns from lending activities, and perhaps to use trade finance as a way of securing other forms of business from clients. The major risk, of course, relates to the possibility of losses linked to trade and supply chain finance activity.

Understanding Export Credit Agencies and International Financial Institutions

The global financial and economic crisis reaffirmed the important – and until late 2007 – nearly forgotten role of export credit and insurance agencies in providing trade finance related solutions.

Export Credit Agencies (ECAs) were established initially in post-war Europe, with the primary mandate of facilitating and enabling export trade through financing, insurance and various forms of guarantee programs. While there are debates about the nature of ECA support, specifically the degree to which such agencies are motivated by political objectives, or commercial mandates, the global economic crisis has demonstrated that they are essential to the smooth flow of trade. This is particularly the case in times of crisis when private sector sources of trade finance may not fully meet the needs of international traders.

As with other entities engaged in trade and trade finance, it is valuable for business executives to be aware of the ECAs that might be inclined to support a relationship or transaction with financing, risk insurance or other solutions on the basis of their specific mandate. Such an understanding can prove invaluable in identifying and securing financing and other forms of support.

In the past, exporters engaged primarily with the ECAs of their home country, as those ECAs were mandated to facilitate and support exports and to enable transactions deemed to be in the national interest. The variation in business models among such agencies today allows for the situation where an ECA might provide financing to a foreign-based buyer, to facilitate export sales. Similarly, ECAs might provide funding to – perhaps even take an equity interest in – a foreign company with the objective of encouraging trade flows beneficial to the ECA's home country or clients. .

International Financial Institutions (IFIs), such as the World Bank's International Finance Corporation (IFC) and numerous others, have developed a variety of trade and supply chain finance programs, including guarantee programs meant to ensure the engagement of financial institutions based in developing or emerging markets, in the provision of trade finance.

The potential scope of a supply chain finance program, extending from sub-suppliers to distributors and to end-clients, is effectively illustrated by Figure 1.6, which presents the IFC Supply Chain Finance Program.

Export Credit Agencies and International Financial Institutions make a very important contribution to trade and trade finance, and can offer both risk mitigation solutions and financing options to businesses of all sizes, in most markets across the globe. Small business or large corporate, if your company is engaged in trade, it is worth becoming familiar with the leading ECAs and IFIs.

IFIs are mandated to support international development efforts in emerging and developing markets and are often specifically tasked to enable trade flows as a means of facilitating poverty reduction and economic development.

While some financing programs are limited in scope and are fairly rudimentary in terms of the options they offer, others, such as the program devised by the IFC, are comprehensive and highly sophisticated. Such programs can provide solutions across the life of a transaction, and to one or more parties involved in a trade deal or relationship.

The support of IFIs can be indispensable in developing and emerging markets, which are typically viewed as higher risk. Banks and other financiers may be reluctant to provide financing for trade involving such markets, and the engagement of an international institution can help mitigate the risk and thereby facilitate access to financing.

Companies based in, or doing business in, developing and emerging markets may benefit significantly from resources available through international institutions. Aid agencies, likewise, can provide access to useful resources, including financial resources, when trade activities support international development.

Ultimately, an understanding of the objectives and priorities of parties engaged in international commerce, including those providing trade finance solutions, will help a company to better manage its business, including the financial dimension of business activities.

Financing solutions are a core element of international commerce, trade and investment. As the global economic system continues to struggle with limitations around access to financing, and liquidity in general, the ability of

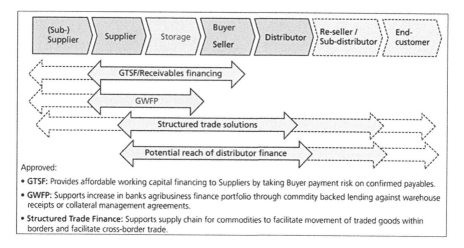

Figure 1.6   IFC supply chain finance program

Source: International Finance Corporation, Short Term Trade Finance, 2011; http:// www.ifc.org/trade

an exporter to offer attractive financing to a buyer is once again a significant competitive advantage.

Trade and supply chain finance solutions are fundamental to international commerce, and any entrepreneur, manager or executive with international aspirations will benefit greatly from an understanding of the role of finance – including the main objectives of each party in a deal or trading relationship – in cross-border business.

Trade and supply chain finance are more than enablers of international business and trade; more than merely transactional solutions limited to the flow of money across borders. Trade and supply chain finance are highly strategic elements of the successful pursuit of business opportunities in international markets, at every stage of a given trade deal, and throughout the lifecycle of a trading relationship.

An understanding of the strategic role of finance, and an appreciation for the financing options, mechanisms and transactions, will serve any entrepreneur, small business manager or finance executive in a large organization.

2

The Fundamentals of Trade Finance

To appreciate the value and flexibility of trade and supply chain finance, it is worth highlighting a few basics about finance in general, particularly those that are relevant and valuable in the context of international commerce.

Cost of Funds

Financing – the use of money – has a price, and unlike other products or services, the price is not fixed by a single supplier, but rather varies among suppliers, and can vary quite significantly depending on the consumer or borrower involved. Put another way, a start-up business led by an entrepreneur with no track record of business, located in a developing economy, will (generally) be offered financing at relatively high cost, in comparison to an established corporation with international experience, solid financials and a base of operations in a developed and secure market.

The same borrower will also encounter variances in costs related to financing or funding, depending on the institution, or the mechanism through which funds are borrowed. Banks will offer financing at rates (costs) that are generally lower than finance companies for example, just as trade bankers will generally provide financing that is less expensive than factoring houses or factors. The cost of financing will vary based on the instrument or mechanism through which financing is accessed, as well. A company borrowing on the basis of an unsecured or partially secured line of credit may pay more in that instance, than might be the case if that same company were borrowing through a fully secured loan.

In trade and supply chain finance, the same dynamics can be encountered by a borrower. An exporter may obtain pre-shipment financing through a bank as a secured facility, or may sign on to a supply chain finance program, and secure financing on the basis of the borrowing capacity of a large buyer that is a client to the exporter, and also happens to be a well-established client of the bank through which a financing facility has been established, for use by approved suppliers.

The cost of financing is a core consideration in effective financial management, in general and in the context of international commerce. Importers and exporters, in assessing financing options, must consider various options, including specialist trade and supply chain finance, and more conventional business finance options.

Financing costs must also be assessed for their impact on the viability of a business transaction. In some markets, financing costs, including necessary risk mitigation mechanisms, can amount to 5–10 percent or more of the value of a transaction. Given that profit margins can be as tight as 2–3 percent or less, it is clear that financing costs must be carefully considered and, where appropriate, factored into pricing.

Time Value of Money

Money and time have a close and direct relationship that is important to effective financial management. Generally, a business will prefer to be paid today, rather than await payment at some future date. The passage of time introduces the risk of non-payment, and implies a cost to the recipient, in that monies cannot be invested to generate a return.

Similarly for a company with a payment obligation, the opportunity to delay payment, and ensure that funds are "working" to create value, perhaps in an investment vehicle, reflects the same reality about the value of money over time.

One of the important but perhaps overlooked advantages of financing in the context of trade is the ability to shift payment and/or settlement to different points on the timeline linked to a commercial transaction. An exporter may agree to sell goods on the basis that payment is due 90 days after shipment, for example, in order to close a sale to a new client. The exporter may, however, face cashflow challenges that make it difficult to wait three months for payment, and therefore, may require the exporter to seek financing for that period of time.

Trade and supply chain finance are specialized and esoteric areas in finance, but fundamentals of finance and credit management remain at the core of the effective financing of international trade.

Trade finance practices and mechanisms have evolved in a way that makes them extremely effective and versatile in nearly every market on the globe, and across a wide variety of legal, commercial and political jurisdictions.

The exporter would assess cashflow needs, identify financing options and the cost of each, and then select the optimal solution, paying the agreed interest and any fees associated with the required financing.

Trade finance is sufficiently mature and versatile to meet the needs of both buyer and seller (importer and exporter) at the same time. Trade and supply chain finance can help an exporter collect payment earlier, while concurrently assisting an importer to pay later than agreed, with the effect of providing liquidity (financing) to both parties. The provider of financing, perhaps a bank, or two banks each acting on behalf of their respective clients, effectively take on the payment obligations in the transaction, for a price.

Money – financing – has a cost, and has value that changes with the passage of time. There is also "opportunity cost" associated with borrowing or lending money, given that it is a resource in limited supply. Financing is about balancing a set of requirements; in international commerce, those requirements can be more urgent, and the costs can be greater, even as business partners seek to manage them across borders.

Trade and Supply Chain Finance

Trade and supply chain finance can involve products and solutions specifically aimed at a single transaction, or can involve comprehensive programs supporting long-standing trade relationships, and complex supply chains with hundreds of business partners working to facilitate the flow of international commerce.

As noted earlier, the business of financing trade involves four elements that typically combine with varying degrees of emphasis ad complexity, as shown in Figure 2.1:

- The facilitation of secure and timely payment across borders;

- The provision of financing for buyers, sellers, banks and other members of the value chain around international trade transactions;

- The mitigation of a variety of risks in the context of international trade;

- The provision of information about a transaction and about related financial flows.

Payment	Financing	Risk Mitigation	Information
▪ Secure	▪ Available to importer or exporter	▪ Risk Transfer	▪ Financial flows
▪ Timely & Prompt		▪ Country, Bank and Commercial Risk	▪ Shipment Status
▪ Global	▪ Several stages in the transaction		▪ Quality of Shipment
▪ Low-cost		▪ Transport Insurance	▪ L/C systems include web & desktop solutions
▪ All leading currencies	▪ No impact in Operating Line for exporters	▪ Export Credit Insurance	

Figure 2.1   Four elements of trade finance

Source: Practical Insights: Documentary Letters of Credit, OPUS Advisory Services International Inc.

Facilitation of Payment

Commerce is about exchange. Exchange of products or services as agreed, against payment in the form and timeframe agreed. In the context of international commerce, the otherwise straightforward process of effecting payment can be complicated and fraught with risk. An exporter invests significant time, effort and money into developing new markets, and even in preparing a single shipment for export to an international destination. As a result, that exporter will seek ways to assure secure and timely payment, and trade finance has evolved a set of proven products, practices and solutions that facilitate precisely such outcomes.

Payment delays can have drastic impact on the ability of a business to maintain operations, especially if a trade deal or transaction is financially material relative to the size of a company's revenues. For many SMEs, and certainly for many start-ups or entrepreneurial ventures, financial exposure in international markets can be so significant as to put the domestic operations, even the overall viability of a company, at risk.

Banks, in their role as intermediaries and providers of trade finance solutions, use their correspondent (partner bank) networks and supporting technology to facilitate payments related to a variety of international transactions, including trade.

The vast majority of banks across the globe are members of SWIFT, the Belgium-based Society for World Inter-Bank Financial Telecommunications.

SWIFT provides a technology platform, formatted messaging and a comprehensive set of processes that enable trillions of dollars of financial transactions across the globe. Formatted messages allow for effective communication between financial institutions.

SWIFT has developed several Message Types (MTs) designed specifically to be used in the conduct of international trade business.

MT400 series messages relate to Documentary Collections, while MT700 series messages are linked to Documentary Letters of Credit – both instruments that are part of the traditional products long used in the finance of international trade.

SWIFT messages are trusted and universally understood across the industry and across the globe, because they are securely transmitted and structured/ formatted in a way that all banks who are members of SWIFT can interpret consistently.

SWIFT messages serve to facilitate secure and timely communication and settlement (payment) between buyer and seller through their respective banks. The right-hand column in the graphic below represents a Documentary Credit, with the left side of the illustration describing each of the fields in the MT700 message. In addition to serving as a means of transmitting instruments such as those used in trade finance, SWIFT messages can be used to send funds in

Explanation	Format
Sender	OELBATWW
Message Type	700
Receiver	AMRONL2A
Message Text	
Sequence of Total	:27:1/1
Form of Documentary Credit	:40A:IRREVOCABLE
Documentary Credit Number	:20:12345
Reference to Pre-Advice	:23:PREADV/130510
Date of Issue	:31C:130517
Applicable Rules	:40E:UCP LATEST VERSION
Date and Place of Expiry	:31D:130730AMSTERDAM
Applicant	:50:ABC COMPANY KAERNTNERSTRASSE 3 VIENNA
Beneficiary	:59:AMDAM COMPANY PO BOX 123 AMSTERDAM
Currency Code/Amount	:32B:EUR100000,
Available With ... By ...	:41A:AMRONL2A BY PAYMENT
Partial Shipments	:43P:ALLOWED
Transshipment	:43T:ALLOWED
Taking in Charge ...	:44A:AMSTERDAM
For Transportation to ...	:44B:VIENNA
Description of Goods	:45A:+400,000 BOTTLES OF BEER PACKED 12 TO AN EXPORT CARTON +FCA AMSTERDAM
Documents Required	:46A:+SIGNED COMMERCIAL INVOICE IN QUINTUPLICATE + FORWARDING AGENTS CERTIFICATE OF RECEIPT SHOWING GOODS ADDRESSED TO THE APPLICANT
Period for Presentation	:48:WITHIN 6 DAYS OF ISSUANCE OF FCR
Confirmation Instructions	:49:CONFIRM
'Advise Through' Bank	:57A:MEESNL2A
End of Message Text/Trailer	

Figure 2.2   SWIFT MT 700 message format

Source: SWIFT Handbook

most currencies across the globe, with a speed that is important to successful international trade.

The majority of trade finance transactions involving traditional products are effected through SWIFT, and huge volumes of payment transactions for trade (and other business) are facilitated through the SWIFT network. SWIFT has been working to devise solutions to the current needs of importers and exporters, and the ways in which they now seek to do business internationally. These developments will be explored in detail later in this book.

In addition to assuring secure payment, the speed with which a payment can be settled through SWIFT can also be important. Speed of payment can help exporters manage cashflow and working capital; likewise, quick payment can help businesses reduce the risk of volatility related to foreign exchange, as well as other commercial and political risks that may be encountered in international trade.

Financing, particularly under current economic conditions, is a strategic aspect of the conduct of business, especially across borders.

Sales cycles, payment timeframes and timeliness associated with the conduct of business are invariably longer in international business and trade, and those extended timelines drive the requirement for an effective financing plan.

Likewise, the ability of a company to package attractive financing represents a significant competitive advantage in the pursuit of opportunities in international markets. All else being equal, attractive financing can close the sale.

There are also situations in international trade, where nations may be short of foreign currency, and may be compelled to impose exchange controls, restricting the use of limited currency for selected, government-approved purposes. In such circumstances, trade flows are generally considered obligations of high priority, and when foreign currency is in limited supply, government agencies charged with controlling the disbursement of currency will require the issuance of a documentary letter of credit to track the uses of foreign currency.

Financing

Trade and supply chain finance products and solutions offer a wide range of options around financing – lending – to importers, exporters and other parties involved in an international trade transaction.

Financing in the context of a trade transaction can be aimed at a particular party, such as an exporter in need of pre-shipment or pre-export finance. This type of financing is designed to assist a seller to meet the cost of production and/or shipment of goods prior to collecting payment (and hopefully earning a profit) as a result. Buyer credit, on the other hand, is offered to the importer, to assist in paying for the imported goods prior to their eventual sale. There is also the option for one bank to offer financing to another bank, with the ultimate intent of supporting the completion of a transaction, and a longer-term trade relationship.

Financing can be extended on the basis of a specific, agreed event such as the creation of a purchase order, the issuance and acceptance of an invoice for payment, or the loading of a shipment onto a vessel. This has been referred to as "event-based financing," and it has been suggested that the number of trigger events in a transaction can vary from a few, to two or three dozen. The need for financing, and the points at which financing can be offered to one or more trading parties, can vary significantly across markets, across trading relationships and even between transactions involving well-established trading relationships.

Importers and exporters may have a variety of options in terms of sourcing financing.

One issue to consider is the relative cost of these numerous sources, and their impact on the balance sheet of a business. In some cases, it may be appropriate to fund short-term needs related to a trade transaction through an existing banking facility such as an operating line of credit. In other instances, it may be better for a company to avoid impacting existing facilities, opting rather to take advantage of financing solutions available through trade finance mechanisms.

A small business with limited financial resources might agree to sell its goods to a buyer overseas, on the basis that the invoice will be settled (for example) 90 days after the shipment date of the goods. A business with good cashflow may have the option to wait for payment on the agreed due date; more typically however, the exporter will seek ways to accelerate that payment.

The exporter might:

- use an operating line of credit to fund its needs over the 90-day period;

- sell its invoice covering the shipment to a third party provider such as a bank or a factor (a company that specializes in various forms of invoice-based finance), collecting perhaps 80 percent of the face value of that invoice immediately, and relinquishing the remaining 20 percent as a fee to the financier. The financier may also opt to make two payments, perhaps 60 percent of face value immediately, with 30 percent upon collection of the payment from the buyer, with the remaining 10 percent flowing to the lender.

- arrange for the shipment to be effected on the basis of a documentary letter of credit with a payment due date set at 90 days after the shipment date, and then asking a bank to discount this obligation for immediate payment, again paying fees and interest for that option;

- join a supply chain finance (SCF) program at the invitation of a large buyer/client, gaining access to financing on the strength of that larger company and its ability to access financing on a cost-effective (often significantly lower) basis.

Each option will be suited to a different set of circumstances, and will imply a different set of financing costs to the exporter. An importer may have similar options, and should, likewise, consider the mechanisms, timing and cost of these financing options prior to deciding which to request/accept.

A company's need for financing may vary significantly at different points in time, and it is worth revisiting financing alternatives and costs periodically, to ensure that business requirements are being adequately met and managed from the financial perspective. In times of relatively abundant liquidity and credit, it will often be worth accelerating settlement of invoices at nominal cost; likewise, in difficult times, the need to financing and liquidity to support and maintain business operations may demand the payment of a significant premium, to secure the necessary funding.

In addition to understanding and appreciating the financing needs of other parties to a transaction, it is valuable to understand the role and value proposition of banks and other financiers in the context of international trade.

Banks are motivated by the need to generate revenues and profit, either directly through the trade finance business, or by using trade finance to capture other, profitable business such as corporate lending.

An important contribution of banks in the context of trade transactions is referred to as credit enhancement. Instead of relying on the credit standing and capacity of the importer, to meet financial obligations to the seller, one contribution of a bank that issues a letter of credit, is to shift the financial obligation from the importer to the issuing bank, acting on behalf of their importer client. In the end, the exporter benefits from the participation of a bank in the transaction, as the financial obligation shifts from a company to a bank, generally, a party with stronger credit standing.

In addition to providing greater comfort to an exporter, the presence of a bank in a trade transaction facilitates financing options that would not be available if a bank were not involved. A financier will be more likely to provide trade and supply chain finance solutions, if the ultimate payment obligation rests with a reputable financial institution with a strong balance sheet, as opposed to a business with limited financial resources, or one whose background is not known or easily verified.

Risk Mitigation

Risk is a reality of business, and its presence and impact are amplified when business crosses borders. This reality is what makes international commerce profitable and attractive, yet it is worth noting that risk is ultimately defined on two levels: objective "reality" and perception.

It is reasonable to attribute higher risk to a country in the midst of significant political turmoil or outright military conflict than to a market advantaged by stability and peace. This is reality. It is no less common, but less easily justifiable, to attribute higher risk to an international market on the basis of gaps in knowledge, or difficulty in securing necessary data or information. This is the element of risk shaped by perception.

Just as with capital market and investment activity, it is the difference in assessment of risk (objective plus perceived), coupled with the variance in risk tolerance and target returns or profitability, that combine to make international commerce compelling to some and frightening to others. Risk is directly related to return, with higher risk (international business versus domestic business) expected to generate more attractive return.

In the end, entrepreneurs, managers and executives assess risk and return, consider their company's tolerance for risk and the impact of a worse-case outcome and decide whether or not to pursue a given opportunity. Risk combines both objective fact and subjective assessment or perception. The subjective, perception-based element of risk can be offset through research, information, greater transparency trusted advice and first-hand experience and observation in an international market. The "information provision" aspect of trade and supply chain finance can be invaluable in this exercise.

The objective aspects of risk can be mitigated or offset at least to some degree through business arrangements, contracting and the selection of appropriate trade and supply chain finance solutions, appropriately structured to include risk mitigation mechanisms.

Trade and supply chain finance offers numerous features, mechanisms and processes intended to assist importers and exporters (as well as lenders and other parties involved in trade) with the effective mitigation of a wide range of risks. More correctly, the tools available through trade finance and financial supply chain management allow a business to optimize risk against the cost of mitigation, the level of risk tolerance of the company, and the target returns linked to the opportunity under consideration.

The principal risks that can be effectively managed and mitigated/optimized through trade and supply chain finance instruments are illustrated in Figure 2.3 and include:

- Commercial risk

- Bank risk

- Country and political risk

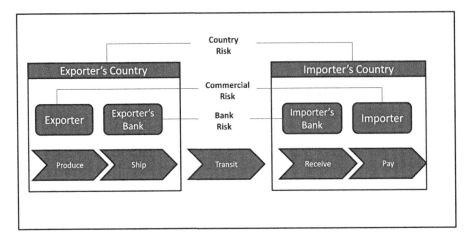

Figure 2.3   Risk in international trade
Source: OPUS Advisory

Commercial risk refers to the risk faced by buyers and sellers as a result of choosing to do business together. Bank risk relates to the possibility that a bank may fail to make payment as agreed, or may face bankruptcy, while country risk includes a wide range of risks – economic, political and otherwise – related to the unique circumstances within and around a particular jurisdiction.

As with domestic transactions, any business undertaking involves the risk of non-payment or non-performance of obligations (in trade, the production and shipment of the agreed goods) by either partner, for a variety of reasons, ranging from financial difficulty to outright bankruptcy, to intentional fraud, and a wide variety of circumstances between those options.

Even when the trading partners act in good faith and attempt to meet their respective obligations to the best of their abilities, factors beyond their control can intervene to prevent production and/or shipment of goods, or timely payment of monies due. Goods may be damaged or lost in transit for example, for reasons that are entirely out of the control of the exporter.

Trade finance instruments, and supply chain finance programs, can be structured in ways that allow parties to a trade relationship or transaction, to manage and mitigate a wide variety of risks. One way this is accomplished in a trade transaction is to shift the risk from one party to another, to match the nature of a transaction to the risk circumstances and/or tolerances of the parties involved.

Importers and exporters doing business together could very easily agree to settle their transaction by check; however, this option leaves the exporter completely exposed and at the mercy of the importer's ability and intention to pay as promised. This is a situation where significant commercial risk is present for the exporter. Likewise, the cashing of a check from a foreign source takes significantly longer than the same transaction involving a domestic check, which further adds to the risk for the exporter.

The conduct of international commerce frequently involves financial institutions as facilitators or providers of various solutions in the context of trade and supply chain finance. As with commercial risk however, the presence of a bank in a transaction does not guarantee that a transaction is secure.

As the financial crisis has clearly demonstrated, there are banks in very poor financial health. Aside from these extreme circumstances, it is a reality that banks fail, or can fail to meet financial obligations for a variety of reasons. Bank risk refers to the risk that a bank will fail to meet its financial obligations and therefore expose other parties to financial risk.

The use of a documentary letter of credit, and the explicit inclusion of certain features of a letter of credit in a particular transaction, allows the exporter to eliminate dependence on their importer/client, by agreeing to settlement of invoices by and through banks acting on behalf of their respective customers.

An exporter can even avoid country risk and largely reduce or eliminate bank risk, by using a particular feature of a letter of credit that allows an exporter to be paid by their own bank, in their own country of domicile, should they deem this prudent. Such options will be explored in detail later.

Country risk relates to the risk of doing business across borders, and encompasses several types of risks related specifically to the conduct of business in the international environment. Country risk involves risks ranging from the possibility of default due to the inability of a country to meet financial obligations, to transaction-level risks, including exchange rate risk, or transfer risk (risk related to the inability to move funds across borders).

Risk is a reality of business and even more critical in the conduct of commerce across borders.

Country risk is a particular type of risk, and involves several components, each relevant to varying degrees depending on the markets involved.

Country risk analysis is part art, part science – a combination of complex economic and financial models, on-the-ground assessments and the judgment of specialists.

There are many credible sources of country risk analysis, which should be reviewed in the context of a trade or investment development effort.

Country risk includes:

- Economic risk

- Transfer risk

- Exchange rate risk

- Location or neighborhood risk

- Sovereign risk

- Political risk

The conduct of business across borders involves risks that are unique to international commerce. Importers and exporters face some element of country risk, simply by virtue of pursuing commercial opportunities together. While certain markets involve a wider range of risks than others, country risk requires careful consideration – and appropriate mitigation – by both importer and exporter.

The majority of trade transactions are conducted in US dollars, which creates foreign exchange risk for any trading partners located in markets where the currency is not the American dollar. While currency risk can certainly be the basis for speculative activity (that is, intentional attempts to generate profit by accurately predicting the direction of currency fluctuations, and structuring a transaction in a way that will be favourable, as the predicted scenario arises), in the context international trade, the objective is generally to reduce uncertainty about the impact of foreign exchange on costs (for the importer) or on revenue and profitability (for the exporter). Trade finance specialists can advise on mechanisms or financing structures aimed at managing foreign currency exposure for each party in a trade transaction.

Political risk refers to the risk of political instability impacting the conduct of business. Certain markets face serious internal issues, including the risk of civil war or other disruptive military action, or political dynamics leading to expropriation or nationalization of foreign-owned businesses, assets or revenues.

It is worth noting again, that trade obligations are generally considered high priority by government authorities. Even in times of economic and political crisis, governments are motivated – and well advised – to respect their financial and trade obligations. Importing countries, bringing in foodstuffs or commodities of various types, benefit in the long term from a level of international confidence related to the timely payment of obligations. The international system and the mechanisms of international commerce rely on this level of priority being assigned to trade obligations.

Country Risk: A Reality of Trade

Trade obligations, particularly those related to the purchase of agri-food, commodities and various natural resources, are generally considered by governments to be high-priority obligations, which must be respected and met even in the most difficult of circumstances. This reality contributes to the high degree of confidence in the international system, around the likelihood of payment of trade-related obligations.

This discipline around trade obligations has proven to be robust and resilient even in the most trying circumstances, with governments facing foreign exchange shortages, but ensuring that even those scarce financial resources were available to honor payment obligations related to key imports.

A recent situation in Kazakhstan provided a striking illustration of the impact to the international system, when a government indicates that they cannot or will not meet outstanding trade obligations:

International banking groups are urging Kazakhstan to ensure trade finance obligations are repaid in full by the country's banks in a timely manner.

The Bankers' Association for Finance and Trade (BAFT) and the International Financial Services Association (IFSA) have written a letter to the Kazakh president Nursultan Nazarbayev expressing concerns over recent proposals for debt restructuring in the Kazakh banking sector, particularly with BTA Bank.

BTA Bank, the largest bank in Kazakhstan, is presently going through a debt restructuring process, following a state takeover earlier this year, and the suspension of principal payments on debt in April.

Although no official debt restructuring plan has been finalised, there are fears that trade debt will be subject to discounts. The joint BAFT-IFSA letter expresses the belief that such an outcome would be "unprecedented in the global markets for banks with overall systemic national importance. (Global Trade Review, August 2009)

This reality of international trade helps to assure that trade-related financial obligations are settled in a timely fashion, even in the context of difficult conditions. When nations fail to place appropriate priority on their trade obligations – and the related financial undertakings – the good faith that underpins international commerce can sustain serious damage.

One important lesson from the global financial crisis that erupted in late 2007 is the importance of appropriate and well-considered risk mitigation in the business of international commerce. The revival of this discipline is well facilitated through long-established trade finance instruments, as well as through newer solutions in the supply chain finance domain.

Information

Trade and supply chain finance is facilitated through increasingly sophisticated technology, including technology provided by the banks, logistics providers and others involved in facilitating trade. Importers and exporters value timely information about the status of their transactions, including specific shipments and the related financial flows.

The use of Radio Frequency Identification (RFID) technology allows real-time tracking of packages or containers at any moment between shipment and delivery. Relatedly, trading partners receive detailed reports about the status of financing and payments. Importers and exporters, and their bankers, can benefit from shipment-related status information, by linking shipment status to financing options, including the event-based financing discussed earlier.

Once financing is put into place, the status of financial flows, from the loan approval/provision to the final settlement of the transaction (repayment of the loan) can be monitored by all parties authorized to do so. Information is linked directly to commercial considerations: the status of a shipment can help a buyer to plan production activities, resale activities and related business decisions; information about the financial side of a transaction, particularly when it is timely, is invaluable in managing working capital and cashflow.

Industry specialists refer to the physical supply chain, which relates to the movement of goods, as well as the financial supply chain, which refers to the related movement of monies between buyer and seller, likely through one or more financial intermediary. More recently, there is recognition of a flow of data and information that relates directly to the transaction.

Trade and supply chain finance can involve the simplest, single-shipment transaction, or it might enable multi-year transactions in the context of complex capital projects; irrespective of the characteristics of a particular deal, the business of trade finance involves some combination of payment facilitation, financing, risk mitigation and provision of information.

3

Understanding Global Supply Chains

Trade, Networks and Globalization

International trade was, for a very long time, conducted, or at least, understood primarily on a bilateral basis: one buyer, seeking a product from a particular supplier, and therefore, the products and solutions devised in support of international commerce often functioned to facilitate transactions between two key parties.

More recently, the focus has shifted from such a bilateral view to one encompassing increasingly complex networks – even ecosystems – of commercial relationships, including international and global supply chains: the series of partnerships and relationships, from suppliers and buyers, to sub-suppliers, distributors, service providers and others, that collaborate to bring a product to market.

Supply chains are not new, nor is it a revelation that supply chains cross national borders or play a fundamentally important role in the conduct of international commerce. The novelty of the last several years is that trade financiers have shifted their focus from a largely bilateral view of trade, to a network and supply chain view of international commerce.

The financing needs of these global networks are, if not more complex, then arguably more intricate and far-reaching in their scope and impact.

Understanding and managing international and global supply chains is a complex undertaking, as illustrated by the variety of topics and disciplines covered in supply chain management, and as shown in Figure 3.1.

Elements of Supply Chain Management - Illustrative
1. Understanding the Corporate Environment
2. Specifying Requirements and Planning Supply
3. Analyzing Supply Markets
4. Developing Supply Strategies
5. Appraising and Short-Listing Suppliers
6. Obtaining and Selecting Offers
7. Negotiating
8. Preparing the Contract
9. Managing the Contract and Supplier Relationships
10. Managing Logistics in the Supply Chain
11. Managing Inventory
12. Measuring and Evaluating Performance
13. Environmental Procurement
14. Group Purchasing
15. E-Procurement
16. Customer Relationship Management
17. Operations Management
18. Managing Finance in the Supply Chain
19. Packaging in the Supply Chain
20. Quality in the Supply Chain…and more

Figure 3.1   International supply chains – illustrative

Source: International Trade Centre, Geneva

The concept of "Integrative Trade," frequently referenced by Export Development Canada, the national export credit agency, recognizes a fundamental change in the nature of international commerce – one where import, export and investment are closely linked and often take place concurrently.

This evolution has direct implications for the way a company of any size undertakes international activity, and has a direct effect on financing options and mechanisms.

The Integrative Trade view of international commerce links very well to the increased focus on global supply chains and supply chain finance.

Global sourcing and trade patterns have been reshaped in several ways, by current economic and commercial realities, including the increasingly globalized and interrelated dynamics of business.

Where activities such as import, export and investment were historically discreet and clearly distinguished, more recent developments are such that an exporter may find it advantageous to source inputs to production from another country – in effect, becoming an importer. Likewise, the historical distinction between trade and investment activity has blurred, with investment and trade often taking place concurrently rather than sequentially.

This evolution, which brings together three forms of international activity – import, export and investment, has been referred to as "Integrative Trade." In addition to conceiving international activity in a more holistic, integrated manner, the Integrative Trade model links very well to the nature and dynamics around international and global supply chains, further supporting a shift from the bilateral view of trade to the network and ecosystem view of international commerce.

In addition, the Integrative Trade model recognizes the central role of outsourcing and offshoring, including the contributions of foreign affiliate firms, as central to the overall sourcing and trade model that must now be supported by trade and supply chain finance.

A view of the Canadian experience in quantitative terms, as determined by Export Development Canada, reflects the following (expressed in Canadian dollars):

- Exports of goods and services (2012) = $510.7 billion;

- Imports of goods and services (2012) = $569.9 billion;

- Canadian Direct Investment Abroad flows (2012) = $53.9 billion;

- Foreign Direct Investment-in flows (2012) = $45.3 billion;

- Foreign affiliate sales (2010) = $462.2 billion.

Taking an Integrative Trade view of international business, and combining that with the definition of global supply chain management developed by the International Trade Centre in Geneva, facilitates an appreciation of the complexities inherent in understanding and managing international supply chains, and in assuring that they are adequately financed, that the relationships and transactions are supported with appropriate levels of risk mitigation, and that payments flow globally in a timely and secure fashion, across the supply chain ecosystem. Similarly, the importance of timely and sufficiently detailed information flow is amplified in the complex environment of global supply chains and the Integrative Trade activity they enable.

Integrative Trade

Global sourcing and trade patterns have evolved over the past number of years, such that traditional distinctions between import, export and foreign investment activity – historically separate and distinct – are now closely related and, in some circumstances, tightly integrated. One outcome of this new reality is that trade and supply chain finance, like the business it aims to support, must evolve to be more holistic and integrated.

Canada's export credit agency, Export Development Canada, describes the advent of Integrative Trade in numerous publications – a model which is illustrated in Figure 3.2.

"One can think of the full integrative trade model as emerging from the growth process of the globalizing firm. In the beginning, the firm is engaged in traditional export sales, with all production taking place domestically. It then begins to import components in order to reduce costs, sharpen its price point and increase its export sales; in other words, the company imports more in order to export more. After a time, it purchases a foreign supplier, or perhaps creates a new one, thereby embedding the global supply chain in its own corporate structure. This creation requires that the company invest abroad – to undertake what the statisticians call "foreign direct investment." Finally, that foreign-based affiliate is in a position to develop export sales to third parties from that foreign location." "The emergence of integrative trade means that there is considerably more international trade involved in producing the next unit of output than in the past."

—Stephen Poloz, Export Development Canada
"Financial Intermediation under the New Trade Paradigm:
EDC and Integrative Trade," January 2007 (Updated, January 2012)

Three Supply Chains in One

Supply chains can be extremely complex, involving, for example, a large global company, perhaps a purchasing or buying unit, multiple related or affiliate firms and hundreds, even thousands of suppliers (or more) across the world. They may also be relatively small, perhaps one buyer with one or two suppliers.

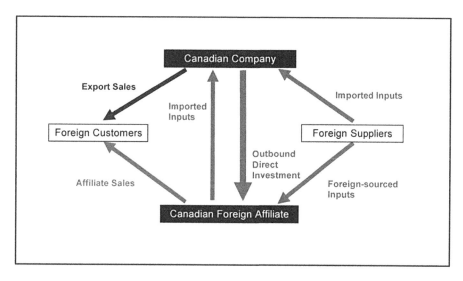

Figure 3.2   Integrative trade
Source: EDC

Irrespective of the complexity of a given supply chain, there are, in fact, three supply chains operating concurrently, as shown in Figure 3.3.

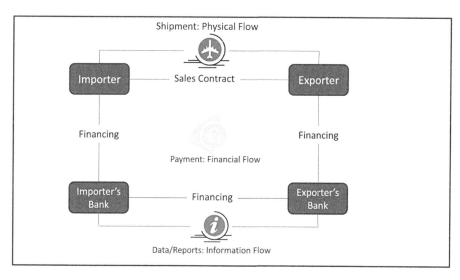

Figure 3.3   Physical, financial and information flow
Source: OPUS Advisory

- The "physical" supply chain, involving the flow of goods (or services) between exporter and importer, buyer and seller;

- The "financial" supply chain, referring to the movement of money – payment – between importer and exporter;

- The "information" supply chain, which relates to the exchange of data and information between various parties (including service providers such as logistics companies, banks and others, and the buyer and seller.

As a company seeking to conduct business, and in need of some form of trade or supply chain finance, it is worth being aware of these three related components of any supply chain, to better understand the mechanisms available, and to identify suitable financing options.

The physical flow generally involves movement of the goods purchased, from the exporter to the importer, through the services of a logistics or shipping company or some form of transport service provider.

Financial flows can involve multiple parties in a trade transaction or a supply chain, and can flow in several directions – payment from importer to exporter through one or more banks, financing from one bank to another, or from a bank to one or both of the trading partners, at various points in the transaction.

Data or information flows, likewise, can run in different "'directions'" between the various parties involved: the shipping company providing updates on the status and location of the shipment, or the exporter providing details on the status of production or shipment of the goods or a bank sending details about the timing of agreed payment or financing transactions.

Each of these supply chains – physical, informational and financial – are intimately connected. The nature of those connections relates directly to the financing options available to a buyer or supplier.

Implicit in the foregoing, is an additional layer of flows – those involving the transfers of risk, liability and legal obligations between the various parties in the transaction or in the supply chain. This dimension is represented by the various legal frameworks, rules and practices around trade and supply chain finance and the related instruments and solutions. Rules governing the use of Documentary Letters of Credit, or the discounting of drafts presented under letters of credit, or practices related to the terms of sale, including definitions of risk and ownership transfer, are all examples of this additional dimension of trade finance.

The Physical Supply Chain

The physical supply chain refers to all aspects of the physical flow of goods from supplier to ultimate end-customer, through brokers and, as may be the case, various intermediaries.

The physical supply chain involves interaction between buyers and suppliers, their various representatives, and service providers such as logistics companies, forwarders and others involved in the transport and delivery of the goods, as well as customs brokers and various government authorities involved in the movement of goods across borders.

The physical supply chain, by its end-to-end nature, involves management of both demand-side and supply-side aspects of a commercial and trade transaction. Whereas supply chains were once commonly linear in nature, involving a supplier and an ultimate buyer, the nature of global sourcing patterns today is such that supply chains can look much more like a network of relationships serving various purposes, than a chain of relationships and processes aimed at facilitating one relationship between importer and exporter.

The physical supply chain encompasses the sourcing of raw materials, components or other inputs required in a production process, along with the production or manufacturing of the goods, and delivery to the buyer.

Management of the physical supply chain is facilitated through increasingly sophisticated technology, from electronic data interchange or EDI (formatted messaging between parties) to the use of materials and distribution planning systems, to RFID technology, which enables real-time tracking of product at any stage of the transport and delivery process.

All of this relates very directly to the business of trade and supply chain finance.

Finance-related risk includes consideration of the duration of financial exposure, as well as concern about loss of visibility, or control, of the shipment while in transit. The processes and technologies around the management of the physical supply chain have succeeded in accelerating delivery (reducing the term of financial exposure) as well as providing greater visibility of and control over a shipment, which can be critical, if a lender feels they must take ownership of the goods as collateral, in order to be able to provide trade or supply chain finance.

The Information Supply Chain

Data and information flow have become increasingly central to the business of financing, in particular, in the context of international commerce.

The ability and the role of banks in collecting and disseminating information of various kinds has expanded to the degree that some have argued, banks are no longer primarily in the business of money, but rather, in the business of information and data. While this suggestion may be counterintuitive, it makes the point about the increasing focus on data collection and information extraction in financial services.

While it is understandable, and prudent, for a company to treat commercially sensitive information as confidential, the reality is that some level of transparency is required by bankers and business partners. Such transparency, carefully provided, will serve to enhance and increase financing options for the buyer, seller or for the entire supply chain.

KYC – the "Know Your Client Rule" has been a requirement of investment bankers and brokers for many years. More recently, a similar legal and regulatory requirement has been imposed on bankers, particularly in the context of international banking and financing activities.

Bankers are compelled to demonstrate adequate understanding of a client's business activities, and even adequate knowledge of a client's buyers or suppliers, regardless of where they might be located.

As a business, understanding some of the obligations of bankers can help secure timely and fairly priced financing.

A reflection of this reality, is in the difficulty businesses encounter in securing financing through banks and other conventional (and legal) means, in markets where information about companies or businesses – such as credit reports, audited financial statements, details about supplier relationships and company structure/ownership – is difficult to access or considered unreliable. If financing is accessible, it will generally be expensive, and the terms of financing, such as the level of collateral required, or the restrictiveness of loan agreements, will tend to be onerous.

Lenders like banks, that are regulated through government agencies, or subject to international regulation or quasi-regulation, are subject to stringent and increasing demands related to international transactions, from detailed reporting and tracking of financial flows, to the requirement that they be familiar not only with the business of their own client (the KYC rule), but also, that they be aware of and have some understanding of their client's buyers, suppliers and other partners.

This can be a challenging requirement for banks, in that it can be difficult to source reliable information about a business located in a remote part of the world many thousands of kilometers away, where communication infrastructure and technology may not be sufficiently robust.

There are, however, a variety of important reasons for requiring financiers to know the transaction and the underlying commercial relationships so intimately. Those reasons range from a desire to assure adequate stewardship and risk management among banks, to the global efforts to combat money laundering and terrorist financing.

Government and law enforcement authorities maintain lists of countries, companies and individuals subject to boycott or other enforcement measures, and financial institutions are required to monitor transactions to ensure they do not – willingly or inadvertently – facilitate transactions that violate these various restrictions.

In this respect, information flow and relative transparency about business activities and commercial relationships can help facilitate the smooth conduct of business, and can help companies avoid unnecessary delays or unintended entanglement in legal matters, or worse, serious errors in the conduct of international business.

Transparency and Information Flow in Finance: The End of Name-Lending?

International trade has been a reality of the human experience for thousands of years. One banker in Lebanon noted, with only the slightest humour, that the Phoenicians had invented the first instrument of trade finance more than six thousand years ago: the alphabet.

Commercial practices related to trade and to financing, likewise, have been in existence for similarly long periods; however, the increasingly integrated and interdependent nature of international financial markets is driving a degree of alignment of certain practices across the world. Banks and businesses in the Middle East and North Africa (the MENA Region) for example, have long engaged in a practice referred to as "Name Lending" – the granting of financing facilities, including trade finance, on the basis of a borrower's reputation, including the reputation of respected, long-established and often wealthy families with extensive business interests.

EIU Predicts End of "Name Lending" in the Region

The Economist Intelligence Unit (EIU) has said in a new report that defaults by Saudi Arabia's Algosaibi and Saad groups could signal an end of name lending, a practice that banks in the region follow whereby loans are extended to influential business families in the Gulf on the basis of their name.

"The defaults in June by the two large Saudi family-owned conglomerates have generated some concern among banks about lending to Gulf family-owned firms, and may herald the end of the unofficial practice of 'name-lending' – lending to influential business families largely on the basis of their name," the EIU said in its latest global forecast.

Credit environment in the Gulf – Saudi Arabia in particular – is expected to remain tight for some time as lending sentiment is depressed. "The known bank loans extended to the two groups stand at around $7.4 billion (Dh27bn), but this figure excludes bilateral loans and letters of credit, and the full amount is likely to be significantly higher," the EIU said.

Such events linked to the global crisis, coupled with the regulatory pressure on banks operating internationally, and the mobility of capital, which can now move freely through many jurisdictions in search of attractive investment (including lending) options, have put pressure on this long-standing but risky practice. (Source: EIU quoted in *Zawya*, International Edition, and July, 2009)

The importance of adequate information flow and transactional transparency is clear in the context of bilateral trading relationships – between one buyer and one supplier, for example, however, it is magnified in the context of complex, far-reaching and highly integrated supply chains, where the relationships may be indirect and only superficially managed.

Whether your company is a start-up, a small business or a large multinational, the issue of information flow and transparency will impact your attempts to secure timely, acceptably priced trade and supply chain finance, and in that respect, it is important to appreciate the role of information in trade relationships and in the context of international supply chains, as it relates directly to trade and supply chain finance.

The Financial Supply Chain

International trade involves the flow of goods between exporter and importer, and the flow of information between various parties and partners engaged in the transaction. Trade also involves the flow of financing between parties; in theory, any company, business partner or service provider involved in international commerce, or any such entity that is part of an international supply chain could, at a given stage in a transaction, require some form of financing.

There is, of course, some form of financial flow between buyer and seller, either directly, as in the case where an importer simply sends funds to be deposited to the exporter's account, or indirectly, where a bank or other provider acts to facilitate the settlement of payments owed in the context of a trade transaction. Institutions such as export credit agencies and international financial institutions are often critically important to the structuring of a trade or supply chain finance solution, and are included in a financial supply chain, as shown in Figure 3.4.

It is possible for one bank involved in facilitating a trade transaction, to require financing from another financial institution. A bank in a developing or emerging market, where financing is expensive, and where that bank may face limitations in its own resources, may find it necessary or simply advantageous from a cost point of view, to seek trade-related finance from another financial institution – usually an established international bank, or perhaps an institution

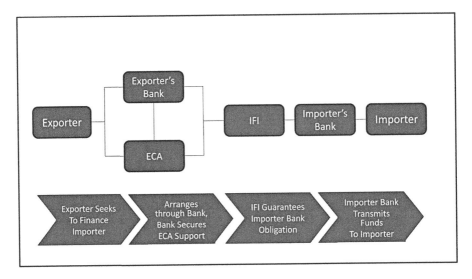

Figure 3.4   **Export credit agency and international financial institution**
Source: OPUS Advisory

such as an export credit agency or one of the international financial institutions with a trade finance program in place to address just such a situation.

As an importer or exporter, it is useful to be aware of such dynamics, in order to be able to identify challenges in sourcing trade finance in a given market or from a particular financial institution. More importantly, this understanding can be helpful in identifying alternative sources of trade finance, or even in better managing the overall cost of financing, by appreciating the ultimate source of such financing.

While a physical supply chain – the flow of production inputs into a final product and its ultimate arrival at a destination market and end-customer can be viewed as relatively linear in nature, with a starting point and an endpoint, the flows in a financial supply chain may mirror the flow of goods, or they may flow in multiple directions, from multiple sources, simultaneously.

Financing can originate from the importing or exporting country, from any one or more of the banks and financiers potentially involved, and can be aimed at supporting one or more of the organizations active in the supply chain ecosystem.

Relationships: Strategic Suppliers

International supply chains are, in effect, a network of relationships. In business as in other situations, all relationships are not created equal.

Certain suppliers within a global supply chain may provide a unique product or service, not easily sourced elsewhere, or perhaps not available on the same advantageous terms from other suppliers. Such unique inputs can be so critical that their absence, or delay in accessing them, can have serious adverse implications for the overall supply chain and for the production of the final product.

There have been numerous instances in sectors as varied as automotive, consumer electronics, aviation and others, where a relatively small supplier contributing what was seen as a minor component in an overall supply chain, proved critical to the point that disrupted access caused major negative impact on production – in some cases even outright stoppage of production lines two continents away.

Such circumstances have motivated a more considered assessment of supplier relationships, and supported an understanding of the critical importance of certain suppliers – strategic suppliers – in the health of a global supply chain and in the success of the supply chain ecosystem, including the buyer.

The notion of a strategic supplier is worth exploring in the context of trade and supply chain finance.

Companies that maintain supply chains across international jurisdictions must manage those supply chains, and ensure adequate risk mitigation and contingency plans, to minimize supply chain disruptions that could adversely impact product, sales and the overall profitability of the buyer companies.

Suppliers located in markets where natural disasters have struck, may be unable to continue to provide components – or services – to a client overseas, and in certain cases, those suppliers provide critical components that, if unavailable, can cause production to grind to a halt, and significant financial loss.

Buyers have learned to ensure adequate risk mitigation and redundancy across their supply chains, with particular attention to strategic suppliers. In addition to the extreme scenarios of natural disaster, the focus on strategic suppliers has evolved to encompass their overall commercial success, including financial strength and viability.

One of the advantages of supply chain finance programs is in the ability of large buyers to use their financial strength and borrowing capacity, to help their suppliers – especially those considered to be "strategic suppliers" – access liquidity in ways that may be much faster and more cost-effective than the supplier may be able to do, directly.

Supply chain finance, in this form, allows a small supplier to access liquidity at lower cost through the buyer's bank, on the strength of that buyer's borrowing capacity and favourable risk profile. Such structures allow the suppliers to avoid using their own (likely limited) financial resources and borrowing capacity to provide working capital in support of their export activity.

The practical application of supply chain dynamics in the financing of international trade is increasingly apparent and is increasingly shifting from evolving practice to mainstream activity.

Analysts and researchers have been suggesting that global supply chains have hundreds of billions, perhaps over a trillion dollars' worth of liquidity trapped in inefficient processes. Estimates suggest that in the UK alone, cash holdings among UK businesses were in excess of GBP 700 billion in late 2011, and that these resources, accessed through supply chain finance and by other means, could fully support the financing needs of SMEs.

Supply Chain Finance Across Sectors

Current global market conditions, characterized by ongoing restrictions on liquidity and capital in trade and in investment flows, have motivated a focus on the opportunities available to unlock working capital and liquidity through more efficient and well-targeted financing mechanisms and solutions.

Supply chain finance is increasingly recognized as one form of ecosystem-based financing that has significant potential to enhance the overall liquidity and financial health of national economies and of the global financial system.

Supply chain finance is clearly shifting from innovation to market practice. Perhaps equally importantly, the mechanisms of supply chain finance developed in the context of international commerce are increasingly seeing application in the context of domestic supply chains. More recently, leading specialists, and senior political leaders, have identified an opportunity to further extract liquidity through supply chain finance, by applying SCF mechanisms in the context of government and public sector procurement – with the objective of generating financial benefit for small and medium-sized enterprises.

The levels of utilization of supply chain finance facilities have increased from about 10 percent just three years ago, to 85 percent or more today. Even "unsuccessful" programs exhibit usage rates of 35 percent or more, with expectations that such rates of use of SCF facilities will increase further in the short term.

Supply chains are not new, and some bankers have argued that supply chain finance is, itself, nothing new.

Perhaps the important thing to note from a commercially practical perspective is that the linkage between the physical flow of goods and services, and the related financial flows, are now well established as a basis for industry practice, and that this approach offers a wide range of payment, financing and risk mitigation options, along with supporting a level of information flow that covers an ecosystem of global commercial relationships.

In addition to having direct and practical implications related to the availability of liquidity and working capital, a focus on supply chains and their network of relationships, provides a practical portal through which small suppliers with limited resources can pursue opportunities in international markets: by becoming familiar with, and pursuing, relationships with companies already linked to global supply chains.

In addition to facilitating the development of new trading relationships, a supply chain-based approach may provide an opportunity to gain access to attractive terms and financing, through participation in an existing supply chain finance program, particularly in cases where such a program is fairly mature and encompassing, extending beyond buyer and supplier, to apply to sub-suppliers and distributors, among other members of that trading ecosystem.

4

Trade and Supply Chain Finance: The Needs of Buyers and Sellers

The financing requirements of corporates and businesses can vary significantly by client segment, just as they vary on the basis of the markets in which companies are based, or operate. While it is difficult to capture nuances in generalization, there is value in understanding financing needs on the basis of a segmented view of businesses, by size and by maturity of the enterprise.

Financing Needs of SMEs

Small businesses generally operate in a reality where cash is limited, liquidity is a perpetual challenge and there are ongoing issues around access to financing. SMEs across the globe, whether in developed or developing economies, consistently identify lack of financing as a major obstacle to growth and success.

Although government agencies promote SME financing, and attempt to encourage banks to finance SME customers, the commercial conditions are such that banks tend to underserve the SME customer segment. Banks are driven by revenue and profitability targets that motivate greater focus on mid-market and large corporate clients.

From the bank point of view, SMEs require significant coaching and "hand-holding," which places demands on bank resources. Additionally, the business volumes and transaction values typically related to small business are not attractive to large financial institutions. Historically, the returns from servicing small business clients have been limited, and the opportunity cost of assigning human or financial resources to small business customers has been deemed excessive.

More recently, as liquidity issues have impacted every client segment (and the financial sector globally), the profitability of SME lending has become more attractive, and governments have increased their demands for banks to provide adequate support to small business.

The experience of SMEs in seeking to obtain trade finance is similarly difficult, though the advent of supply chain finance, with its focus on reducing the overall cost of borrowing across a global supply chain while assuring adequate liquidity for all, will mitigate the perennial financing issues faced by SMEs, particularly as they seek opportunity in international markets.

Brokers, often referred to as middlemen that leverage their contacts to help importers source goods, have specific financing requirements. Such brokers are often small businesses, perhaps one-person operations with limited financial resources; these entities play an important role in the facilitation of trade flows, and often seek financial resources through trade financing instruments and mechanisms.

Financing Mid-Market Clients

Mid-market businesses are generally in better financial state than SMEs, and generally shield their domestic operations from international ventures. The requirements of these larger, more established enterprises will tend to focus on financing and capital efficiency, as opposed to cashflow and working capital.

Mid-market companies tend to look for financing solutions in the context of international business, that offer liquidity at competitive cost, perhaps avoid impacting the company's balance sheet or eliminate the need to utilize banking facilities such as operating lines of credit.

As a company engaged in international commerce, an appreciation for the common motivators of business partners, trading counterparties and others in the trade supply and value chain can be valuable in managing relationships and in using tailored financing solutions as a competitive advantage.

Financing Large Corporates

Large corporates and multinationals, generally, are cash rich and will have optimized cashflow and working capital through sophisticated treasury and financial management strategies.

Most commonly, the largest companies are focused on effective risk mitigation perhaps more than on other aspects of trade and supply chain finance, and this includes assuring steady and trusted supply of components through effectively designed supply chain finance programs aimed at smaller suppliers.

The Impact of Time

The need for companies and businesses to secure financing relative to the conduct of international trade, relates not only to the individual financial situation of a business, but also to the timeframes involved in sourcing, producing, selling and collecting payment for goods secured in foreign markets, or shipped to a foreign market.

The conduct of business in many sectors today requires a producer and exporter to become an importer, sourcing components to production from cost-competitive markets across the globe. This reality automatically extends the order to cash cycle for exporters – the time it takes for a company to receive and order, and to be paid for that order by the buyer.

The distances involved in international commerce can result in situations where a manufacturer must halt production, incur significant cost and ill-will from customers and absorb additional losses due to legal action or the payment of penalties provided for in a commercial contract with a client, all as a result of issues or delays involving, potentially, a single small supplier in a remote location.

Understanding the potential impact of such delays, a company sourcing internationally may seek to make up for the impact of such circumstances on the importing side of their business, by seeking favourable settlement terms, or financing options resulting in accelerated payment, on the export side of their commercial activity.

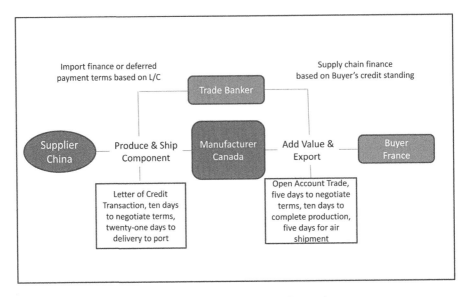

Figure 4.1   Financial flow and timeframes, L/C and open account
Source: OPUS Advisory

Buyers, ultimately required to pay for goods sourced in an international market, may conduct business on the basis of razor-thin margins, and as a result of this reality of their industry, may not have the cashflow or working capital available to make immediate payment for a shipment received from a foreign supplier.

A manufacturer may be in need of financing on both the import side and the export side of their business, as illustrated in Figure 4.1, due to cashflow constraints and extended production and settlement timeframes. The procure to pay side of the transaction, where a component is sourced from a foreign supplier, may need to be financed until the manufacturer has sold the final product to its own customer, and the order to cash side of a deal may necessitate pre-export financing, so that the exporter can cover the cost of producing and shipping the final product to its ultimate destination.

To the extent that businesses benefit from significant and multiple sources of cashflow, and can finance operations on that basis, the urgency in obtaining trade finance may be reduced; however, trade and supply chain finance options may be both compellingly efficient and cost-effective.

Competitive Realities

Exporters are once again facing a global market where competition is not only intense in terms of business development, product quality and after-sales service, but one where the shortage of liquidity engendered by the crisis has impacted companies of all sizes, in all markets.

The ability to package attractive financing proposals with a competitive product is once again a significant competitive advantage. At the same time, even the largest global buyers are becoming increasingly sensitive to the importance of a robust, secure and dependable supply chain, populated with strong, financially viable suppliers.

These developments are directly relevant to the need for companies of all sizes to engage expert assistance in structuring appropriate trade and supply chain finance solutions to meet their unique requirements.

Exporters will wish to consider options related to financing their foreign buyers, either simply by agreeing to payment at an agreed future date, or through more complex forms of financing combining numerous options. Buyers, including large importers in excellent positions in terms of cashflow, liquidity and working capital, will look to trade and supply chain finance to support the needs of key suppliers, potentially dozens of them, in multiple markets across the globe, concurrently.

Cost Constraints

Global competition, sourcing patterns and the increasing reach of international supply chains combine to create commercial scenarios where margins and profitability can be extremely thin. Under such conditions, the cost of pursuing international opportunities is an important factor for businesses of all sizes to consider.

In addition to domestic pricing strategy, an exporter must carefully assess the total cost of getting a product to the foreign market. Landed cost calculations can reveal that a product that is profitable and competitive at home becomes unviable in certain international markets.

Landed cost refers to the cost of production domestically, plus the added costs incurred in delivering the final product to the destined foreign market, which can add significantly to the total cost of the product by the time it reaches a foreign consumer.

Landed cost calculations include elements such as freight charges to destination, insurance to secure the cargo, any applicable duties or excise taxes imposed by the importing jurisdiction, fees paid to local distributors and numerous other factors, which, combined, are likely to have significant impact on the final price of the product at destination.

In some circumstances, even the fees and interest associated with the financing a trade transaction can add significant costs to the product being exported.

This is particularly true in industry sectors such as textile and garment trade and other sectors, where margins are already thin, and companies from such sectors seek to engage in business in high-risk markets.

Under certain circumstances, trade finance can be a significant contributor to the cost of conducting business in international markets. Financing costs should be carefully considered in determining the landed cost of a product in a given international market.

Successful Conclusion of a Transaction

Despite the competitive nature of international commerce, and the sometimes win/lose or zero-sum approach taken by some short-sighted executives, the majority of business leaders and entrepreneurs take a long view and aspire to success in individual trade transactions, as well as in the development of longer-term trading relationships with trusted suppliers and valued clients.

Fraud is certainly a risk, as is unethical business conduct, and attempts to use various forms of leverage in order to gain commercial advantage. In some cases, the conduct of business with companies and individuals driven by competition and the win/lose view of international commerce, may be unavoidable, and in those instances, due diligence, adequate research and appropriate risk mitigation strategies will be critical.

Cost of Financing

A specialty telecommunications technology company closed a multi-year, multi-million dollar export transaction to a new client in North Africa. Although the buyer was a government agency and therefore should have been considered a strong counterparty, the country and political risk situation, including the stability of the government itself, were in question at that time.

The company, under advice of its trade finance bankers, wisely insisted on the use of a documentary letter of credit (Letter of Credit, or L/C), and further, sought confirmation of the L/C through its own financial institution.

The size of the transaction, associated country risk and the payment timeframe of 180 days from date of shipment of the equipment, proved unacceptable to the confirming bank's central risk and credit committees as a standalone transaction. The bank succeeded in obtaining export credit insurance from the national ECA, securing 80 percent of the transaction, and was able to entice three other financial institutions to enter into a risk-sharing agreement.

The exporter had been keen to close the sale, and had agreed to be paid on a term basis, 180 days after shipment, however, the impact on cashflow and working capital was significant, and the company requested their bankers to consider discounting the receivable and to provide payment immediately upon agreement that the documentation was in full conformity with the terms and conditions in the letter of credit.

The transaction was lucrative for the exporter, however, the necessary risk mitigation measures, coupled with the characteristics of the trading relationship and the request for financing, combined in a way that the costs represented about 7 percent of the value of the transaction. The contributing factors included:

- High cost of ECA cover due to country risk
- Fees paid to other banks engaged in risk-sharing
- Expensive Confirmation Commission due to risk profile and 180-day tenor
- Expensive Acceptance Commission due to risk profile and tenor
- High interest on the discount, again due to risk and tenor

Trade finance, including traditional mechanisms such as documentary letters of credit, and supply chain finance, is most effective when trading partners are working together, in good faith, to conclude a transaction that is mutually beneficial, and to develop a positive trading relationship.

The importance of this type of goodwill cannot be overstated, even in the financial context. Likewise, the adverse impact of bad faith can be significant for one or both of the trading partners.

There are numerous ways for banks and companies familiar with the intricacies of documentary credits, for example, to take advantage of less experienced counterparties. While such practices may create short-term advantages, in the long run, they do a serious disservice to the conduct of international commerce, and very likely, raise the cost of future transactions or of the trading relationship overall.

Documentary letters of credit require an exporter to prepare and submit documents demonstrating that the transaction between buyer and seller has been executed as agreed: the goods are of the type and quality promised, the shipment has been effected in the timeframe and by the mode of transport agreed, and any other terms and conditions reflected in the letter of credit have been fully complied with.

In many cases, exporters initially submit documentation that is in some way discrepant against the terms of the Documentary Letter of Credit (also referred to as a Documentary Credit, and abbreviated as L/C or, less commonly, D/C). Estimates suggest that 60–80 percent of the time, initial presentations of documents are in some way non-compliant. While certain discrepancies can be corrected (if the exporter is provided an opportunity to make such corrections), others cannot be corrected. Examples include errors involving documents that cannot be revised, or conditions that cannot be changed once they have not been met, such as shipment of the goods after the agreed date.

When documents presented under an L/C are deemed non-compliant, the importer has the option to refuse the goods; however, by the time documents are produced, the shipment is commonly already en route, and a refusal of the shipment results in significant expense to the exporter. Refusal of the shipment requires the exporter to store the goods at the port of destination and find another buyer – generally on the basis of a significant discount aimed at minimizing losses, or imply incurring the cost of returning the goods to the port of origin. The latter option is of course not available if the shipment is perishable.

Some importers have been known to intentionally complicate L/C terms in the hope of creating discrepancies, with the objective of threatening refusal of the shipment, then demanding a significant discount to waive the discrepancies and accept the shipment.

The process of managing discrepancies is time-consuming and costly, and can delay payment, impacting cashflow and working capital. Exporters eventually become familiar with buyers who engage in such practices, and, either cease to do business with them, or simply adjust their pricing to account for the possibility of having to offer a discount on a shipment to this buyer.

Emerging practices in supply chain finance, likewise, illustrate that goodwill and the desire to conclude successful transactions – and to build high-value relationships – is fundamentally important to international commerce and to the financing that enables it.

The approach in which each party looks after their own interests and financing requirements is old school, and would be a significant competitive disadvantage compared to the more collaborative practices in evidence in many markets today.

Large buyers based in consumer markets such as the US and Europe are increasingly conscious of the opportunity to support their supplier communities in numerous ways, including through the provision of supply chain finance options. Suppliers located in remote, developing and emerging markets may encounter particularly acute shortages of liquidity, or scenarios where financing is available, but the cost is so onerous as to be commercially impractical, or so high that the final price to the buyer is adversely impacted. Importers can alleviate such issues through supply chain finance, and are increasingly prepared to do so.

Expertise and Advisory Support

Trade and supply chain finance is a technical and esoteric area of finance, and is generally not well understood, even among senior bankers.

Trade finance can involve products and transactions that are fairly routine and transactional in nature, such as basic letter of credit transactions, and some of the financing that can be arranged on the basis of an L/C. It is equally true however, that trade and supply chain finance offers numerous features and options that can be combined to meet the most complex financing and risk mitigation requirements that a company can encounter, in almost any market around the globe.

Advisory support and access to expertise is an undervalued advantage in dealing with specialists in trade and supply chain finance. Small businesses and global corporates alike can benefit from a trusted advisor relationship with their trade financiers.

Importers and exporters, even those with extensive international experience, can benefit greatly from the expertise and advisory support of trade bankers and trade financiers. Small businesses and entrepreneurial ventures are known to be actively seeking such support; however, it is increasingly the case that bankers involved in international transactions are sought after for more than the particular combination of products offered by their financial institution by clients of all sizes.

Bankers often speak of a relationship approach to their clients; in the trade space, one indicator of the sophistication of such an approach, and of the commercial acumen of trade bankers, is the degree to which they demonstrate a willingness and capability to provide tailored advisory support for importers and exporters.

Regional Variations in Financing Needs

The needs and expectations of importers and exporters can vary significantly by region, on the basis of local conditions and of common commercial practices. It can be a competitive advantage – or an effective element of a comprehensive risk management approach – to understand the practices and expectations in markets of interest.

NORTH AMERICA

North America, which includes Mexico, is a region that has long operated in the context of a free trade agreement, and one where the three neighboring countries are on positive political and commercial terms in most respects. The Canada-US border has held the distinction of being the longest undefended border in the world, and both countries have enjoyed a history of relative economic stability and growth. While Mexico did endure several crises, severe currency devaluation and currently faces a protracted drug war, the three trading partners are relatively well positioned. The ongoing crisis in the US has driven both Canada and Mexico to seek alternative markets for their exports, and to secure investment from other jurisdictions, with the intent of diversifying commercial activity and reducing dependence on the US.

The majority of trade is conducted on open account terms, and Mexico was, in the period just before the global economic crisis, making significant advances in developing supply chain and technology/platform-based trade finance options. Some export activity to Mexico has necessitated the use of export credit cover and other risk mitigation options

Canada/US trade flows involve two jurisdictions with low political and country risk; however, the significant appreciation of the Canadian dollar relative to the US currency (to parity or above at one point over the course of the global economic crisis) reshaped the trading environment significantly, forcing Canadian exporters to compete on factors other than a price advantage. While the US dollar did regain a relatively stronger position eventually, the long-familiar 35–40 percent difference that provided a competitive advantage – or a source of attractive margin – to Canadian exporters evaporated in relatively short order.

The dynamics and context around international commerce can change significantly, even among established markets and trading partners.

EUROPE

Europe, and particularly the European Union, is both a political union and an economic union, with numerous infrastructure elements increasingly integrated and centralized, however, the EU is far from homogenous, and far from fully integrated. Local jurisdictions and commercial practices continue to have significant impact on the conduct of trade, and recent figures indicate that about 65 percent of trade flows are intra-EU.

Importers and exporters in the region tend to favour trade on open account terms, and the role of SMEs is perhaps more central to certain economies in Europe than elsewhere. The export-driven German economy relies heavily on the *mittelstand*: small to medium-sized family businesses, widely recognized as the engines of the German economy, so successful in weathering the global economic crisis that other jurisdictions have sought to emulate the model.

Post-global crisis, the EU has faced a very serious sovereign and country-risk crisis, with several economies on the brink of collapse, requiring decisive, unprecedented financial support and intervention from other members of the EU and from the European Central Bank. The future of the euro, and of the European Union itself was in question at the peak of the sovereign crisis, and corporate finance executives spoke publicly about the reality that certain EU economies had become the equivalent of high-risk emerging markets.

The EU crisis served to once again bring the risk mitigation aspect of trade finance very much into focus, and to help reaffirm the importance of the contributions of export credit agencies in enabling global commerce.

The trade finance executive at a major European automotive manufacturer noted that it was the norm, pre-crisis, to consider OECD markets to be relatively low-risk, but that more recently, certain OECD countries had taken on risk profiles comparable to those of developing economies. This shift has had direct impact on trade and supply chain financing strategies.

ASIA

Asia encompasses a variety of markets with a range of experience and requirements around trade finance. Hong Kong has long been a centre of expertise in traditional trade finance, and Indian banks, likewise, are adept at the mechanisms of trade finance, as are other markets.

Financing has been a core element of value in trade finance, with financial institutions in Japan and elsewhere, prepared to accept documentary L/Cs as collateral for other finance facilities. South Korea was an early adopter and leader in terms of online and technology-based trade activity, including financing.

Japan and South Korea are economies characterized by groups of affiliated companies engaging in a wide range of commercial activity, including international commerce, and the needs of those entities relative to the financing of international activity can be significant, but may also be unique in their affiliate character, as well as in the close connection to a company's primary financial institution.

Indonesia, Trade and the Asian Flu

The more difficult the macroeconomic environment and the more precarious the situation of the financial institutions, the more risk averse they become. In this sense, an unstable macroeconomic environment is an additional barrier for SME access to finance. The experience during the Asian crisis of the late 1990s illustrates this difficulty, which is now being experienced in other countries.

For trade finance instruments that rely on banks, such as L/Cs, financial crises that affect trust among financial counterparties can have a paralyzing effect on trade. L/Cs are important in enabling trade in certain markets, and their proper functioning depends on a level of trust between financial institutions. L/Cs represent a payment undertaking, and all parties to a transaction must trust such undertakings for the process to function. In higher-risk markets, a second level of undertaking, referred to as confirmation of an L/C, requires even greater trust between financial institutions. Confirmation of an L/C has similar effect to a guarantee in that the confirming bank accepts to make payment, trusting it will be able to recover funds from the issuing bank.

But when financial institutions do not have confidence in the stability of the importer's country or in the standing of the financial institution issuing the L/C, confirmed L/Cs become very difficult and expensive – sometimes impossible – to obtain. During the Asian crisis, Indonesian banks had difficulty getting foreign counterparties to confirm the L/Cs they issued on behalf of Indonesian importers because of doubt over the stability of the entire Indonesian financial system.

In times like these, national or multilateral support in terms of export credit guarantees can help break the logjam. In the case of Indonesia, the central bank had to step in to guarantee Indonesian bank-issued L/Cs by depositing US $1 billion of its foreign reserves offshore and using it as guarantee. Some relatively stable Indonesian banks, likewise, made deposits in foreign banks and used those deposits as cash collateral for their L/Cs. Without these steps, foreign banks would not confirm L/Cs from Indonesian banks. Without confirmed L/Cs, Indonesian importers could not import needed raw materials. (Source: "How to Access Trade Finance," ITC Geneva)

China has emerged as a global economic power, and the financing needs of businesses have shifted significantly over the last 15 years or more, from being largely L/C driven due to perceived risk, to being increasingly conducted on open account, due partly to the commercial leverage of Chinese authorities and companies, including numerous state-owned enterprises that are very active in trade and in foreign investment.

The rise of the renminbi (RMB) as currency of regional and international commerce has had – and will continue to have – direct impact on trade financing options, and the related currency risk profile of such transactions. The growth rate of RMB adoption is significant, though government policy in China has been to take a gradual and deliberate approach to the appreciation of the currency and its adoption as a currency of international commerce.

Trade financing requirements involving markets in Asia will cover the full range of options. While certain economies are export driven, and recognize the central role of their SME sector, others exhibit strong contributions from large corporates and multinationals.

The asset quality of Chinese banks is an area of concern that is being monitored, and as such, while the banking sector is clearly in growth mode, and in international expansion mode, there may be a need to ensure adequate mitigation of bank risk, particularly when dealing with second-tier financial institutions. The offsetting reality, of course, is that the role of the government offers a degree of assurance that banks are less likely to fail in meeting international obligations.

The emergence of economies such as Indonesia, Malaysia and Vietnam, among others, will drive the next phase of growth in the region, and trade finance requirements will vary with each market, with international institutions such as the Asian Development Bank continuing to play an important role in the facilitation of trade flows and trade financing, covering a wide range of markets, including newly emerging Myanmar.

MIDDLE EAST AND NORTH AFRICA (MENA)

The Middle East, including North Africa, has exhibited an enduring loyalty to the traditional mechanisms of trade finance, in particular, the documentary L/C.

While most of the globe showed a clear shift to open account terms, the MENA region stood out, pre-crisis, as an area where traditional trade

> The fundamentals of trade and supply chain finance may be consistent on a global basis – hence the success of these mechanisms in such a wide range of markets and commercial conditions, however markets do exhibit certain differentiating characteristics, and by extension, differing nuances in terms of trade finance needs.
>
> Entrepreneurs and business executives must be aware of the unique requirements of the markets in which they aim to conduct business – including the general level of expertise and competency around trade finance.

instruments and practices remained robust – perhaps even the preferred option for the conduct of international trade.

Leading economies in the region are shaped by businesses and commercial ventures that are family owned and/or closely linked, and the region has long relied on name lending and financing based on reputation and various networks and linkages.

As international banks and other institutions are becoming more active in the region, and as financial norms and practices continue to evolve and align on a global basis, certain traditional practices are giving way to modes of doing business that are more consistent with those in other parts of the world.

Local events in the last several years, including large defaults by prominent families and businesses, have motivated a call for greater financial and commercial transparency, and for the introduction of credit bureaux and for credit analysis and reporting disciplines, together with greater reliance on audited financial statements and other objective and verifiable financial information.

At the same time, the disciplines and practices of Islamic finance, including specifically, Islamic trade finance, have shielded the region from direct exposure to the toxic mortgage assets originating in the US, and have allowed businesses in the MENA region to develop robust regional trade flows as one dimension of their growth and recovery strategy.

The MENA region provides an excellent illustration of the near-universal applicability to trade financing mechanisms and practices, including global rules such as the Uniform Customs and Practice for Documentary Credits, or the UCP. Numerous markets in the MENA region (and Asia) are governed by Islam-based Shari'ah law, in the context of which, a specific form of Islamic finance – including Islamic trade finance – guides the conduct of business.

The disciplines and practices of Islamic banking and finance are best left to specialists in this domain; however, at a high level, we can observe that jurisdictions where Islamic finance governs banking relationships, the impact of the global financial crisis (and the questionable financial instruments that triggered it) was significantly lower than elsewhere, because of the guiding principles of Shari'ah law, including the imperative that a financial transaction be linked directly and clearly to an underlying flow of goods or services and that speculative transactions are discouraged, even deemed unacceptable by Islamic finance standards.

Purists will point out that Islamic finance, including Islamic trade finance, does not permit the charging or collection of interest, and that the nature of the lender/borrower relationship is perhaps more akin to a commercial partnership or merchant banking arrangement than such relationships in other jurisdictions. Whether a transaction is structured on the basis of a mark-up (*murabaha*) or on the basis of profit or loss-sharing (*musharaka*), the practices, products and solutions of trade and supply chain finance are applicable and effective in the context of Shari'ah-based transactions.

Trade and financial flows, and the opportunity to undertake attractive business, are such that numerous non-Islamic banks and institutions have demonstrated a desire to develop competencies and capabilities in Islamic banking and Islamic trade finance.

AFRICA

Africa, like the MENA region, exhibits strong post-crisis growth rates particularly in leading economies, driven partly by regional trade activity and partly by a significant influx of resource-aimed inward investment from China and elsewhere.

The use of traditional, particularly risk-mitigated, trade financing mechanisms remains prevalent in business involving markets in Africa. The relatively recent launch of a trade finance program at the African Development Bank illustrates the growing appreciation for the importance of robust trade in the region.

Access to affordable liquidity and to timely risk mitigation remains a perennial challenge in Africa due to the risk profile of many markets – a combination of sovereign risk, bank risk and commercial risk – and as such, specific efforts have been made to assist businesses in Africa to link to international supply chains as a means of developing export markets, and as a way of accessing relatively affordable financing.

Trade in Africa is often linked to poverty reduction and international development activity, and as such, may benefit from an additional layer of financing support through development finance institutions or international development agencies, including the International Trade Centre in Geneva, that has developed financing programs aimed specifically at sectors of economic value creation in selected markets.

5

Financing Trade: Selected Concepts and Traditional Solutions

Trade finance has remained largely unchanged for decades, until a near-global shift to open account trade settlement motivated – even forced – banks and other major providers to reconsider their approach and their value proposition to clients.

Traditional trade finance products and mechanisms remain relevant, even important, to the flow of international commerce. At the same time, new propositions have been developed around the preferences of importers and exporters, and devised specifically in light of business needs in the context of international supply chains.

Some industry specialists have argued that "new" trade finance solutions offered in response to open account trade, and labeled "supply chain finance" involve nothing more than a re-packaging of existing and long-familiar banking products. Others suggest that the approach to trade financing has evolved, and that even a re-packaging of existing products in new ways, offers additional options to importers and exporters.

Traditional trade finance versus supply chain finance: Which is a subset of which? How do they relate? Ultimately, the key for companies pursuing opportunities in international markets is that there are a variety of potential products and solutions available to meet a wide range of business needs. The name of the solution and the way one solution relates to another, may evolve, and may even differ among banks or other providers. The key is to be aware of the options and to be sufficiently conversant about them to determine which best meets business requirements at a given moment.

In any event, a review of traditional and emerging trade finance solutions and the various propositions around trade finance is a worthwhile exercise, and has practical implications for the way businesses of all sizes approach trade finance.

The fundamental questions around financing international commerce remain the same, and are shaped by the same business objectives.

Barring any imbalance in a trading relationship, or some form of advantage held by one partner over another, importers and exporters generally agree on financing and settlement terms prior to contracting, and tend to reflect such agreement in contract terms.

The maturity (and therefore trust) of a relationship between buyer and seller is a critical factor in determining how best to structure a trade financing and settlement solution; likewise, the experience and expertise of a trading partner in the conduct of international business can influence the agreed structure of a transaction. Macro-factors, such as country risk, will also contribute to decisions around the most appropriate trade financing approach, as shown in Figure 5.1.

Long-established trading partnerships involving (what are deemed to be) lower-risk markets, for example, will tend to suggest trade finance solutions that emphasize cost-effective financing and timely settlement, whereas newer relationships, or those that exist in the context of high-risk markets, will put significantly more focus on effective (and potentially expensive) mitigation of risk.

Every relationship is different, and every deal can have unique characteristics, however, general observations can be instructive.

Established relationships underpinned by trust, which has been developed over time and as a result of multiple successful transactions, where both trading partners exhibit competence (even expertise) in international commerce, and where the markets involved are relatively low risk, will tend to come together to motivate a focus on payment or financing, as opposed to risk mitigation.

It is true that certain circumstances – well-established, expert and trusted relationships – will combine with high-risk context and still demand a sharp focus on risk mitigation: the specific, optimal combination of trade and supply

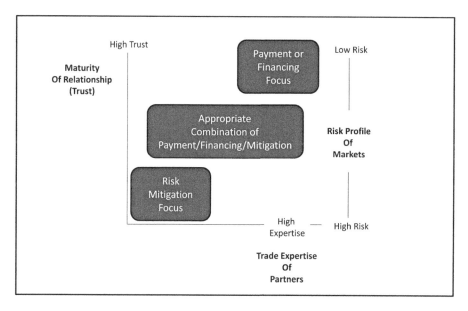

Figure 5.1   Trust and expertise in trade relationships
Source: OPUS Advisory

chain finance features will vary and are best tailored to the conditions around a particular transaction or relationship.

Traditional trade finance offers a series of mechanisms and solutions to importers and exporters, to meet a wide variety of commercial circumstances, in the widest variety of contexts, including nearly every economy on the globe, every legal jurisdiction in existence and the full spectrum of economic conditions encountered in history.

As noted earlier, there are circumstances where one partner may exercise greater influence or leverage in shaping a business relationship: a large global importer dealing with small suppliers, and as a result of sheer relative size, in a position to define commercial terms; a supplier with a unique, patented or difficult-to-access product, likewise, can make demands about the terms of a trading relationship.

Certain traditional instruments such as LCs have evolved a series of features that have made these instruments very effective across a wide variety of circumstances, and have made them resilient despite decades of prediction that these long-established tools of trade were nearing "extinction" as a trusted mechanism of international commerce.

Numerous settlement options are available to companies engaged in international commerce, and each option, typically, implies a different level of protection and therefore, a different level of risk for each trading partner. Before exploring some of those traditional mechanisms, it is worth reviewing certain concepts and definitions commonly used in trade and supply chain finance.

Selected Concepts/Definitions

Established trade finance instruments are effective in part because of their use of widely understood and accepted practices, language and techniques. A few such common definitions and concepts are worth exploring to set some context around traditional trade financing instruments and mechanisms.

MARKET PRACTICE/CUSTOMS AND PRACTICE

Certain instruments and mechanisms such as Documentary Collections and Documentary Letters of Credit are effective because their use and interpretation is guided by a common set of rules, to which countries, organizations and businesses, have agreed to be bound. The International Chamber of Commerce (ICC) in Paris has played a fundamental and longstanding role in drafting such quasi-regulations and in promoting widespread adherence to related commercial practices.

The ICC began publishing the "Uniform Customs and Practice for Documentary Credits" since 1933. This set of rules, referred to as the UCP, are adhered to by most countries on the globe, and set out in detail, the roles and responsibilities of parties agreeing to use documentary letters of credit (explicitly issued subject to UCP).

The UCP are now so central to the use of documentary credits that the articles that comprise the UCP have effectively been granted the force of law in numerous jurisdictions, by being incorporated in legal precedents, decisions and judgments. This is particularly the case in common law jurisdictions such as the UK and Canada among others, but the articles of the UCP are equally important in guiding the use of documentary letters of credit in legal traditions ranging from Shari'ah law to legal systems across every continent on the globe.

Specialists at the ICC, particularly the ICC Banking Commission, publish guiding commentary to assist bankers, international traders, courts and other interested parties in interpreting the intentions of the ICC and of the various articles of the UCP. The process of managing these articles, updating them roughly every 10 years and otherwise assuring the effective functioning of documentary letters of credit, involves significant effort, wide-ranging consultations and extensive financial and legal expertise.

The latest version of UCP, version 600, came into effect in July of 2007, following a drafting process that began in 2003, and involved a nine-member drafting committee, a 41-member consultative committee from 26 countries, a review of 15 drafts and over 5,000 sets of comments. Copies of the UCP can be obtained directly from the ICC, or through most financial institutions involved in the provision of trade finance.

The ICC publishes similar sets of rules for other instruments important in the conduct of international trade, including the Uniform Rules for Collections, the Uniform Rules for Demand Guarantees and numerous others, most recently agreeing with SWIFT to collaborate on the publication, promotion and adoption of a set of rules governing the use of a technology-based trade mechanism referred to as the Bank Payment Obligation (BPO).

TIMING OF PAYMENT

Timing is a fundamental concept of finance, and one of the important factors in planning adequate financial resources in the conduct of international trade.

The pursuit of commerce across borders tends to extend the time required to close a sale, as well as the time required to complete a transaction and finalize payment. Commercial and payment terms are consequently, even more important considerations than they are in purely domestic transactions.

The timing of payment can be arranged to suit the needs of importers and exporters, and can be varied over the course of a transaction to meet otherwise conflicting objectives, such as the desire of exporters to be paid as soon as feasible, and the preference of importers to delay disbursement.

An exporter requiring payment 30 days after an invoice has been taken up for payment by the importer or buyer must be aware of various financing options and mechanisms to meet their objectives, if the importer proposes payment at 120 days after the bill of lading date.

Both parties can simultaneously achieve their respective objectives by effectively structuring the transaction, and utilizing various financing and settlement mechanisms available through trade and supply chain finance. The exporter can be paid within 30 days, while the importer can delay their obligation to pay by 120, through the support of financiers and intermediaries like trade finance banks.

PAYMENT AT SIGHT

The expression "Payment at Sight" is used in the context of trade finance, particularly in relation to traditional instruments such as letters of credit, to mean that payment is made when a bank receives compliant documents (sees them, hence the expression "At Sight") under a letter of credit. In practical terms, banks are permitted a reasonable time to conduct the customary verifications and to complete internal processes before issuing payment, so that an exporter may still wait a few days, perhaps a week, before typically receiving funds due.

TERM (USANCE) PAYMENT

An exporter may offer favourable terms to a buyer or importer, by agreeing to payment at some future date, such as "60 Days Sight" or "60 Days After Sight" of the documents by a bank, which then sets the due date or "Maturity Date" for payment.

Payment may also be agreed on the basis of a triggering event, such as the loading on board of a shipment onto a vessel for transport to the importer, or the date of issuance of a bill of lading or other transport document, again evidencing that the shipment has been taken in charge and is or has been shipped.

Generally, documents presented by the exporter will include a legally recognized instrument called a Draft (similar but not identical to a bank draft) that represents the existence of a financial obligation. When buyer and seller agree to settlement at a future date, the Draft is endorsed and a due date for payment, or a Maturity Date, is determined according to the agreed terms of the transaction. Such a draft is deemed to have been Accepted, creating a Banker's Acceptance which can then be discounted, sold into the market for such instruments or held for payment at maturity.

A Term Payment in effect allows the importer to delay payment as agreed; the exporter may ask that such an obligation be discounted for immediate payment, and in so doing, will incur fees and interest according to the risk assessment and practices of the bank effecting the discount.

RECOURSE VERSUS NON-RECOURSE

Financing can be extended With Recourse or Without Recourse. A loan or financing provided With Recourse implies that the lender can come back to the borrower to claim the money leant, in the event that the lender cannot collect from the party ultimately responsible for payment of the financial obligation. If a bank finances an exporter by providing immediate payment, but is unable for some reason to collect the monies from the importer on the due date, for example, the bank can revert to the exporter to claim the monies back.

A loan provided Without Recourse, or on a Non-Recourse Basis is one in which the lender takes the full risk of non-payment by the party that owes the funds being advanced or financed, and that the borrower, having paid the agreed fees and interest, faces no further risk from any downstream complications.

The distinction is critical to a borrower; while financing with recourse is typically less expensive, since the lender can come back to the borrower, it may be worth the extra fees and/or interest to the borrower, to arrange non-recourse financing, in order to avoid any subsequent liability in the event of non-payment by the party that ultimately must settle the invoice or financial obligation.

In Non-Recourse financing, an exporter can be financed, and need not worry about whether the importer will ultimately pay the lending institution, or whether the importer might be forced into bankruptcy, causing the lender to seek a refund from the exporter. The lender takes these risks directly.

Factoring is a type of financing where an exporter can sell an invoice that has been accepted for payment by an importer to a third party called a factor.

The invoice is typically sold at a discount to its value, perhaps as much as 20 percent, when an exporter requires cashflow and prefers to avoid any risk (or recovery costs) associated with non-payment of that invoice. The cost of a factoring transaction can be significant, but may be worthwhile, particularly if the factoring transaction is concluded Without Recourse.

The structure and cost of factoring transactions can vary significantly by market; this type of financing is more common in Europe than in some other markets, for example, and may involve a flat fee plus some amount based on the tenor of the financed receivable, and may in the end represent a margin of 3–8 percent per annum for the factor.

GOODWILL AND TRADE

Goodwill and a sincere desire to do business are fundamental to the effective and efficient functioning of the mechanisms of trade and trade finance. Even the most secure instruments rely to a significant extent on a desire between buyer and seller to work together to ensure the successful conclusion of a transaction.

In the context of documentary letters of credit, for example, banks have an obligation to engage in a process of verification of documents against the terms and conditions of the letter of credit, but the verification process is limited to checking documents on their face – only in very specific circumstances, such as apprehension of fraud, or suspicion of money-laundering, terrorist financing or related issues, are the banks expected to undertake greater scrutiny.

Certain processes in trade and trade finance are subject to manipulation by one or other trading party: practices that some view as "street smart" and commercially competitive, and others perceive as short-sighted and self-sabotaging. In the end, such practices slow the process and often result in inflated costs, to questionable net benefit.

INCOTERMS

International Commercial Terms, known commonly as INCOTERMS, play an important role in defining the basis upon which a trade transaction is concluded, particularly the points at which ownership of (and therefore the risk related to) the cargo shifts from seller to buyer, the party responsible for arranging insurance, and the point to which delivery must be effected.

INCOTERMS are published by the ICC in Paris and updated periodically to reflect evolutions in business practice. The latest version of INCOTERMS was published in 2010.

The definition of the point of transfer of ownership of a shipment – perhaps as early as at the production facility of the exporter, or as late as the final point of destination in the importing country, can have direct implications related to financing options, particularly if the bank or financier wishes to retain control of the cargo to secure a financing facility. In the event the exporter is being financed through to receipt of final payment and the bank wishes to maintain control of the cargo; for example, it would be unlikely that the INCOTERM selected, would be one that transfers ownership of the shipment to the importer, early in the lifecycle of the transaction.

A CONTINUUM OF SETTLEMENT OPTIONS

Trade and supply chain finance provide a variety of payment, settlement and therefore financing options for companies engaged in international commerce. The following graphic, Figure 5.2, illustrates the common options on a continuum, showing which tends to be more risky for one partner and less for the other, as illustrated.

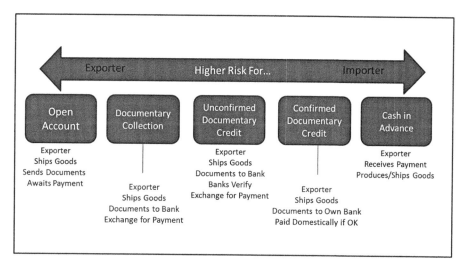

Figure 5.2   Settlement options
Source: OPUS Advisory

TRADE ON OPEN ACCOUNT

Trade on Open Account typically involves high risk for the exporter, because the contracted goods are produced and shipped to the buyer, with all production and shipping costs incurred by the exporter. The exporter then sends shipping documents to the importer, in effect, relinquishing control of the goods, as the documents typically include the commercial invoice, the (Marine) Bill of Lading and other documents that represent control and/or ownership of the goods shipped.

Once the documents are sent across, and the exporter has effectively lost control of the shipment, upon receipt of the shipping documents, the buyer/importer typically has everything necessary to claim the goods from customs and take possession of the shipment. In the end, trading on Open Account offers zero protection to the exporter, and exposes the exporter to fraud in the form of non-payment.

The importer, by contrast, incurs no cost and no risk, gains early control and ownership of the goods, and has an opportunity to inspect the goods in great detail, ensuring that the shipment was precisely as contracted.

It is a near-global shift in trading patterns to open account terms that motivated (forced) banks to devise trade settlement and financing solutions related to trade on open account terms, under the umbrella of supply chain finance.

DOCUMENTARY COLLECTIONS

Trading partners with a certain degree of trust, in markets involving acceptable levels of risk for both parties, but still wishing to engage bankers as intermediaries, can avail themselves of a long-established instrument called a Documentary Collection, the flow of which is shown in Figure 5.3.

In this instance, importers and exporters seek to better balance the protection available to each trading partner, by using their respective bankers as intermediaries, facilitating an exchange of shipping documents, for payment or for a promise of payment at an agreed (and legally binding) future date. It is worth noting that Documentary Collections do not obligate a bank to make payment, in the way that Documentary Credits do.

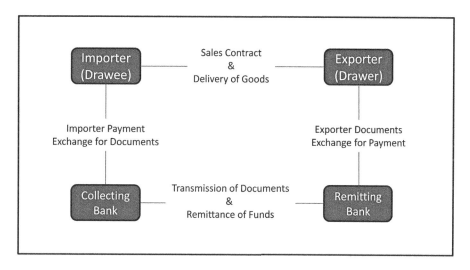

Figure 5.3   Documentary Collection
Source: OPUS Advisory

Documentary Collections are relatively affordable banking instruments, where financial institutions play a limited role in facilitating trade-related settlement and financing, with limited focus on risk mitigation. It must be noted that banks do not engage in any verification, other than to assure the correct number and sets of documents have been presented by the exporter.

In some instances, the process can be accelerated by using a Direct Collection where only one bank serves as intermediary, taking on both the role of Collecting Bank and Remitting Bank.

Documentary Letters of Credit are legally binding financial obligations of the issuing bank.

In some cases, the Issuing Bank will be required to honor the payment obligation despite the fact that the commercial interests of their client – the importer – would be better served if the payment were not affected. One such situation arises in the trade of highly price-volatile commodities: if the commodity suddenly became significantly less expensive, an importer might actively seek ways to avoid completing a transaction. If an Exporter has met all conditions in the L/C however, the Issuing Bank must respect its obligations.

The importer and exporter sign a contract covering the shipment of goods, defining the specific characteristics of the goods, timing of shipment, payment and other commercial terms, including agreement to transact on the basis of a Documentary Collection.

Once the goods have been produced and readied for shipment, the exporter collects all the documents necessary/agreed to trigger payment or a commitment to pay at an agreed future date. The exporter presents documents to the collecting bank, where the documents are counted to ensure the correct set (and the agreed number of originals and copies) have been submitted.

The collecting bank then sends the documents to the remitting bank, requesting payment (or acceptance/agreement to pay at an agreed future date). The remitting bank ultimately sends monies due to the collecting bank, and passes the shipping documents along to the Importer. In this way, the Importer receives documents (and control/ownership of the goods) at the time a payment has been made or the timing for payment has been agreed, based upon the sales contract.

Documentary Collections and their use are guided by the ICC-published Uniform Rules for Collections.

DOCUMENTARY LETTERS OF CREDIT

Documentary Letters of Credit, also referred to as Documentary Credits, Letters of Credit or L/Cs, provide a balance of security for both the importer and the exporter. The use of a feature called Confirmation, or a Confirmed Letter of Credit, provides even further security to the exporter, by adding an additional payment promise to the basic instrument, to the benefit of the exporter.

As illustrated in Figure 5.4, a Letter of Credit is applied for by the importer through their bank, and issued in favour of the exporter, typically transmitted through the exporter's bank (or at least, a bank located in the exporter's home country). Once issued, the L/C represents a legally binding payment undertaking of the issuing bank, to the exporter.

The instrument is popular, because it provides the exporter with the comfort of a bank's financial obligation, in lieu of an obligation from a foreign-based buyer – the conventional view being that a bank will be more financial stable and perhaps more trustworthy, as a party on which to rely for payment.

The notion of Credit Enhancement is based on the expectation, largely accurate in pre-crisis times, that banks are financially stronger than many commercial ventures.

The addition of a Confirmation to a letter of credit is the process whereby an additional and legally separate payment undertaking is added to the L/C, with the objective of providing additional security to the exporter. There are (many) situations where an exporter may be uncomfortable with a payment promise from a foreign financial institution. This includes discomfort with the standing and/or reputation of the foreign financial institution, or concern about the political stability of the buyer's market, where payment might be delayed or prevented outright, in the event of some form of local crisis. The exporter may ask that the Letter of Credit be issued with the option of adding a Confirmation – this would be a payment promise by a trusted financial institution based in the exporter's country – most often the exporter's bank.

While a Letter of Credit has numerous features, there is in many situations, an ultimate reliance on the Issuing Bank for final payment to take place. A confirmed L/C allows the exporter to obtain payment domestically from a trusted financial institution, avoiding all of the risk linked to doing business with the importer, the foreign Issuing Bank and the importer's home market.

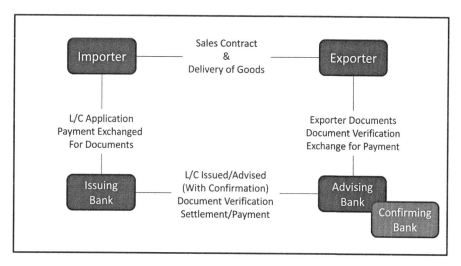

Figure 5.4   Documentary letter of credit
Source: OPUS Advisory

L/Cs can be expensive relative to the profit margins of many types of business. They involve paper and a poorly understood process that is perceived to be complex and prone to error. These instruments, while resilient, effective and long-used in international commerce, are unpopular among most companies engaged in trade.

The importer and exporter agree the terms of their transaction in a sales contract, including the mode and specifics of payment and financing. Having agreed to the use of a letter of credit, the Importer completes an application for a letter of credit, specifying the terms and conditions of the letter of credit in the application form. Such terms include the documents to be prepared and presented by the exporter for payment, and things like the latest shipment date, and the routing of shipment as well as the mode of transport, and any insurance to be arranged.

An L/C is a payment undertaking by the bank that issues the instrument. Accordingly, the bank will review the application (often assist the Importer in completing the application form) to ensure that they, as an institution, are comfortable with the instrument – and related terms and conditions – once issued on the basis of the application process.

It is critical to note that the L/C is an obligation of the Issuing Bank, and there are circumstances where the Issuing Bank, in meeting its legal and industry-level obligations under the L/C might well act in a manner that counteracts the interests of the Importer, despite the fact that the Importer is a client of the Issuing Bank.

Once the application is approved and the L/C is issued, it is typically transmitted via the SWIFT network, to another financial institution referred to as the Advising Bank – the bank selected (typically by the exporter) to receive the transmission, confirm its authenticity and ultimately advise it or make it available to the exporter.

The advising bank is expected also to review the terms and conditions of the Letter of Credit, and to work with the exporter to ensure that its terms can be successfully met, or if there is some doubt, that the terms be revised through an Amendment to the L/C. In some cases, for example, the issuance of an L/C may be unexpectedly delayed, such that the exporter is unable to arrange shipment by the specified latest shipment date, or is unable to avail of the L/C prior to its expiry date.

A Letter of Credit: Just Like Cash?

It has been suggested that once an exporter holds a Documentary Letter of Credit in their favour, this is the equivalent of holding cash, so familiar are these instruments and so trusted are the related processes.

The reality however, is that L/Cs provide protection to exporters only in the event that all the terms and conditions enumerated in the L/C have been fully met. Absent this reality, such instruments provide protection only to the extent that the importer continues to seek successful conclusion of the transaction.

Exporters must take an active role in defining and agreeing to the terms of an L/C to maximize their chances of fully meeting those requirements. Globally, it is estimated that 60–70 percent of drawings (requests for payment) under L/Cs are non-compliant, and therefore leave the exporters fully exposed to financial loss, perhaps amounting to the full value of the shipment. In the Nordic region, the rates of non-compliance have been reported to be as high as 80 percent or more.

Letters of Credit ought not to be treated as cash: exporters must understand the strengths and the limitations of such instruments.

It is worth noting, however, that in some markets, Japan being one example, letters of credit are sufficiently trusted by bankers to be used by the Beneficiary as collateral for other facilities or financing.

If all is well, the credit is advised to the exporter, and the exporter proceeds to prepare the goods, ready them for shipment, and gather the documents necessary to demonstrate that the terms of the L/C have been fully met, so that payment may be claimed. Documents typically required of the exporter include:

- Draft

- Commercial invoice

- Ppacking list

- Bill of lading/transport document

- Customs invoice

- Inspection certificate

- Insurance certificate

It is critically important to the exporter that all terms and conditions specified in the L/C be fully and clearly complied with. The description of the goods on the commercial invoice, in particular, must match – verbatim – the description in the Letter of Credit. A typographical difference between the two descriptions, even if the L/C is incorrect and the invoice is accurate, is considered a discrepancy, and the drawing, or request for payment is deemed non-compliant.

Proper practice requires the banks verifying documents to make the determination about whether documents are compliant or discrepant. Where discrepancies can be legitimately corrected within the applicable deadlines, the advising bank may work with the exporter to identify such issues and provide an opportunity for corrected documents to be presented.

Though discouraged by the ICC and others, it is also fairly common practice for the importer's bank (the issuing bank) to receive documents from the advising bank, and invite the importer to check the documents prior to communicating a finding to the advising bank. The importer can then influence the settlement process, either waiving frivolous discrepancies and expediting settlement, or deeming the documents discrepant. In the latter case, the importer can refuse the shipment outright, or use the threat of refusal (and significant expense to the exporter) as a way to demand significant discount from the exporter.

Banks can, and often do, disagree on what constitutes a discrepancy; the high rates of discrepancy globally have prompted banks and other service providers to develop automated solutions to the preparation of shipping documents.

The verification of documents presented under a Letter of Credit is the purview of trade finance operations specialists, and involves a combination of clear guidelines and professional judgment. Certain banks follow an approach referred to as Strict Compliance, where any discrepancy is identified and called by the bank. Other institutions are guided by the principle of Material or Substantial Compliance, where only discrepancies deemed significant to the commercial undertaking are identified, and frivolous discrepancies are ignored.

SPECIAL TERMS/FEATURES OF LETTERS OF CREDIT

Documentary Letters of Credit are extremely versatile in their ability to address a wide variety of commercial requirements for both the importer and the exporter. Several special terms or features that can be incorporated into an L/C are worth exploring, to illustrate the flexibility of these long-established instruments of trade finance.

CONFIRMATION OR CONFIRMED LETTER OF CREDIT

As noted earlier, an L/C can be issued with the instruction/option to confirm the credit.

This process involves a bank, typically the Advising Bank in the exporter's country, adding its own separate and distinct payment undertaking (Confirmation) to the letter of credit. The purpose of this is to provide the exporter with the right to present documents to the Confirming Bank, and, if they are fully compliant, to claim payment directly from the Confirming Bank, avoiding any risk associated with the importer, the Issuing Bank and any country risk issues linked to the importing country.

Confirmation also removes the exporter from any impact of disagreement between banks, about whether a set of documents are compliant or not: the decision made by the Confirming Bank is the one that concerns the exporter, provided documents are in order.

Requesting a Confirmation can be seen as a sign of lack of trust or confidence on the part of the exporter, and as such, may be offensive to a new importer client.

Relationship issues of this nature may motivate an exporter to seek a "silent" or "blind" Confirmation from their bankers – a Confirmation that is added to an L/C without the knowledge of the Issuing Bank or the importer.

This is a risky proposition for the Confirming Bank, and the option is not widely offered, and is generally only provided to well-established customers of the Confirming Bank.

A Confirmation involves the Confirming Bank assessing and accepting the risk associated with the importing country and the Issuing Bank, since the Confirming Bank ultimately claims monies back from the Issuing Bank, and must be comfortable about the likelihood of being repaid by that institution.

This is a credit/risk decision for the Confirming Bank; in many cases, a bank requested to add its Confirmation to an L/C will have limits or lines of credit available covering the importing country, as well as the issuing bank, and can promptly indicate its willingness to confirm the credit, indicating the fees associated with doing so. Confirmation charges are generally borne by the exporter.

Banks maintain credit facilities – or "lines" for other banks with which they have correspondent relationships, as well as for countries with/in which they expect or aspire to do business. The limits on those facilities are typically set and managed by central credit groups, or may be managed on a delegated basis, by business areas such as trade finance units.

In certain cases, where the country risk or the Issuing Bank risk are unacceptable to the bank requested to provide Confirmation, the bank may decline to do so. Where country or bank limits have been fully utilized, or cannot accommodate the value of the L/C, the confirming bank must make the case in favour of doing the deal, and secure internal approval, typically from a central credit committee at the bank.

This is relevant to an exporter, because such considerations impact the speed with which a Confirmation may be provided, and by extension, the speed with which an exporter can begin to prepare the shipment, and present the relative documents to the Confirming Bank. In the worst case, a refusal to confirm an L/C may require the exporter to approach another financial institution to ask about the possibility of confirming the L/C, or perhaps to make the business decision of accepting the risk of using an unconfirmed L/C.

In the event that a bank or country risk is deemed elevated, a confirming bank may purchase risk insurance from an export credit agency or a private underwriter. The cost of such coverage, which protects against non-payment to the confirming bank, is passed along to the exporter, and can be quite significant, therefore, should be accounted for in the exporter's pricing to the importer.

Silent or Blind Confirmation

The initiation and development of a trading relationship can be a sensitive process, requiring a combination of commercial acumen and diplomatic finesse.

While banks and companies understand the need to adequately manage risk, and most experienced parties appreciate that risk is a combination of objective reality and subjective perception, it is possible to unintentionally offend a new trading partner by suggesting that risk mitigation in the form of a Confirmed Letter of Credit is a requirement of doing business.

The trading partner may take offense at a request from an exporter to allow for Confirmation of a Letter of Credit, interpreting this as a form of mistrust, and a negative reflection on their bankers and/or their country.

The desire to maintain a positive tone in the trading relationship, and avoid causing offense, is one motivation for an exporter to request a silent confirmation – one where their trade bankers add a separate but secret payment undertaking to a letter of credit. The confirmation is arranged between exporter and banker, without the knowledge of the importer or the Issuing Bank.

Such arrangements are not supported under the ICC rules, and a bank extending a Silent Confirmation does so generally only for well-known and valued clients, given the relative risk and exposure involved.

TRANSFERABLE AND BACK-TO-BACK CREDITS

International trade is often facilitated by brokers or "middlemen" whose contribution is to maintain extensive international networks, and in so doing, to be able to source goods on behalf of importers, from suppliers that are unknown to those importers. The brokers generally keep their suppliers' identities confidential.

Letters of credit that are issued as "Transferable" allow for such transactions to take place. The transaction flow is shown in Figure 5.5. An importer issues a letter of credit in favour of the broker who is the beneficiary of the credit, taking the position of the exporter in the basic transaction flow, except that the broker (the first beneficiary) can request a bank – the transferring bank – to mirror the terms of the credit and transfer it to the ultimate exporter/supplier. The identity of the ultimate exporter or supplier is typically not known to the importer or buyer.

The transfer is typically for a smaller amount than the original, Master L/C, since the Master L/C would include the broker's fees to be paid by the importer, and the transfer covers only the supplier's portion of the value of the shipment.

In transferring all or some portion of a letter of credit, the broker may require certain terms to be revised, in order to ensure compliance with the transfer portion and with the Master L/C. The supplier must then prepare documents and present them according to the terms of the transfer, and the broker must present documents in compliance with the Master L/C.

Keeping in mind that the master and transfer refer, in the end, to the same shipment(s) of goods, sent by the supplier to the importer via the broker, it stands to reason that only certain terms in the transfer can be modified, specifically:

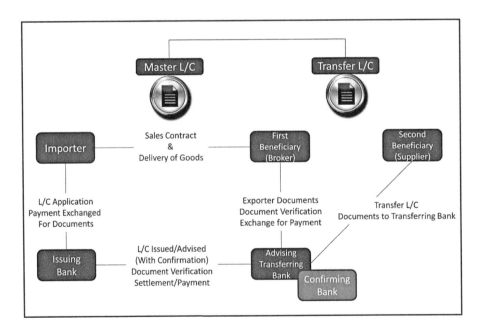

Figure 5.5   Transferable documentary letter of credit
Source: OPUS Advisory

- Amount of the transfer;

- Unit price of the goods;

- Insurance coverage, since it is usually quoted as a percentage of the value of the shipment;

- Latest shipment date;

- Expiry date.

A Master L/C might be issued for US $260,000 expiring on December 31, 2013 with a latest shipment date of December 15, 2013, for example, covering 100 units of the goods sold at US $2,600 each. The transfer might be done for US $220,000 covering 100 units at US $2,200 each, expiring December 15 and with a latest shipment date of December 1, to account for the broker's fees of US $40,000, and to allow the broker enough time to make final arrangements for delivery to the importer.

It should be noted that an L/C can be transferred to as many second beneficiaries as necessary (in the example above, the broker could request one transfer to one supplier for US $220,000, or 10 transfers to 10 separate suppliers, for US $22,000 each), but that the second beneficiaries cannot, themselves, transfer the credit further.

The broker, or first beneficiary, typically wishes to keep the identities of the importer and the supplier from each other, given that they might then prefer to transact directly and make alternate financial arrangements. Documentary credit practice allows the broker, upon receipt of documents from the supplier, to substitute certain documents such as the commercial invoice and packing list, among others, and to direct that other documents such as the transport document be prepared and issued in a manner which masks the identity of the supplier.

Note that the Master L/C is issued on the basis of the financial standing of the importer or buyer, and an existing credit/banking relationship with the issuing bank. The broker offers no collateral or other security and can arrange such a structure with little in the way of financial resources, though most banks are cautious about accepting the role of a transferring bank, and in so doing, will generally try to minimize their own exposure.

Transferable credits are a flexible and effective mechanism of international trade; however, the risk is significant, in that a discrepancy under the transfer can often be an automatic discrepancy under the Master L/C, which leaves the entire arrangement at the mercy of the importer's decision to waive discrepancies and accept the shipment, authorizing payment, which only then flows to the broker and the supplier.

Back-to-back credits serve a similar purpose to transferable credits – allowing a broker with limited financial resources to facilitate trade between a buyer and an ultimate supplier, but this time, on the basis of two separate, but generally quite similar letters of credit.

The broker requests an L/C from the importer, ensuring that the terms and conditions are as agreed and can be fully met. The broker, as Beneficiary to the first or Master L/C, approaches their bank, and asks that the Master L/C be accepted as collateral, on the basis of which the second L/C, or the back-to-back L/C, is to be issued, with the broker as applicant, and the supplier as beneficiary. Some banks will accept this type of arrangement, generally for a well-known and trusted client.

In the case of back-to-back credits, the terms and conditions in each instrument stand separately, and a discrepancy in the back-to-back transaction need not lead to a discrepancy under the master or original instrument.

These variations or features of letters of credit are presented to demonstrate the flexibility of such instruments and their usefulness in a variety of commercial transactions. As with all commercial transactions, it is advisable to seek appropriate expert advice before agreeing to certain terms or the use of certain mechanisms, including transferable or back-to-back letters of credit.

Letters of credit can also include special provisions such as allowing for "revolving" facility to support multiple identical shipments over an agreed period of time, or special clauses referred to as Red Clause or Green Clause, which, in the case of red clause credits, allow the exporter, for example, to obtain an advance payment against the L/C at the full risk of the importer in the event of non-shipment.

It is also possible for a Beneficiary to assign the proceeds, in whole or in part, to a third party in order to meet an existing obligation, such as payment to a supplier or service provider.

STANDBY CREDITS AND GUARANTEES

Standby L/Cs and Guarantees are also used in the context of trade and trade financing activity, though these instruments can, and often do, serve to facilitate various types of domestic commercial transactions and relationships.

There are legal and technical distinctions between standby L/Cs and guarantees, primarily related to the entities (banks, insurance companies and surety companies) that can issue them, and related to the obligations of issuing institutions in the case of potential fraud.

At the highest level, and for purposes of introduction in the context of trade and supply chain finance, however, these instruments are sufficiently similar to be presented as nearly interchangeable. Standby L/C and Guarantee expertise is often maintained in trade finance groups within banks, and the staff handling standbys also typically handle the guarantee needs of the banks' clients, along with transactions requiring the issuance and processing of various forms of bid bonds and performance bonds.

Standby L/Cs and Guarantees are extremely versatile instruments, and can protect against a wide variety of risks related to non-performance or non-payment in the context of a commercial relationship. They can support domestic and international transactions, and can be combined with other legal and financial instruments to facilitate complex arrangements, agreements and financing structures.

The mechanics and transactional processes related to standby L/Cs (SLCs) and guarantees mirror those described earlier in relation to documentary credits, as shown in Figure 5.6. The same parties are involved – an Applicant, requesting that the SLC be issued to a Beneficiary whose rights are meant to be protected by the SLC, and banks acting in support of their respective clients, but, as in the case of a documentary credit, compelled to respect and act on the terms of the standby when the terms and conditions of the credit require it.

As with documentary credits, it is possible to have a standby L/C Confirmed to provide additional comfort to the Beneficiary.

In its simplest form, an SLC can be a straightforward document identifying the Applicant and Beneficiary, and stating that the Beneficiary can submit a simple statement or demand for payment, indicating that the Applicant has failed to meet the terms of an agreement entered into between the two parties.

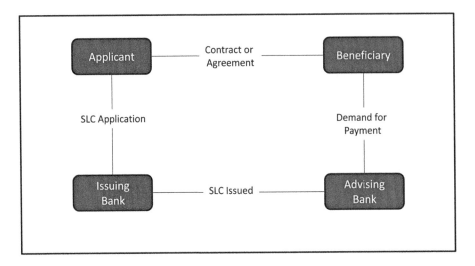

Figure 5.6   Standby letter of credit
Source: OPUS Advisory

Some standbys will require the submission of supporting proof or documentation, but very often, SLCs are issued in a way that allows the Beneficiary to simply make a statement indicating non-performance or non-payment by the Applicant, and the Issuing Bank is committed to pay the agreed sum.

Standby credits can serve to protect a beneficiary against non-payment of a financial obligation by the Applicant, or they can protect against non-performance of an agreed activity, action or service by the Applicant, in either case, allowing the Beneficiary to draw under the standby credit by submitting the appropriate request, as specified in the terms of the standby L/C.

Standby L/Cs and Guarantees can be subject to the UCP, or the counterpart Uniform Rules for Demand Guarantees (URDG), published by the International Chamber of Commerce in Paris. They typically have an agreed expiry date, but, in recognition of the long-term nature of the commercial agreements they often protect, they may be issued with an auto-renewal or evergreen clause included in their terms.

Such a clause has the effect of automatically renewing the credit for an agreed period, unless the Applicant advises the Beneficiary of their intent not to renew the instrument, within a set number of days prior to the expiry of the instrument. Such a notification may trigger a demand for payment by the Beneficiary, unless the obligations covered under the standby have been discharged as agreed.

The level of protection potentially provided under an SLC – amounting to a payment on demand – can seem skewed in favour of the Beneficiary, and sometimes, that is the case, particularly when the leverage in a commercial relationship clearly rests with the Beneficiary.

Governments departments, may, for example, require a contractor or service provider to arrange for the issuance of a standby credit in their favour, to protect against non-performance (or inadequate performance) of services by the contractor. The provision of a standby L/C may be a condition stipulated by the government client in its procurement practices, and any provider wishing to pursue such business is compelled to apply for a standby L/C, often with the full text of the credit – including the condition(s) under which payment can be demanded – provided by the Beneficiary to the Issuing Bank.

Standby L/Cs can take many formats, and can be of low value, as straightforward as requiring a single-sentence demand for payment, or extremely complex, covering obligations in the hundreds of millions of dollars in a single SLC or Guarantee.

Standby L/Cs may be used to cover a traditional, cross-border trade transaction, paralleling the mechanics (and terms and conditions) of a documentary credit, or they can be combined with documentary credit or supply chain finance structures, to protect the interests of one or more parties in such transactions.

An exporter's bank, for example, may agree to finance their client's buyer in a foreign market to assist in closing the sale. Doing so on the basis of a documentary credit or a supply chain financing option, the exporter's bank may insist on a guarantee from the importer's bank to protect against the case where the importer fails to repay the monies financed.

CASH IN ADVANCE

Finally, on the spectrum of settlement options, cash advance is the most favourable alternative for the exporter. In this instance, the exporter requires payment prior to shipping (perhaps even prior to producing) the goods. This option may be required if the exporter possesses access to a unique product, or holds a patent or intellectual property related to the goods, that make them difficult, more expensive, or impossible to source from an alternate supplier.

The foregoing discussion illustrates clearly, the flexibility and adaptability of trade finance in meeting a range of requirements for both importer and exporter.

The selection of payment and financing options links directly to the nature of a trading relationship, including the relative leverage of one party over another, or an asymmetry of information between the two partners. Information asymmetry may be as complex as inaccurate analysis of risk, incomplete information about settlement and financing options, or risk mitigation solutions.

Trade finance has also evolved processes and mechanisms meant to facilitate international commerce in a wide variety of contexts. Small business managers, entrepreneurs or finance executives will benefit from an understanding of the financing of international commerce.

Other Financing Mechanisms

There are numerous other products and mechanisms used in the facilitation of international trade.

FACTORING

Factoring is a mechanism whereby a company can sell its invoice(s) to a third party provider called a Factor, that purchases the invoice(s), providing immediate but discounted payment against the amount due under the invoice. An exporter can negotiate a factoring arrangement for a single invoice, or for a series of invoices payable by the same buyer.

Some factors are prepared to extend this service to exporters, providing immediate payment against invoices payable by foreign-based importers.

Factoring can be done with or without recourse to the exporter – in the former case, the factor reserves the right to reclaim funds from the exporter in the event of non-payment. In the latter scenario, non-recourse factoring, the factoring company accepts the risk of non-payment and is prepared to undertake collection activities if necessary.

Factoring helps to accelerate settlement, and to improve cashflow and working capital for the exporter; however, it can be a relatively expensive financing option, particularly if other options are available.

FORFAITING

Forfaiting, or forfait financing, is sometimes defined as a medium-term form of financing provided to exporters by trade banks. In that model, a financier agrees to purchase and discount, on a fixed-rate basis, promissory notes payable to the exporter by the foreign importer, with terms ranging up to five to seven years.

A forfait transaction can be supported by a guarantee from the importer's bank in favour of the exporter's bank, and typically involves financing without recourse to the exporter.

Some financial institutions will combine a forfait structure with a documentary letter of credit, or even a short-term trade receivable. As with other areas in trade finance, the definitions and transaction characteristics around forfaiting can vary by market and even by provider.

Factoring and forfaiting may be effected on the basis of a single invoice, or on the basis of a portfolio of receivables and a flow of business. Specifics again will differ by market, though forfaiting is most typically associated with a portfolio of receivables.

AVAL

The act of having a third party, usually a bank or lending institution, guarantee the obligations of a buyer to a seller per the terms of a contract such as a promissory note or purchase agreement. The bank avalizes the document by stamping the words "By Aval" on the document, to demonstrate that the underlying obligation bears the support of the financial institution. The bank effectively becomes a co-signer with the buyer in the transaction.

WAREHOUSE RECEIPT FINANCING

Warehouse receipt financing is a pre-shipment collateralized loan, using goods stored in independent warehouse as security. Such storage may be effected by the exporter prior to shipment, in which case, the exporter may require and arrange financing on the basis of a warehouse receipt. Likewise, an importer may need to store goods into a warehouse upon their arrival and prior to taking possession of the shipment, because of an inability to pay immediately. The importer can then arrange for financing until, for example, the goods have been sold and the importer can settle the loan.

Warehouse receipts may be negotiable or non-negotiable, with the former made out "To Order" of a specified party or to bearer, the latter is made out to a specified party, and only that party may authorize release of the goods.

TRUST RECEIPT FINANCING

This type of financing involves financing provided to the importer, after release of the Bill of Lading and the goods, against the signing of a trust receipt by the importer, based on an established and trusted commercial relationship between the importer and the financier. The importer is expected to repay the loan after sale of the goods.

FINANCING BASED ON A BANKER'S ACCEPTANCE

A bank can Accept a draft presented under an L/C or a collection, for example, indicating that the monies due at an agreed future date, will be paid by the accepting bank at maturity. In trade finance, acceptances mature within 30, 60 or 90 days most commonly, but may extend out to 360 days or longer. The discounting of such financial undertakings for immediate payment to the beneficiary (typically the exporter) is a form of financing; the Banker's Acceptance, created when a bank commits to payment at maturity, is a negotiable instrument that can be traded in the capital markets.

FINANCING OF FOREIGN RECEIVABLES

Financing of receivables, including invoices approved for payment, can be done on a transactional basis – one invoice at a time – though lenders may prefer to finance a pool of receivables, particularly in the case of foreign receivables. Such financing is commonly provided with full recourse to the borrower, in the event of default.

BUYER CREDITS

A Buyer Credit provides financing directly to the importer or buyer, with the explicit intent of facilitating an export sale. The exporter's banker may extend credit directly to the foreign buyer in support of the exporting customer. As in most forms of trade finance, when analyzing importer credits, the bank must consider the economic and political risks associated with the importer's country, as well as the commercial risks associated with the transaction.

SUPPLIER CREDITS

A bank or financial institution purchases the debt of an importer to an exporter, providing immediate liquidity to the exporter in exchange. Such structure may be more cost-effective and more quickly arranged, as the financing bank is dealing with a known borrower located in the banker's country, where due diligence and negotiation can be more easily conducted.

Supplier credits are generally suited to transactions with a value between US $100,000 and US $5,000,000, or the equivalent thereof, with terms of payment ranging from six months to five years.

COUNTERTRADE

Countertrade is an arrangement in which trading partners agree to a non-monetary exchange such as the exchange of wheat for steel of equal value, or product for service. Countertrade involves some form of payment in kind, with variations such as barter, counterpurchase, advance purchase, buybacks, bilateral and offset arrangements.

INTERNATIONAL LEASING

Exporters can propose the use of cross-border leasing arrangements as a form of financing, when dealing in markets that prohibit the purchase and outright ownership of foreign equipment. Such financial structures are used in support of exports of aircraft, machinery, industrial equipment and motor vehicles, among others.

Leasing may also prove to be advantageous from the perspective of local tax treatment in the importing country, and can therefore be an attractive way for buyers to obtain capital equipment on cost-effective terms.

6

Financing Trade: Supply Chain Finance

The business of trade finance, including the traditional mechanisms such as documentary collections or documentary credits, have been in use for at least several hundred years. There are sample letters of credit from the sixteenth century at the museum of the Banca Monte dei Paschi di Siena in Italy. These traditional instruments have endured and served the facilitation of international commerce; over a relatively short period prior to the global economic crisis, the business of trade finance evolved as a direct response to the changing needs and commercial practices of importers and exporters.

In the late 1990s, technology advanced sufficiently to allow the conception, design and development of electronic or web-based solutions related to the finance of international trade. These solutions took years to gain traction, in part because existing solutions were robust and deemed effective, and in part because major banks and providers of trade finance were, at that time, reticent about adopting new business models.

In the end, exporters and importers operating in a period of global growth and high levels of affordable liquidity determined that trade could be conducted largely on open account terms, with minimal risk mitigation even in markets once considered relatively high risk.

Banks, perceiving the risk of losing their role in facilitating trade through financing, were compelled to devise and deploy new products, propositions and business solutions in response to open account trade, which ultimately led to the development of a series of propositions related to the financing of global supply chains.

Understanding Supply Chain Finance

Supply chain finance is still a relatively new proposition in the business of financing international commerce, at least to the extent that it is being developed, marketed and deployed as a solution based upon complex international networks and global supply chains. As noted earlier, SCF solutions are equally applicable in the context of domestic supply chain transactions.

Some senior bankers have suggested that the early versions of supply chain finance are little more than a re-packaging of long-established financing mechanisms, and a repositioning of such mechanisms in the context of cross-border supply chains. Others argue that there is in fact something new in the supply chain finance proposition. The novelty of the concept is illustrated by the current reality that banks are taking very different approaches in the organizational positioning of traditional trade finance, supply chain solutions and related elements such as working capital and liquidity management, or broader activities such as transaction banking.

What is important at this juncture in practical, commercial terms is that the primary global providers of trade finance – the banks – are responding to the emerging needs of importers and exporters.

Financial institutions committed to the business of financing international trade are developing new products and offerings under the banner of supply chain finance, or repackaging and marketing familiar financial instruments into more elaborate, strategic financing programs. Leading banks are also accelerating their adoption of new business models and technology platforms designed to provide alternatives, or complements, to traditional trade finance. It is worth noting also, that smaller, boutique financing firms have taken the opportunity to engage in the financing of international commerce through various flavours of supply chain finance programs.

For some providers, trade finance is a subset, or a component of supply chain finance, where others perceive supply chain finance as an outgrowth and subset of trade finance. Others still prefer to position trade finance and supply chain finance as complementary elements of a broader working capital or liquidity management proposition. Some financial institutions have gone so far as to articulate a supply chain finance proposition that encompasses both international and domestic transactions, blurring the line between import/export and purely domestic financing requirements.

This is an area that will continue to evolve over the coming several years, however, even at this early stage, it is important for finance and treasury specialists to appreciate some similarities and distinctions between traditional mechanisms and supply chain finance, as well as the position of one relative to the other.

One useful way to view trade and supply chain finance is illustrated in Figure 6.1 below.

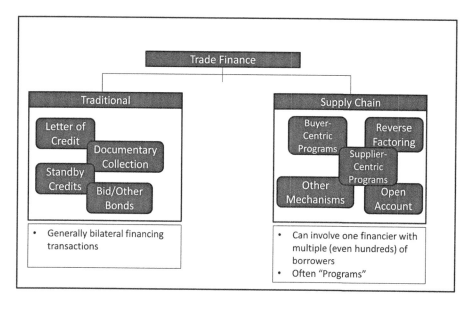

Figure 6.1   Traditional trade finance and supply chain finance
Source: OPUS Advisory

In broad terms, the financing of international trade is evolving along two dimensions: first, trade finance providers are recognizing the need to develop solutions and propositions linked to the trading preferences of importers and exporters, with such preferences shifting decidedly away from traditional mechanisms such as letters of credit, to trade on open account terms. Secondly, there is a shift related to the evolution of technology, which is clearly contributing to a move away from paper and process-intensive mechanisms such as the letter of credit, to technology-based options that aim to (and have succeeded to varying degrees) reduce or eliminate paper flow in favour of data.

> Supply chain finance represents an important evolution in the proposition around the finance of international trade, not so much because of the products and solutions available, but, at this early stage at least, because it represents a clear shift in the thinking of bankers, from product and transaction to solution and relationships.
>
> Supply chain finance looks at international trade as more than a bilateral activity between buyer and seller – seeing instead an ecosystem of relationships that support and enable trade across borders.
>
> Such a view opens up significant additional opportunity for accessing financing and liquidity.

Technology solutions and platforms purporting to facilitate trade and supply chain finance are gaining traction and credibility, and are increasingly viable as alternatives to traditional mechanisms.

As noted earlier, there has been an increasing focus over the last 15 years or so, on the important linkage between the Physical Supply Chain, and its complement, the Financial Supply Chain, and more recently, in line with technological developments, the role of a parallel Information Supply Chain.

Financial executives and entrepreneurs leading small businesses must appreciate the direct connection between the movement of components and goods through a supply chain, and the corresponding movement of capital – money – through the same supply chain, and the relationships that sustain it. Similarly, supply chains generate, and rely on, tremendous amounts of data and information related to both the movement of the goods and the flow of money.

Physical Supply Chain

While the conventional view of a supply chain may be somewhat linear, current sourcing patterns are such that many businesses – from global retailers to small suppliers – are part of a web or network, even an ecosystem of relationships that constitute an international or global supply chain.

Complex businesses develop, manage and work to optimize extremely complex sets of supply chain relationships, with service and supplier communities often numbering in the thousands or more, and geographic reach extending to the four corners of the world. The management of these ecosystems includes efforts to ensure the financial viability of the supply chain, including the health of small suppliers in far-flung, often developing or emerging markets.

Leading analysts are looking at important characteristics of supply chains, including the role of strategic suppliers, whose contribution is so critical that any disruption in their ability to assure supply can cause the entire production process to grind to a halt. Similarly, service providers and others that support a supply chain and enable its activities can be critical to its ongoing operation, and as such, ought to be considered strategically important.

One of the implications of this notion of strategic suppliers relates directly to trade and supply chain finance.

Financial Supply Chain

In the two decades or so prior to the eruption of the global financial crisis, access to capital and liquidity – including financing – was relatively easy and affordable for established businesses, especially those at the mid-market and large corporate end of the spectrum, perhaps less so for micro, small and medium-sized enterprises, particularly those located in developing or higher-risk markets.

Post-2007, the realities of global liquidity and access to financing have been drastically reshaped, with the effect that the ability to access financing is both critically important, and increasingly, challenging to the point of representing a demonstrable competitive advantage for businesses.

Trade finance has been shown to be critical to the support of international commerce, and various forms of trade finance, in particular pre-shipment or pre-export finance, which allow access to capital for exporters, to support sourcing, production and shipment, have proven to be particularly important.

Supply chain finance is typically viewed and positioned as a financing program, in contrast to traditional trade finance mechanisms that are typically transaction focused and bilateral in nature: one deal, with financing arrangements involving the buyer and seller and other parties involved directly in that deal.

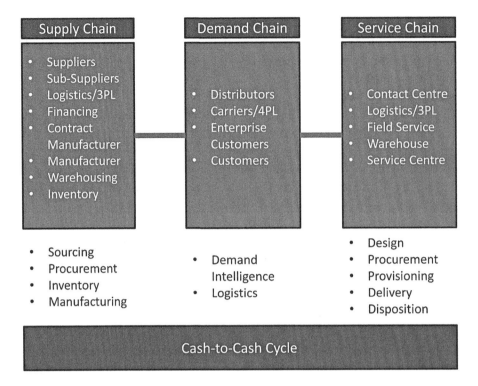

Figure 6.2   Supply, demand and service chains
Source: Adapted from Infosys

Financing a supply chain might involve, for example, providing access to financing and liquidity to a subset of the supply chain (or even the entire supply chain) on the basis of the credit strength and borrowing capacity of a large global buyer at the center of that supply chain. Such programs will often specifically seek to provide financing to strategic suppliers.

Figure 6.2 illustrates the ways in which various elements of a commercial ecosystem can be combined to understand the relationships and dynamics at play: Infosys recognizes the physical supply chain, covering demand and supply, as well as related services, while also linking in the related financial flows. The information supply chain is implicit – the graphic originates from a technology provider promoting the importance of technology, visibility and reporting and tracking, around global supply chains.

Information Supply Chain

The physical and financial supply chains are supported and enabled by a critical flow of information related to the business, relationships and dynamics of these supply chains – a flow that has been dubbed the information supply chain.

Visibility and transparency are critical in the conduct of international trade, as much to assure effective management of the process, as to respond to increasingly stringent demands related to compliance and regulatory requirements. These demands apply to both the physical side of the transaction, and the associated financial flows: international sanctions, anti-money laundering, terrorism finance monitoring and a wide variety of related laws and regulations have direct links to trade and trade/supply chain finance.

Demand and Service Chains

The overall commercial ecosystem also depends on a chain of demand, and a network of relationships and capabilities related to servicing of the ecosystem and related products, including procurement and related activities.

Supply Chain Finance

Just as the majority of international trade takes place with the direct support of trade finance, it is equally notable that the most complex and efficient global supply chains are increasingly looking at liquidity – financing – as an important enabler of business.

Global supply chains cross many borders and can involve hundreds, even thousands of commercial relationships, as partially illustrated in Figure 6.3. Some (or most) of the companies in such supply chains can be based in emerging markets, where financing can be difficult and expensive to secure, and in such cases, financing can be provided through the access and borrowing capability of another member of the supply chain, ultimately to the benefit of the overall system.

While there are numerous variations of supply chain finance, and within that, numerous individual products and solutions, the scope and flexibility of

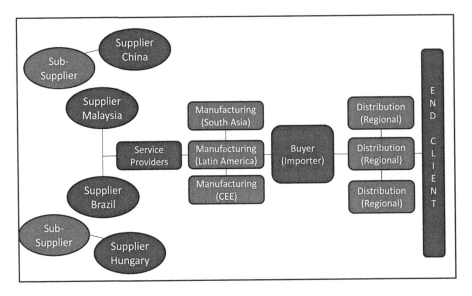

Figure 6.3   International supply chain, end-to-end
Source: OPUS Advisory

supply chain finance programs can be illustrated by considering the nature of buyer-centric supply chain finance (SCF) programs.

These programs typically involve a large global buyer, perhaps in retail, automotive, aviation or consumer electronics, for example. Such programs will aim to provide liquidity to large supply chain, including downstream suppliers and upstream distributors.

These programs are generally offered through the buyer's primary trade finance bank, as the facilities and liquidity provided, are most commonly extended on the basis of the credit standing, borrowing capacity and risk, of the buyer.

Buyers are often headquartered in consumer economies such as the US and Europe, though typical sourcing and consumption patterns are changing quickly: China, seen as the world's manufacturer for many years, is shifting upward along global value chains, increasingly involved in design, development and value-added manufacturing, while at the same time, taking an increasingly important role as a consumer economy, and a position at the downstream, customer, end of supply chains.

Buyer-centric programs generally involve supply chains where the importer is financially and commercially stronger than most or all of its suppliers, such that the proposition of extending credit and liquidity to those suppliers is seen, generally, as a desirable proposition from the supplier point of view.

Ultimately, the purpose of supply chain finance programs is to enhance the overall financial health of an international or global supply chain by assuring adequate liquidity throughout, which enables suppliers and various service providers to access much-needed working capital. Working capital is typically used to financing sourcing and production activities that, in the end, enable the buyer to secure the desired goods.

An SCF transaction, part of a larger program, might work as follows:

- A buyer issues a purchase order and transmits the data to the supplier through a trade finance or supply chain technology platform;

- The supplier accepts the purchase order and produces the agreed goods;

- The supplier delivers goods and submits an invoice to their buyer/importer customer;

- The buyer approves the invoice for payment, creating a legal obligation to settle the payable according to the terms agreed, typically at least 30 days after the approval date;

- The supplier, having received confirmation that the invoice is approved for payment, requests immediate settlement of that invoice from the financial institution facilitating the SCF program;

- The bank effects payment to the supplier (generally, with recourse to the buyer under the terms of the SCF program);

- The bank collects reimbursement of from the buyer, at the time the invoice becomes due.

This mechanism allows a buyer to propose payment terms of 60 or 90 days or longer, extending their settlement timeframe, while enabling the supplier to collect funds immediately, on the basis of the approved invoice. This variation of SCF is often referred to as approved payables financing.

Supply chain finance programs can enable buyers to extend payment terms from the typical 30-day timeframe to 90 or 120 days, and can reduce the cost of borrowing for suppliers – even for extended periods, by 70 or 80 percent. Globally, the impact of supply chain finance programs can be significant, providing access to several hundred billion dollars or more in additional liquidity through acceleration of the cash conversion cycle.

Supply chain finance, just like traditional trade finance mechanisms such as documentary letters of credit, can provide financing solutions concurrently to importers and exporters. A supplier (exporter) can borrow through an SCF program, on the strength of their customer's credit, while at the same time, the buyer can arrange financing directly through their financial institution, in the form of an agreed delay in payment due date, which is financed by the bank.

Supply chain finance can be a powerful vehicle for the delivery of solutions and products of great value to importers and exporters.

These solutions can include foreign currency risk hedging, various forms of financing, as well as cross-border cash management.

SCF programs would seem to be intuitively attractive to both the buyers and the suppliers involved, given the ability of such programs to meet important commercial needs for both parties.

There have been, however, persistent challenges in the setup and launch of such programs, and beyond that, in the rate of usage of such programs as well.

Some of the issues include:

- The complexity of due diligence, including "Know Your Client" requirements around the setup of supply chain finance programs;

- The cost and complexity of completing adequate due diligence on a group or subset of suppliers, often located in remote markets where objective and reliable commercial data is limited if at all available;

- The limitations of information and communications technology (ICT) in certain supplier markets, that make communication, and IT-driven participation in an SCF program, difficult at best;

- The (understandable) concern of suppliers at having to deal with their buyer's bank to secure financing, along with concerns among suppliers at having to disclose their financial circumstances to the buyer and/or the SCF bankers;

- Absence of clarity around the value of participating in an SCF program.

Trade finance specialists have evolved their SCF capabilities and propositions, to the extent that supply chain finance programs originally developed to facilitate cross-border commerce, are increasingly adapted for use in purely domestic transactions. In those cases, numerous challenges related to bringing foreign suppliers into an SCF program, do not arise.

Leading practitioners of supply chain finance note that a major requirement for success in the design and launch of SCF programs is the proper and comprehensive socialization of these programs. This effort must engage all interested parties, including the supplier community, and must clearly demonstrate the value of participating in such a program, in concrete financial and commercial terms.

Suppliers who recognize the positive impact of a supply chain finance program on their working capital, through reduction in days sales outstanding, and the impact of reduced borrowing costs, are far more likely to cooperate in the due diligence process, sign on to a program, and actually use the facilities available.

Buyers, similarly, undertake a significant investment of time and effort in working with their bankers to identify qualified suppliers, assist in the due diligence process, and support the bank in ensuring the smooth operation of the program. Over time, the buyer and the financial institution may seek to invite additional suppliers to the program, and can do so more successfully by demonstrating the value of the program to the initial set of participating suppliers.

SCF Programs: Market Adoption

Trade finance, and particularly supply chain finance, is deemed increasingly to be of strategic importance in the management of company finances and treasury operations. C-level executives are focusing on supply chain finance, and bankers as well as corporate executives are engaging in increasingly sophisticated discussions around the commercial value of SCF Programs.

Carrefour, the French retail giant, implemented a supply chain finance program in Indonesia in 2011. The program was aimed at supporting the liquidity and financing needs of local suppliers, and was aimed initially at a subset of 150 suppliers, with monthly volumes of at least US $100,000. The program was launched on the basis of an initial facility of US $20 to $50 million available for four years, and was to be extended to 250–400 suppliers per year after the initial year.

The number and complexity of supply chain programs has increased exponentially since the early days of SCF and even since the announcement of the Carrefour facility. While early programs reflected only limited usage by suppliers, the rate of adoption of SCF programs over the last three years or so, has been significant.

As noted earlier, industry estimates suggested that early SCF programs, some with facilities in the hundreds of millions, even up to US $2 billion, achieved utilization rates in the 10 percent range: modest result for bankers given the effort required to launch such programs, and the cost (financial cost plus opportunity cost) of keeping the credit lines available to support such large facilities.

More recently, SCF programs are less an exceptional achievement, and more industry norm, with utilization rates among the more successful programs reaching 85 percent or more of the facilities offered.

Supply chain finance programs offer an excellent context within which banks can provide a suite of solutions of great value to companies engaged in international trade activities. The proposition is evolving.

In addition to financing options and solutions, a well-designed supply chain finance program can leverage the capabilities of global financial institutions, to provide access to a range of high-value products, services and solutions.

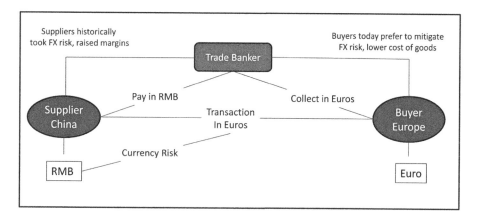

Figure 6.4   Supply chain finance and FX risk
Source: OPUS Advisory

Foreign currency exposure, or FX risk, is inherent for at least one or both trading partners in the majority of international transactions, as shown in Figure 6.4, and may extend to impact a whole group of trading partners in the context of an international supply chain.

The majority of international transactions are denominated in US dollars, with the euro gaining in influence, and the renminbi accelerating its internationalization, and its use in cross-border transactions.

Traditionally, suppliers were faced with the foreign exchange risk, as buyers exercised leverage in selecting the currency of a transaction; however, those same suppliers developed the rational practice of simply increasing the cost of their products, to absorb any anticipated adverse volatility in exchange rates.

Buyers have noted the significant impact on cost, and have opted, as part of the SCF programs offered through their trade bankers, to provide suppliers with the option to settle invoices in local currency. The banks, in effect, "bundle" a trade or supply chain finance solution with some form of currency hedge, be it spot conversion to the currency of the supplier at time of settlement, or conversion on the basis of an FX contract, assuring settlement in local currency on the due date.

Similar options may be offered to the buyer, in the event that the currency of the transaction is also foreign to the buyer. This approach eliminates currency

Supply Chain Finance State of the Market: Coming of Age

Supply chain finance (SCF) is poised to become 'the next big thing' in trade-related financing. And for some, it presents an opportunity to blur the lines between domestic and international banking, by linking the financing practices applied in the context of cross-border business, with finance related to primarily domestic supply chains, and vice versa. SCF is positioned as a model which provides value and solutions for large multinationals, concurrently supporting the international aspirations of small suppliers in remote parts of developing and emerging economies. For large global banks, SCF may even offer an opportunity to build bridges between operating units or lines of business, such as transaction banking groups and investment banking units – recent crisis-motivated rhetoric on the differences between these areas notwithstanding. Finding the perfect balance, however, remains a challenge. Thought leaders are developing several flavours of the SCF value proposition – some with limited impact on organization, business model and required investment, and others with broad-ranging implications, from the need to develop custom technology platforms, to the requirement to ensure adequate operational and transaction-processing support for what amounts to a new offering. In short, supply chain finance, broadly viewed, is an area brimming with potential.

[...] Senior bankers from institutions fully engaged in developing SCF businesses describe a ramp-up in demand for supply chain-related financing solutions. As the question of credit availability and liquidity recedes gradually, the need for producers to respond to increases in demand is driving a commensurate demand for supply chain finance, particularly from larger or global financial institutions. Reference to supply chain finance today can translate to a one or two-product offering centered on factoring, more evolved programmes of buyer or supplier-centric financing programmes, anchor client, onboarding and all, or full-scale, multi-country, multi-currency programmes aiming to address the needs of buyer, supplier and global supply chains overall. Likewise, an SCF programme today could be primarily a platform-driven technology proposition, or a solution based on financing and liquidity. (Source: *Trade Finance Magazine*, cover, April 2011, by Alexander R. Malaket)

risk for one or both parties, by providing hedging solutions linked directly to a specific transaction.

The UK Prime Minister David Cameron has announced an SCF scheme in which the region's largest companies are being asked to leverage their strong credit ratings to encourage banks of the smaller firms that supply them to lend against the invoices approved for payment.

Using the SCF scheme, a funder is automatically notified by a large company that an invoice has been approved for payment. Ideally, at that point the bank then offers a 100 percent immediate advance to the supplier at a lower interest rate, secure in the knowledge the corporate will eventually pay the invoice.

Cameron has also announced that the UK government will look to where it can, implementing this with its own suppliers, starting with the first UK government SCF scheme for community pharmacies in England. This would unlock up to GBP 800 million of new credit for 4,500 pharmacy businesses, many of which are SMEs. A number of large corporates have committed to the SCF program, including Rolls Royce, Kingfisher, Siemens, Tesco and British Airways. (Source: *Trade & Forfaiting Review*, 2012)

SCF can assist program participants with optimizing cash management, including enhancing visibility on trade-related cash positions, and, increasingly, SCF programs are being designed with appropriate risk mitigation components, including foreign accounts receivable insurance, and/or various forms of guarantees aimed at securing the interest of one or more parties and participants to the SCF programs.

Emerging Solutions in Trade and Supply Chain Finance

There have been numerous attempts since the late 1990s to dematerialize traditional letter of credit transactions, shifting trade finance transactions from paper-based models to electronic, data-driven and web-based approaches.

While such emerging models have varied in scope and in the rate and success of uptake, it is clear that technology, and commercial practice, have evolved in the last decade to allow for a significant shift in business model around trade finance.

More than the enhancement of long-familiar transaction processes, the solutions that will impact trade finance in the future are likely to involve significant and material innovation, and may come from unexpected sources. Online invoicing and settlement services that aim to greatly reduce lag times, and thereby improve working capital, along with electronic payment platforms that can facilitate the sending of monies across borders from the via computers, tablets and mobile devices – these are the technologies and business models that hold the promise of transformational change.

The critical importance of trade and supply chain finance is illustrated in part by the profile around this element of international commerce. Trade and supply chain finance have demonstrably reached the highest levels of global leadership.

7

Engaging Effectively with Finance Providers

Trade and supply chain finance is provided (estimates suggest well over 70 percent or more) by a small group of banks that possess the necessary expertise, global footprint and appetite to engage in the financing of international commerce. Despite this high degree of concentration, which was exacerbated by the global economic crisis, there are a variety of sources of trade finance, including local and regional banks, some credit unions or cooperative banks, boutique financing firms and, of course, various public sector entities, government programs and international institutions such as the World Bank's International Finance Corporation, among others.

Bankers

Bankers are often a target of derision, and the recent global financial crisis, as well as various illegal activities uncovered in the global financial system through 2012, have done little to enhance the image or public perception of banks and bankers as pillars of society or supporters of growth and economic prosperity.

The reality of the moment is, however, that no matter how flawed, the banking systems of the world play an important role in facilitating commerce, in enabling growth and prosperity and in raising the standard of living of many millions of people and of communities across the globe.

The conduct of international commerce is one area where the role of the banks, and the leverage of their unique expertise, capabilities and capacities, is quite natural and well matched.

The global financial and economic crisis of 2007 and beyond has resulted in pronounced reaction in leading financial centres – the imperative for banks to "get back to basics" in their activities – to shift away from complex financial engineering and high-risk, high-leverage (high-return) investment banking activity, to the more conventional, core activities around deposit taking and lending, and related areas now often grouped under lines of business called Transaction Banking.

Bankers are wrestling with the challenge of responding to political pressure to serve small businesses, and to assure adequate supply of trade finance, while at the same time, maintain appropriately low levels of risk and loan losses, ensuring the preservation of shareholder value. This dynamic has a direct and positive impact on the way a bank will engage in trade and supply chain finance.

Senior bankers have been focusing on greater engagement in "real economy" activities – activities linked to the creation of concrete and demonstrable value, in contrast to financial engineering through complex and poorly understood investment finance mechanisms.

With major banks, particularly in the US, the UK and Europe having availed themselves of public funding, either in the form of bailout funds, preferential borrowing or in numerous cases, effective nationalization, those same banks now face political pressure to engage in activities that were, pre-crisis, low priority activities.

Greater emphasis on supporting small business is one such activity. The provision of trade finance in support of international trade is, arguably, another such activity – one in which most banks engaged solely for the purposes of attracting or maintaining certain corporate relationships.

Supply chain finance allows the banks to fulfill several objectives at once:

- Demonstrate engagement in and support of real economy activities linked to the flow of goods across borders;

- Demonstrate a desire to service the SME sector, through programs that facilitate access to financing and liquidity for small business;

- Show commitment to the back-to-basics mantra of the post-crisis financial environment;

- Maintain activities in a business with an attractive risk profile and very low loan-loss experience, balancing low risk with steady, conservative returns;

- Traditional trade finance possesses a set of characteristics that make it well-suited to the current business and political environment, including the following:
  - Short-term exposure;
  - Financing linked directly to an underlying flow of goods;
  - Contingent and self-liquidating obligation for banks;
  - Effectively risk-mitigated;
  - Negligible loan loss history.

While trade (and more recently, trade finance) enjoys significant profile in business and political circles, as a driver for global recovery and growth, it is worth noting that trade finance is poorly understood within financial institutions. Until recently, the business of trade finance was poorly championed within banks, and very few outside the international divisions of banks had more than a cursory understanding of the financing of international commerce.

These realities have been problematic for many banks, as the trade business typically relies on non-trade specialists to identify opportunities to finance trade, or to approve credit lines and facilities in support of trade finance. Internal pressures related to compliance and risk management originate from areas in the banks where trade and supply chain finance are poorly understood. Additionally however, regulatory requirements imposed by local and international authorities are a significant factor.

While banks often enjoyed disproportionate leverage pre-crisis, the reality post-2007 has been that large corporations and multinationals possess better credit ratings than some of their banks. While certain financial institutions have undergone a process of downsizing and rationalization – covering lines of business, geographic scope and client relationships – it is equally true that the global financial system has witnessed a flight to quality, where corporate clients have opted to exit certain bank relationships seen as unstable or risky.

In addition to looking at credit standing and the strength of a bank's balance sheet, companies have also considered intangibles such as reputational risk, and the potential damage to their own brands, of being associated with certain financial institutions. This reputational dimension is proving increasingly central to discussions around bank-corporate relationships, both in the domestic context, and perhaps more acutely, in the context of international business activity.

Understanding the motivations of trade bankers and the characteristics of the trade and supply chain finance business, as well as the context within which trade finance operates, can enable corporate executives and leaders of small businesses to interact effectively with bankers and trade finance specialists.

Engaging Effectively

Executives and entrepreneurs pursuing opportunities in the international marketplace ought to appreciate the commercial value of an effective relationship with bankers and other financiers, including, and perhaps particularly, bankers specialized in trade and supply chain finance.

There is a long-standing debate about whether companies are better advised to maintain a core banking relationship covering key requirements, including domestic and international financing needs, or whether the prudent approach is to diversify among two or more providers, in some cases, separating bank relationships between those focused on domestic needs and those addressing the requirements of international transactions and operations.

The rationale parallels the discussion about whether to spin off international business and operations from domestic business, in order to insulate the domestic venture from the ostensibly higher-risk international activity. Maintaining separate banking relationships, some would argue, reduces the leverage of banks against the company, in the event there are difficulties in either the local activity or the international activity. Credit or liquidity issues on one side of the business will not disrupt the other dimension of the company's activity, in the event a banker decides to restrict liquidity or call any outstanding obligations or liabilities.

There is no single correct approach, and it is common for large enterprises to maintain several core banking relationships, and numerous second-tier relationships on the basis of specific requirements, differentiated areas of expertise, price competitiveness and other considerations.

Banks and trade financiers are concerned about where to recover funds in the event a payment is made or a financing solution is extended to one or more parties. Sometimes, that party is a corporate client, sometimes, that party is another bank, an insurer or an international institution. The nature of a financial obligation can provide flexibility in some cases, in terms of the source of a payment or financing solution.

Importers remain constrained in trade finance transactions in that the issuance of a letter of credit requires that a relationship – and a credit facility such as a line of credit – is in place between the importer and the Issuing Bank. An importer cannot typically request any bank to issue a letter of credit on behalf of that importer, as the bank will want to be assured of adequate protection – including the ability to recover payments made under the credit by debiting the importer's account or line of credit.

An exporter enjoys somewhat more flexibility in most markets, because any financial risk or liability on the export side traces back to the issuing bank and/or the importer's country of domicile. A financial institution providing services on the export side of a letter of credit transaction will look to the issuing bank for reimbursement of any payments made or financing offered to the exporter, and will, from a risk perspective, be concerned with the standing of the issuing bank and of the country in which the letter of credit is issued.

The exporter's credit standing is, in many ways, not relevant from the perspective of the recovery of funds. In the event that a transaction is covered by some form of risk insurance, the ultimate source of reimbursement may be a private insurer or a public sector (government) export credit agency: once again, the standing of the exporter is incidental.

The implication of this for an exporter is that there are often options related to the selection of a bank (or other entity) as a provider of trade finance. This is perhaps less the case in certain markets in Asia, as noted earlier, due to the nature of the corporate-to-bank relationships and their close interconnectedness.

There are transactional advantages to exporters in selecting their provider of trade finance under traditional instruments such as letter of credit. Likewise, certain forms of supply chain finance, including buyer-centric programs in which the supplier community is financed on the borrowing strength and capacity (and therefore through the banking relationship) of the importer, will create situations where an exporter may transact with a bank other than their own primary banker.

KYC and KYCC: it is no longer sufficient, from a regulatory perspective, for banks to know their own clients.

They are now expected to know the buyers and suppliers of their customers, particularly when a cross-border transaction is involved.

Trade financiers must monitor transactions to ensure that no individual, organization or country on official boycott lists or on the US "Office of Foreign Assets Control," or OFAC list, benefits from a transaction.

Regulatory and compliance requirements on banks are significant, expensive and time and resource intensive. Companies that facilitate transparency and visibility will benefit.

There are, despite the foregoing, compelling reasons to take a longer-term relationship view of banking relationships, and sound arguments for maintaining close and comprehensive relationships with a company's lead banks. Those reasons include:

- the importance of a supporting relationship with bankers;

- the development of a solid understanding of a company's business over time;

- the likelihood that a relationship bank will work through difficult periods with a client in ways they are unlikely to do when the approach is purely transactional;

- the opportunity to exercise leverage and influence in the relationship, depending on the size and profitability of the client;

- the enhanced ability to develop complementary and appropriately tailored financial solutions across the business, reducing duplication of facilities, and potentially reducing cost.

Banks seek profitable client relationships in most cases (unless the prestige of banking a particular client is deemed sufficiently important to accept a break-even or even a loss-making position), and are often guided by revenue and profitability targets, by product and on the overall relationship.

Understanding the motivations of a banker and relationship manager can be extremely valuable in ensuring the most positive and valuable relationship, and can also facilitate a dialogue where the banker(s) become familiar with the unique challenges, needs and opportunities related to a particular business.

Transparency and open communication with bankers is important from a couple of perspectives – the need to facilitate adequate understanding about the business of a company, to ensure adequate support from the bank and the imperative to assist banks in meeting their various regulatory and compliance obligations, again, to ensure that the bank supports company activities and does not inadvertently create issues for the business.

Communication and transparency with bankers – particularly trade and international bankers – may be difficult for some executives and entrepreneurs to envision, however, an understanding of the various obligations of banks will quickly demonstrate the value of such an approach when appropriate.

The conduct of international trade, including the movement of funds across borders, brings with it some unique and high-profile issues for bankers – particularly around regulatory issues, compliance and boycott requirements. In this respect, a business is best served by ensuring transparent, open and regular communication with bankers on the state of the company, and on specific transactions or commercial relationships, as deemed appropriate. The frequency of communication with bankers can be adjusted based on prevailing circumstances.

Bankers, including trade finance bankers, are expected to be aware of, and monitor various aspects of the relationships they manage for the financial institution. These include:

- KYC or KYCC: "Know Your Customer" and "Know Your Customer's Customer";

- anti-money laundering and anti-terrorism and terrorism finance;

- OFAC and boycott lists;

- capital adequacy and reserve requirements.

Trade finance, including traditional instruments such as documentary letters of credit, are often used to launder illicit funds, or to facilitate access to liquidity and foreign currency, to parties ranging from criminals to terrorists to governing regimes deemed illegitimate by the international community. As such, trade finance transactions are meant to be subject to stringent screening processes and oversight measures.

> "We take a long-term view of our banking relationships, considering whether the strategy, long-term direction and corporate values of our financial institution align with our own. Such considerations form the basis of a partnership between our company and our financial services providers, including our trade financiers."
> (Source: OPUS Advisory)

To the extent that a company can facilitate visibility around its business, including buyer and supplier relationships, to bankers and trade financiers, such visibility will assist the bank in fulfilling compliance and regulatory requirements, and will prevent unintended delays and other negative impact on the conduct of legitimate business.

Appropriate levels of transparency will facilitate informed, often faster decisions related to the granting of credit and financial facilities, and to the general support of a given commercial relationship or transaction. In the pursuit of opportunities in the international marketplace, where speed is often critical, the responsiveness of a company's bankers, based on adequate visibility, can translate to an important competitive advantage. Similarly, an exporter pursuing a sale in a foreign market can gain advantage by including attractive financing or payment terms – an option that generally requires the support of a financial institution.

Effective interaction with bankers and trade financiers depends to a large extent on effective communication – about the business of a company, the various commercial relationships involved and the markets in which the company pursues and intends to pursue opportunities. Regulatory and compliance requirements are one reality facing trade bankers.

Another reality, perhaps equally challenging, is the lack of understanding of trade and supply chain finance in most financial institutions, and the need to explain the business and its characteristics to internal partners and decision makers, such as credit committees, risk analysts and relationship managers among numerous others.

This gap in knowledge and understanding represents another strong argument in favour of communication and transparency. The greater the clarity available to a trade finance banker, relative to the business needs of a client, the more effectively – and promptly – the trade specialist can make the case internally to provide the support and facilities required by the corporate client.

It is often prudent to inform and engage trade finance specialists early in the development of a trade relationship, or a particular transaction, given that internal adjudication can take time or be subject to various levels of review and approval. The same partnership-based approach can be very effective in managing the regulatory requirements around trade finance, which, though aimed primarily at bankers, have a direct impact on the business of importers and exporters.

Regulatory demands on trade finance may have the unintended impact of raising the cost and reducing the availability of trade and supply chain finance; accordingly, an informed and collaborative approach by bankers and corporate clients around this issue will be the most effective in assuring appropriate and equitable treatment of this form of financing, by various regulatory bodies.

Bankers and the Cost of Borrowing

Accessing liquidity through trade finance is often commercially sound and cost-effective; however, engaging effectively with bankers also involves ensuring that company interests are well managed, and that requires finance and treasury executives to consider corporate finance and funding strategies in a holistic manner, ensuring that overall sourcing strategies and costs of borrowing are optimized.

In some cases, it may be optimal to finance on the basis of a trade-related solution, such as discounting of a draft under a letter of credit, or the sale of a foreign receivable to secure immediate payment.

There are instances, however, where the cost of trade finance may be elevated relative to other sources of liquidity, and it may be optimal to leverage a corporate operating line of credit or other facility, to provide working capital or financing in support of a trade transaction – provided the terms of the operating line allow such usage.

Circumstances may also arise where trade finance is more economical than other facilities available to a company; in such cases, trade finance specialists may promote this cost advantage, or they may downplay it, in order to avoid cannibalizing other bank business, or otherwise setting an expectation with a client that material differences in the cost of borrowing can arise.

A similar validation exercise in terms of financing options and sources should be undertaken in the context of trading ecosystems and supply chain relationships, given the fact that supply chain finance programs can facilitate access to finance on very attractive terms.

Exporters may incur significant costs related to trade risk mitigation and financing. An adequate estimate of the expected costs associated with trade finance fees and interest ought to be developed, so that such costs can be incorporated appropriately in the pricing strategy related to international transactions.

Detailed analysis, with the assistance of trade finance providers, should be an integral part of a company's efforts to engage effectively with bankers and trade financiers.

Non-Bank Providers: Boutique Firms

Importers and exporters can avail themselves of the services of non-banks in seeking to obtain support in trade and supply chain finance.

Several boutique or specialist finance firms focus on providing solutions to companies engaged in international commerce, some particularly focusing on supporting the aspirations of small and medium-sized enterprises.

The SME focus of certain boutique firms may make them particularly attractive as alternative providers of trade and supply chain finance, as much because of their domain focus, as their willingness to support small businesses with transactional advice, and their preparedness to assess risk and viability on a bespoke basis, as opposed to on the basis of rigid credit models that do not typically allow for the unique positive factors shaping the opportunity pursued by an SME.

Exporters: Choose Your Trade Bankers?

A documentary letter of credit is an undertaking by the issuing bank to provide payment to the exporter, provided documents presented by the exporter demonstrate full compliance with the terms and conditions outlined in the letter of credit.

The L/C is typically sent (authenticated and advised) to the exporter by an advising bank – often but not necessarily, the bank of the exporter, and that L/C may provide for payment to be made to the exporter at the counters of the advising bank, or may request or allow for that L/C to bear a confirmation – a separate and distinct payment promise to the exporter, extended by the confirming bank.

Under a documentary letter of credit, any bank that acts (appropriately and as provided for in the L/C) to facilitate payment to the exporter will seek reimbursement of monies paid or financing provided, through the issuing bank, or through a provider of credit insurance if the transaction is insured and the issuing bank is unable to make payment.

An exporter could (and this happens with some degree of frequency) select a bank other than their primary banker, to act on their behalf in the context of a trade finance transaction.

The "House Bank" or lead banker of the exporting company may have limited experience in international trade finance, or may not wish to undertake a transaction involving a market that is perceived as unacceptably risky, due to the weak standing of the issuing bank, or perhaps the high level of political or country risk associated with the country of the importer or the issuing bank.

As with any type of assessment of risk, opinions will vary between banks. Another financial institution may possess extensive experience in the market and/or industry sector involved, may have specialists located in the importer's home market and may know the issuing bank very well owing to the nature of an existing bank-to-bank relationship, and may be perfectly willing to participate in the transaction, even extending financing to the exporter at acceptable rates.

Additionally, certain investment pools, such as hedge funds, have been active in providing liquidity in support of trade flows and trade finance, focused in the pre-crisis timeframe, on developing and emerging market trade.

Boutique firms may specialize in certain types of transactions or by industry sector or market, and may be more disposed to provide support and financing in those specialized contexts, than the banks. Specialist firms might focus on manufacturing, green energy, commodity trade and any combination of sectors and markets, developing in-depth expertise and understanding of the risks and opportunities in those areas, allowing such firms to be responsive in ways that banks perhaps cannot.

Engaging Effectively

The mechanics of interacting with specialist boutique firms can vary from the more conventional bank-provided trade finance, for several reasons.

- The focus of boutique firms is significantly narrower;

- Such firms are not subject to levels of regulation comparable to the banks;

- The level of technical understanding of trade finance among boutique specialists is high relative to the broader banking community.

Company executives and entrepreneurs seeking the support of specialist firms relative to trade finance, can engage effectively on a transaction basis, or can pursue a more relationship-based approach; in any event, reputable, established and solvent firms in this business can provide viable alternatives to bank-provided trade finance.

The key to effective engagement with specialist firms is to provide sufficient information about the borrowing company and its business, including its international experience, and the very specific characteristics of a particular transaction to be financed. Boutique firms may be more open to understanding the unique advantages and requirements of a small business client, however, they may likewise, be more demanding relative to commercial and transactional transparency than banks – largely as a risk assessment and mitigation measure.

Effective engagement with specialist firms is likely to require appropriate levels of due diligence on the strength and unique specialties of the firm itself, in order to ensure that the transaction – and the relationship – will be supported in the event of unforeseen challenges.

While it can be argued that trade finance offerings and competencies are fairly comparable across the leading global banks, the same cannot be said about boutique trade and supply chain finance providers, and it would be risky for a company to seek commodity trade finance from a specialist firm with a core competency in manufacturing-related exports, or to approach a boutique firm whose principals possess extensive trade finance experience in Latin America, to do a deal in Africa.

Non-Bank Providers: ECAs and IFIs

Importers and exporters can also access – directly or indirectly – trade and supply chain finance facilities through export credit agencies and through various international financial institutions (IFIs), including the World Bank's International Finance Corporation, and various regional development banks.

ECAs were originally public sector entities mandated to enable economic recovery through support for export trade. ECAs provided financing and various forms of guarantees, insurance and other forms of risk mitigation, linked directly to the export aspirations of their sponsoring national governments.

More recently, ECAs have evolved a wide variety of operating models, some remaining public sector entities driven largely by policy priorities, while others have adopted hybrid models, combining public sector drivers to their mandate, with private sector dynamics shaped by market forces and requirements. Others still have shifted decidedly toward a private sector, market-based model, relegating policy considerations to largely exceptional elements of their approach and mandate.

While ECAs were historically very directly and narrowly linked to transactions supporting the national interest of their sponsoring jurisdictions, mandates have evolved today to the point that ECAs can be involved in providing trade finance or risk mitigation support, on transactions where the driver is purely commercial, and may not involve consideration of national interest.

Importers and exporters seeking trade finance, or some form of risk mitigation associated with a financing transaction, can look well beyond the offerings of their home country's ECA (be it public sector, hybrid or private sector in character), quite legitimately approaching other ECAs for support in their trade activities.

International institutions, likewise, have developed various favours of trade finance programs, some elements of which can be accessed directly by companies engaged in international commerce, and other aspects of which are accessed through the participation of a group of local and international banks, in those trade finance programs.

It is sufficient at this time to note the existence of these sources of trade and supply chain finance, and to consider how importers and exporters can engage with these organizations, to secure the necessary support.

Engaging Effectively

IFIs are primarily focused on activities linked to international development, though the International Finance Corporation (IFC) was given a far broader mandate in assuring access to trade finance, over the course of the global financial and economic crisis.

Most IFIs have a relatively clear regional focus, and will identify priority markets, as well as priorities in terms of the types of activities they will engage in and support. International trade, through trade finance facilitation and otherwise, tends to be a shared area of focus among IFIs, as does private sector engagement and the development of effective public-private partnerships.

There are significant opportunities for companies of all sizes to engage usefully with IFIs both in the pursuit of commercial opportunities and in the search for support related to accessing trade and supply chain finance. Effective engagement with an IFI requires alignment with the objectives and priorities of that institution, and an understanding that such organizations are, quite appropriately, sensitive to the priorities and objectives of their donor communities.

Export credit agencies, likewise, are specialist organizations; however, there is a wide spectrum of mandates, priorities and business models related to export credit and insurance agencies. Effective engagement demands an understanding of that spectrum of mandates, and requires the ability to identify those ECAs best positioned to support a particular international venture, market or a specific trading relationship.

The key to engaging effectively with an export credit agency is to understand its mandate and priorities and to approach that ECA for support on transactions that align well with those objectives – including transactions that may not qualify for support on commercial terms, but that may align well with the politically connected, public sector dimension of an ECA's overall mandate.

General Guidelines

Trade finance providers are, in most cases, fundamentally lenders.

They are highly specialized financiers adept at meeting complex requirements in support of international commerce, at times in the most challenging business environments across the globe – but in the end, they are financiers, and their core objective is to successfully deploy financial resources to generate target returns (be they financial returns like fees and income, or outcome based returns like the initiation of a new commercial relationship).

Successful engagement with trade financiers requires a prospective borrower to demonstrate an understanding of the proposed trading relationship or transaction, including a sober assessment of associated risks, as well as the commitment and ability to repay funds advanced or provided under a financing arrangement. A borrower may also demonstrate the ability to perform a related contractual obligation (production and shipment of an agreed export), which then triggers the basis for repayment of funds.

Trade finance, perhaps more than other forms of financing, can involve significant effort in terms of internal risk assessment and the securing of necessary approvals, and as such, early engagement with a trade banker or trade financier is generally advantageous. Likewise, the provision of as much transactional detail and information as possible can assist trade financiers in appropriately assessing related risk, and thereby ensuring adequate mitigation measures.

While conventional credit decisions in many markets are influenced, even driven, by complex credit models and automated assessment algorithms, it is worth noting the traditional elements that shaped credit adjudication procedures in the past, and still do so in markets where decisioning is not fully automated.

Lenders refer to the "Five Cs" of credit:

1. Character: Assessment of the way in which a prospective borrower conducts business, manages relationships and meets financial and other obligations.

2. Capacity: Assessment of borrowing capacity – including how much of that capacity is already utilized – to arrive at a view on likelihood of timely repayment. This element can also encompass the capacity of a borrower to successfully carry out the activities necessary to meeting commercial obligations under a trade transaction.

3. Capital: Analysis of the financial health of a business, including the level of investment of a prospective borrower, in the venture or transaction.

4. Conditions: Analysis of the prevailing economic and commercial conditions, locally and in the foreign markets where a business seeks to engage, along with the condition of the company, the trading relationship and the proposed venture.

5. Collateral: Analysis of the hard assets and security available to provide a secondary source of repayment of the loan, in the event that the borrower encounters difficulties with cash flow and is unable to arrange repayment as agreed.

One approach to communicating effectively with bankers and trade financiers may be to develop a message that touches on each of the five components listed, specifically addressing the unique opportunities and challenges related to the transaction – or trading relationship – under consideration.

Given the added complexity and risk around international activity, the five Cs can be augmented to include consideration of aspects specifically relevant to international commerce, and to the market in which a particular transaction is to take place.

Certain transactions may require significant preparation from the perspective of a trade banker, to secure the necessary approvals and credit facilities; in such cases, it may prove advantageous to engage trade financiers early, as a transaction begins to take shape and appear probable, in order to maximize the likelihood of approval.

It is true that different banks and trade financiers will have different levels of comfort – or risk appetite – related to certain markets and transactions. One bank may have been present in a given market for decades and may have tens or hundreds of millions in available facilities and credit limits, while another institution may have little or no experience in that same market and may therefore require a protracted approval process to provide even modest financing.

Similarly, two providers, otherwise largely comparable, may have very different partnerships related to a particular market, with one provider able to quickly mitigate risk to internally acceptable levels, and another so differently positioned as to be unable to assist.

Engaging effectively with trade financiers is as much about knowing a market and transaction, and communicating sufficient detail about it to assist a financier in being responsive, as it is about knowing the capabilities and capacities of various financiers, and where possible, selecting a provider that is well-matched to the financing needs under consideration.

8

Financing in Context: Trade Transaction Flow

Financing can be arranged at any number of points in the typical lifecycle or flow of an international trade transaction. Historically, as providers sought to respond to the emerging needs of importers and exporters, and looked for ways to offer value in the context of open account transactions, the notion of "event-based financing" gained significant traction.

Financing can be offered, or triggered, on the basis of the occurrence of a specific event or events in the course of an international trade transaction, such event typically linked to a potential need for liquidity or capital by one or more of the parties involved.

Trade financing can be linked to or offered on the basis of specific "events" in the trade transaction flow: events that typically offer a basis on which a bank or trade financier can prepare and package a financing solution aimed at meeting the needs of one or more parties.

An event on which financing can be based may also involve a legal change of status relative to the goods or the financial flows underlying a transaction. A change of ownership of the goods or shipment from the seller to the buyer, or a change of status of an invoice, from issued to accepted for payment: either of these changes could enable a trade finance provider to offer financing, in the former case, to the importer, with the goods now serving as security, and in the latter case, to the exporter, on the basis of the legal obligation represented by an invoice that has been accepted for settlement – a financial obligation referred to as an "Approved Payable."

Trigger or Event	Financing	Comment
Purchase Order Issued	P.O. Financing	Banks linking to client PO and ERP systems
Goods Stored in Warehouse	Warehouse Receipt Financing	Title controlled by the Bank or a trusted third party
Invoice/Title Documents Issued	Receivables Purchase	Banks, Factors and others can provide
Documents Presented for Payment	Post-Shipment Financing	Includes transport document evidencing shipment
Documents Deemed Compliant	Approved Payables Financing	Invoice approved for payment
Maturity Date or Due Date	Settlement of Financing, or Financing for Importer/Buyer	Financing reimbursed, or bank/other financing for importer, delay repayment until sale of goods

Figure 8.1   Event-based financing
Source: BAFT-IFSA, Adapted by OPUS Advisory

Financing can be arranged by the most sophisticated of providers, at almost any stage of a transaction, whether prior to the shipment of the goods, or following remittance of monies from the importer to the exporter.

Finance executives or entrepreneurs may not be fully aware of the range of financing options available, and therefore should consult trade finance specialists to identify potential products and solutions that could be of help in assuring adequate liquidity and financing throughout the course of the transaction and perhaps beyond that, over an extended timeframe, based on the strength of the trading relationship.

Trade Transaction Flow: Selected Elements

A trading relationship may begin in several ways, including a specific decision by one company to pursue opportunities in an international market, following the completion of appropriate due diligence and feasibility analysis, and perhaps attendance at an in-market trade show. Increasingly, however, companies are nudged into international activity as a result of receiving an unsolicited order, perhaps via the Internet.

While feasibility analysis funding is not trade finance, it is often available through public sector sources, along with support to offset the costs of initial travels to a target market, or specifically to attend relevant trade shows.

When an international transaction is initiated on an unsolicited basis via the Internet or by referral, a company will typically seek to secure adequate cashflow to support the completion of the transaction; however, uninitiated businesses often underestimate the costs, risks and timeframes involved, and as a direct outcome, often underestimate the level of liquidity required to support international activities.

The first step in ensuring appropriate levels and types of financing in support of international activities, is to obtain competent advice, either from internal specialists or from trade bankers or other domain experts, ideally, even some initial high-level advice to assist in the planning process while the relationship and commercial opportunity is being developed.

Once these elements are appropriately managed, and a sales contract is drafted, finalized and signed, specifying the Terms of Trade and the agreed mode of delivery and payment – including the timings thereof – parties can begin to explore financing alternatives and options.

Discounting a Banker's Acceptance

A textile exporter had been dealing with the same trade finance bank for 20 years or more, and with the same trade finance contacts in that bank for over a decade. The company was understood to be in good financial health and considered to be an excellent credit risk, with ample liquidity and proven ability to finance its international activities.

The company had long accepted, for competitive reasons, to be paid via documentary letter of credit, 90 days after shipment date, and had always awaited payment at maturity.

Standing instructions at the bank were that the company was to be paid at maturity (plus the legally mandated three days grace period available to the bank post-maturity), and this practice had been followed without discussion.

Internal reorganization within the bank resulted in a change of staff assigned to manage this client account within the trade bank operations group. On receipt of the first transaction following the reorganization, a trade operations specialist was reviewing documentation with the company's credit director, and noticing the tenor of the draft, mentioned that it was possible to discount the transaction and arrange for immediate payment.

The credit director had just accepted her new role and was not aware of the mechanics of letters of credit, nor had the bank been aware that their client was in some difficulty due to market conditions, and had been experiencing cashflow challenges.

The bank and the company promptly agreed to discount all acceptances under letters of credit for the foreseeable future, with the effect that the company's cashflow issues were largely resolved, and the bank earned substantial revenues, while ensuring the continued viability of a long-time client. (Source: OPUS Advisory)

Event-based or trigger-based financing is well illustrated in Figure 8.2 by a graphic developed by the Bankers' Association for Finance and Trade/International Financial Services Association, known as BAFT-IFSA, a leading banking industry association whose members include leading trade finance banks, technology providers and others engaged in trade and supply chain finance.

The range of options illustrated begins when the buyer/exporter warehouses goods prior to shipment, and run through the transaction lifecycle to the stage where any outstanding financing is reimbursed. Several event triggers are identified as being linked to financing opportunities, in between these endpoints.

Signature of Sales Contract

The sales contract will typically define the INCOTERM and the method of payment that will apply to a trade transaction, both important elements in helping to define the range of possible financing options and the triggers that might apply, to initiate financing solutions.

While the signature of the contract, on its own, may not facilitate access to financing, its terms will provide an initial basis upon which to undertake

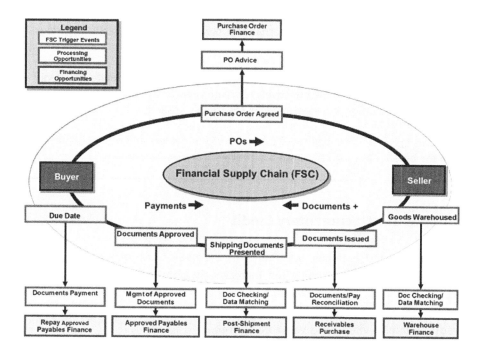

Figure 8.2   Supply chain finance trigger events, financing and processing
Source: Product Definitions for Open Account Trade Processing and Open Account
Trade Finance, BAFT-IFSA, December 2010

a discussion with potential trade finance providers, including banks, export
credit agencies and boutique or specialist firms.

Issuance of a Purchase Order

Once a buyer and seller have agreed to undertake a transaction together, and
the sales contract has been executed, a typical next step might be the issuance
of a Purchase Order. A purchase order, once issued by a buyer and accepted by
a seller or exporter, represents a contractual undertaking, and an obligation to
ship by the exporter, and to pay, by the importer.

In the event the various risks associated with the transaction are acceptable,
a financial institution may choose to offer financing to a seller on the basis of an
accepted purchase order.

> Financing options related to international commerce are available at various stages or steps in the lifecycle of a trade transaction.
>
> Traditional trade financing mechanisms and emerging solutions related to supply chain finance can combine effectively to create value and benefits for importers, exporters and other parties involved in the trade transaction.
>
> Financing is also potentially available to service providers and other supporters of the broader trading relationship.

Issuance of a Documentary Credit

An importer and exporter may agree to the use of one of several payment and settlement options, including increasingly popular open account terms; however, in the case of new relationships and in the event that higher-risk markets or circumstances are involved, a traditional documentary letter of credit remains a viable and valuable option.

Once a documentary credit is issued in favour of the exporter, it is possible in some markets to lodge the letter of credit as security in support of some form of loan or financial facility.

In the event that an exporter requires immediate access to a portion of the funds available under the letter of credit, buyer and seller can agree that the instrument will be issued with a special clause included in the terms of the credit to allow the exporter to draw what amounts to an advance under the L/C.

Production and Preparation for Shipment

An exporter may require cashflow or working capital to assist with sourcing of production inputs, or to finance the shipment and delivery of the final product according to the terms of the sales contract.

In the event that an exporter is sourcing some portion of the goods to be sold to the buyer, through a supplier unknown to the ultimate buyer, a letter of credit may be issued with the option to transfer that letter of credit, or a portion thereof, to the supplier. In this instance, the letter of credit is used as a basis upon which to finance and pay for the portion of the goods sourced from a supplier.

If the exporter is producing and shipping the goods, it is conceivable, even likely under credit-constrained economic conditions, that the exporter would have agreed to favourable payment terms for the buyer, to help close the sale. An exporter may have agreed to have a letter of credit issued on the basis that drawings with compliant documents would be paid, for example, 90 or 120 days after the On Board date of the Ocean Bill of Lading, showing that the shipment had been loaded onto the vessel in the agreed timeframe, for shipment to the importer. In the event that such terms are agreed, an exporter facing cashflow challenges, or simply seeking to manage or optimize working capital, might choose to request financing from a bank or trade financier, for the period from shipment, to the agreed payment due date.

This type of financing requires that the exporter prepare and present shipping documents related to the export of the agreed goods, demonstrating that the terms of the letter of credit have been fully complied with. Additionally, the extension of this type of financing requires that the bank or financier be comfortable with the risk profile of the transaction and the parties ultimately responsible for payment.

An exporter can secure post-shipment financing on the basis of export/shipping documents prepared and deemed to be fully compliant with the terms and conditions of the documentary letter of credit.

Once the shipping has been prepared, and shipping documents relative to the exports have been created and gathered, it follows that the commercial invoice would have been produced by the exporter. In the event that the documents are deemed to be compliant – that is, fully in line with all of the terms and conditions in the letter of credit, an exporter can seek to obtain post-shipment financing, either on the basis of the documents and the letter of credit, or on the basis of the receivable represented by the commercial invoice.

Some banks offer receivables financing and factoring services in addition to traditional trade finance solutions, or as part of an emerging supply chain finance offering. Receivables discounting is also available through factoring companies and other providers, and can be arranged on the basis that the lender holds the exporter accountable for non-payment by the importer (with recourse), or in a way that the lender pursues any required collection activity with the importer, in the event of non-payment (without recourse).

An exporter may warehouse goods locally in preparation for shipment, and depending on the timelines involved, it may be worth arranging financing on the basis of the conditions of warehousing, where the goods are controlled by a trusted party – or consigned to the bank or lender while awaiting shipment. Warehouse receipt financing is an option at this stage of a trade transaction.

Bank-to-Bank Financing

Traditional mechanisms such as letters of credit provide an opportunity for stronger financial institutions, or those located in markets where liquidity is affordable and accessible, to provide financing to other financial institutions involved in a trade transaction. This can be commercially advantageous to an importer, for example, in that such financing can then be used by an Issuing Bank to allow the importer to delay payment to that Issuing Bank under a letter of credit transaction. Banks can also provide financing to foreign financial institutions supporting exports from their countries, or can support each other – and their respective customers – through various channels such as the trade finance programs of various international institutions.

Financing on Settlement

When buyer and seller agree to conduct business on the basis of a term or usance letter of credit, the exporter may receive immediate funds against compliant documents on the basis of a discount provided by a bank or trade financier. The lender then typically awaits the due date or the maturity date, at which time funds are used to repay the amount financed, plus whatever fees and interest are applicable.

Funds due at maturity are generally paid by the buyer or importer, however, importers may also require financing in order to ensure adequate cashflow. In such circumstances, the Issuing Bank may choose to extend financing to the importer, by remitting funds due under the letter of credit, but postponing the debit to the importer's account for an agreed period, perhaps 60 days or 90 days.

This approach allows the amount financed in favour of the exporter to be repaid, while also extending financing to the importer – delaying repayment until the importer has received the goods and sold them at a profit – enabling repayment of the monies due under the letter of credit, on the basis of the sale of goods. The purchase and delivery of the goods is effectively financed end-to-end using the mechanisms of a traditional letter of credit.

Supply Chain Finance

The same trade transaction conducted on the basis of open account terms, with support in the form of supply chain finance on the basis of the borrowing capability of the importer, can be supported in similar fashion, though in this case, the exporter/supplier obtains financing from the importer's bank, based on approval of invoices by said importer. The creation of an approved payable serves as the basis upon which the exporter secures funding, with the trade finance bank relying on the risk profile of the importer, and on the country and political risk profile of the importer's (typically also the bank's) country of domicile.

An exporter can be financed through a supply chain program, based on the issuance of an invoice and its approval for payment by the importer. The trade financier relies on the borrowing capacity and risk profile of their importer client, providing financing directly to a supplier, previously invited to participate in the supply chain finance program.

Complementary Enablers/Sources of Finance

Financing or complementary services such as various forms of guarantee or insurance can be accessed, and in some cases, such support is a pre-requisite to obtaining the necessary financing.

Export credit insurance providers may or may not offer financing, but in certain circumstances, involving high-risk markets or counterparties, a bank may insist on export credit insurance as a means of mitigating its own exposure, prior to extending any financing.

An export letter of credit involving a transaction in a high-risk market, with an Issuing Bank of questionable stability or risk profile, will typically provide the option for that instrument to be Confirmed by another financial institution; however, if the transaction risk profile is deemed to be beyond the risk tolerances of a Confirming Bank, that institution will seek insurance cover from private sector sources or from an export credit/insurance provider.

Absent such mitigating cover, there is little chance of any financing being extended under such a letter of credit, unless another bank can be found, that is prepared to take on the associated risk without such insurance.

Trade-Related Factors

The conduct of international commerce is typically in US dollars, euros or, increasingly, renminbi, with the majority of transactions still denominated in US dollars, and other currencies playing an all but negligible role in such international transactions.

Managing the risk and cost related to currency exposure is an element of financial oversight and management in the conduct of international commerce, and it is one element of an effective trade financing strategy. Whether an importer or exporter seeks to manage currency volatility and risk at the level of an individual shipment, a trading relationship or an overall portfolio of international commercial activity, trade financiers can facilitate access to solutions around management of foreign exchange.

It is also an option with certain global banks to link supply chain finance solutions with various forms of foreign currency exposure management, including forward contracts or spot trades bundled with trade settlement transactions.

Leading financial institutions, particularly those with global presence, have been working for a number of years, to develop integrated transaction banking businesses, with the objective of offering comprehensive commercial and corporate banking solutions to their clients, which encompass trade finance, cash management, foreign exchange and other similar elements.

This trend has direct implications for the way in which companies can interact with their bankers: businesses engaged in material amounts of international business can seek advisory support and business solutions that address the major transactional needs likely to be encountered.

The integration of trade finance and cash management businesses has become something of a trend, although some banks have been challenged in developing a truly integrated organization, and have had to revert to internal structures where trade and cash businesses are separate, even if they exist under a transaction banking umbrella. Internal organization issues aside, the importance of this from the perspective of bank clients, is that such an approach motivates banks and bankers to look at a client's business in a more holistic and commercially meaningful way.

Leading trade bankers are increasingly capable of offering bundled solutions to meet the various transactional needs of companies of all sizes, from SMEs to global multinationals. Trade and supply chain structures can include elements aimed at addressing the foreign currency risk management and the cash management needs of clients.

Trade finance transactions, including those executed on the basis of supply chain programs and solutions can incorporate foreign currency solutions as well as cash management solutions, allowing businesses to optimize not only their financing, but also their cash position across multiple accounts and countries, while simultaneously ensuring appropriate levels of currency hedging.

Practical Transactional Considerations

The overarching principle to note is that trade and supply chain finance offers a wide variety of financing options, either directly linked to transaction flow, or paralleling the trade transaction. Financing solutions are available to importers, exporters and financial institutions, and can be structured to provide end-to-end support over the lifecycle of a trade transaction.

The complete suite of financing elements may be provided by a single trade financier, or it may be the combination of components obtained from several sources, depending on the nature of the trading relationship or transaction, and depending on the specific requirements of the parties involved.

While the uninitiated may approach a financial institution or trade finance provider on an *ad hoc* basis, as a specific financing need becomes apparent, more seasoned finance specialists may take a more complete view of their trade relationship(s), coupled with an understanding of the range of financing mechanisms and options available, actively seeking to optimize the combination, ideally in consultation with their trade financiers.

It is conceivable that existing, non-trade facilities such as operating lines of credit, may prove to be cost-effective as a source of liquidity under certain circumstances, and it is advisable for businesses of all sizes to consider their liquidity requirements holistically, and to access various sources to meet those requirements.

Likewise, it is good practice for entrepreneurs and finance executives to be aware of various trade finance related programs and support mechanisms available at home and in the international markets being developed, given that trade bankers and other specialists may not be fully aware of all the options – and supporting mechanisms – available.

While bankers remain primarily focused on selling products, there is a growing realization of the importance and value of expertise and advisory support. Entrepreneurs and finance executives in large multinationals, likewise, will benefit from actively leveraging the expertise of their trade financiers: it is both appropriate and worthwhile for a client to insist on adequate levels of domain expertise and advisory support from their trade finance providers.

Bankers have not yet fully understood the value of their expertise, and many are of the view that such advice and support is included in the product and transaction-level pricing already linked to the trade finance business. Put another way, trade finance advice, along with some excellent supporting resources and publications, are available to a commercial and corporate client at no extra charge.

Entrepreneurs and finance executives are best positioned to extract maximum value from trade and supply chain finance, when aware of the many options and variations available from banks, specialist firms and related service providers, including features and options unique to specific international markets.

While the foregoing section illustrates that there are clearly a variety of financing mechanisms and options available across the lifecycle of a trade transaction, it is worth noting that a market study conducted some years ago, concluded that there might be as many as 40 potential event-based triggers in a trade deal, based upon which financing could be offered to one or more of the parties involved.

Financing is indeed the oil that lubricates the engine of global commerce, and business leaders and finance executives pursuing opportunities in international markets will benefit greatly from an understanding of the range of settlement, financing and risk mitigation options available in the context of international commerce.

9

Export Credit Agencies, International Institutions and Non-Bank Providers

The financing of international trade is an activity that is heavily concentrated among leading global banks, however, other institutions and organizations play an important role in facilitating access to trade and supply chain finance, particularly (though not exclusively) in higher-risk, developing or emerging markets.

ECAs, originally public sector entities created in post-war Europe to support reconstruction efforts, have made important contributions to global trade, economic growth and prosperity, by providing a wide range of risk mitigation and financing solutions across the globe.

While there was serious debate, just before the global financial crisis of 2007, about whether ECAs had become anachronistic in a period of high and affordable liquidity, the effective evaporation of trade and export finance at the peak of the crisis demonstrated the critically important role of ECAs in assuring access to trade finance in times of crisis.

Several IFIs and development-oriented organizations have devised trade finance programs – mostly aimed at encouraging the provision of trade finance through local and international banks on the basis of various guarantee programs – that have proven, like the support of ECAs, to be critical to the continued conduct of international commerce. This was clearly illustrated, when the World Trade Organization, the G-20 and others determined that the World Bank's International Finance Corporation (IFC) and other institutions together should oversee a process of injecting US $250 billion in liquidity into the global trade finance market, at the peak of the crisis.

Debates about the value of the contributions of ECAs and international institutions, including IFIs, have all but evaporated, given the roles they played in enabling ongoing access to trade finance, at a time when many banks – including leading international banks – were forced to reduce or retreat from their activities in international markets.

ECA and IFI play a crucial role in ensuring access to financing, risk mitigation and high levels of expertise in the conduct of international trade in the highest-risk markets across the globe.

These organizations support billion-dollar multi-year transactions, but are also important partners to small businesses in the conduct of international commerce.

An understanding of ECA and IFI programs can be a significant commercial and competitive advantage for businesses of any size.

Export Credit and Insurance Agencies

ECAs have been in existence for many decades, initially as public sector organizations mandated to support the export and international market aspirations of companies headquartered in their home countries.

While the original, public sector models of ECAs have evolved into various forms, including full privatization, public/private partnerships and hybrid model ECAs, there are concerns in the international community around ensuring that ECA support does not become some form of *de facto* subsidy, thereby distorting tradeflows and adversely impacting efforts to promote free and equitable international commerce.

These concerns are at least partly linked to the reality that ECAs have been, and are still involved in the facilitation of transactions that may not be commercially viable, but are somehow seen to be in the national interest of their home countries.

The Arrangement is a "Gentlemen's Agreement" amongst its Participants who represent most OECD Member Governments. The Arrangement sets forth the most generous export credit terms and conditions that may be supported by its Participants.

The main purpose of Arrangement is to provide a framework for the orderly use of officially supported export credits. In practice, this means providing for a level playing field (whereby competition is based on the price and quality of the exported goods and not the financial terms provided) and working to eliminate subsidies and trade distortions related to officially supported export credits.

The Arrangement came into existence in 1978, building on the export credit "Consensus" agreed among a number of OECD countries in 1976. Prior to this time, the lack of rules set the stage for competition amongst governments to provide the most attractive financial terms in support of exporters competing for overseas sales; the end result being financial subsidies and potential trade distortions.

The Arrangement places limitations on the terms and conditions of officially supported export credits (e.g., minimum interest rates, risk fees and maximum repayment terms) and the provision of tied aid. It includes procedures for prior notification, consultation, information exchange and review for export credit offers that are exceptions to or derogations of the rules as well as tied aid offers.

The Participants to the Arrangement are: Australia, Canada, the European Union, Japan, Korea (Republic of), New Zealand, Norway, Switzerland and the United States. (Source: OECD Website: The Arrangement on Export Credits)

ECAs now exhibit a wide range of mandates and operating models, as well as a wide spectrum of financing, risk mitigation and other products and solutions, supporting the international activities of small businesses, mid-corporates and global multinationals. While some ECAs have significantly narrowed their mandates and the focus of their activities, others have deemed it appropriate and necessary to define mandates that extend far beyond the historical role of export credit and insurance agencies.

Given the wide variety of business models – and the range of mandates – of ECAs, it is wise for companies pursuing business in international markets to look beyond their own national agency or ECA, to identify organizations that could support specific transactions or trading relationships that may not otherwise be enabled by the national ECA.

The mandates, priorities and capabilities of ECAs and IFIs can vary significantly. It is worth the investment of time and effort to become conversant with the programs of several ECAs and some key international institutions, based on their respective focus on market of interest to a company or small business.

The impact and importance of ECA activity in supporting and enabling international commerce can be evaluated by taking a view of the exposure and new business levels reported by ECAs at the industry level, through the Berne Union – an industry body that counts most of the leading ECAs of the world among its members. Figure 9.1 illustrates.

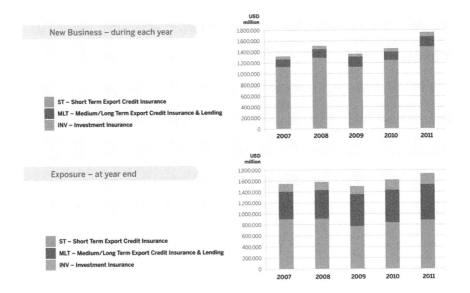

Figure 9.1   Highlights of ECA business
Source: Berne Union, 2012 Yearbook

Certain ECAs will take a competitive posture in the marketplace against other providers of trade finance and risk mitigation solutions, depending on the nature of their mandate, and the degree to which they are commercially oriented or revenue driven. ECAs that have been privatized, or those that are public/private partnerships, are likely to be more commercially focused; however, other ECAs that remain public sector entities have also adopted decidedly commercial perspectives on their business.

The Export-Import Bank of the United States (US Exim Bank) is very much in a non-compete posture relative to banks and private sector providers, to the extent that the agency must not only avoid competing, but must back out of a deal or an area of activity, if a private sector provider decides to provide the necessary support to businesses.

Other ECAs have been, or are today, direct competitors to banks and other providers, which can also prove advantageous to companies seeking favourable pricing. At the same time, however, banks and other providers recognize the indispensable role of ECAs, particularly in helping to mitigate risk and reduce exposure.

As noted earlier, there is a spectrum across which various ECAs can be positioned, as shown in Figure 9.2 and it can be valuable for a finance executive or entrepreneur to understand the options available, in order to have the best chance of identifying an ECA that matches the requirements of a particular deal or market.

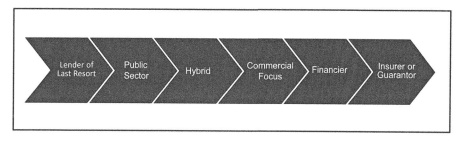

Figure 9.2   Spectrum of ECA models
Source: OPUS Advisory

Certain ECAs operate across the spectrum, providing a comprehensive set of services and aiming to address both the commercial aspect, and the public sector or national interest dimension of an ECA's potential mandate. While some ECAs focus on credit and financing, others may prefer to focus on risk mitigation, and still others provide services and solutions covering both categories of activity.

Transactions that are seen by governments to be in the national interest but that may not necessarily be commercially viable can be finance and supported by an ECA on the basis that they will generate some form of benefit for a country. Such benefits might include the advancement of political objectives or the fulfillment of international development commitments, among numerous others.

Export credit agencies can play a unique role in such contexts, and companies pursuing such business and transactions, may obtain support through an ECA that would certainly not be available through a bank or specialist trade finance provider.

ECAs with a full or partial public sector affiliation, likewise, may be more open to supporting the needs of small businesses, largely as a result of political directive, while fully privatized ECAs, like many banks, will be less inclined to provide trade finance to SMEs, unless such support is clearly profitable.

A high-level understanding of the mandate and operating models of ECAs is important; additionally, each ECA will offer a unique set of products, services and solutions suited to its priorities and the needs of its client base. It is worthwhile for a company or small business to appreciate and understand the specific proposition and product offering associated with the ECAs that may meet a company's requirements.

Export Development Canada (EDC), Canada's national ECA, is among the most highly regarded agencies in the world, and provides an excellent example of the breadth of solutions potentially accessible through an ECA (see Figure 9.3).

In addition to providing services on a standalone basis, ECAs can work closely with banks to support the ability of trade financiers to provide financing solutions to their clients. Companies engaging in international trade on the basis of documentary letters of credit, in higher-risk markets or transactions, may request that the letter of credit be Confirmed. A Confirmation, as described earlier, involves a bank adding its own payment promise to an L/C to provide risk mitigation comfort to their exporter client.

Banks are constrained by limits to the country risk and bank risk exposure they can accept, and in seeking to pursue additional business, as well as to mitigate against the possibility of financial loss, the banks may seek insurance cover from an ECA.

Profile of Export Development Canada
Founded 1944, Owned by Government of Canada
Major Facilities
Insurance: Credit Insurance for export transactions, including policies issued to financial institutions to cover foreign bank payment obligations and purchased receivables. Contract Insurance for capital goods, service contracts and projects. Political Risk Insurance for equity investments, assets and debt, as well as comprehensive insurance policies issued to financial institutions for payment default on sovereign or quasi-sovereign debt obligations
Financing: Flexible financing solutions including Buyer Credits, Supplier Credits, Bank Guarantees, Equity Products and Financing to support Foreign Direct Investment.
Bonding: Guarantee and Insurance products to support Performance Bonding and Surety Bonds as well as Foreign Exchange Facilities.
Corporate Description
EDC is Canada's export credit agency, established to support and develop, directly and indirectly, Canada's export trade, as well as Canadian capacity to engage in that trade and to respond to international business opportunities. EDC is financially self-sustaining and operates on commercial principles. In addition to being a direct lender and insurer, EDC acts as a catalyst to leverage private capital and establishes partnerships both domestically and abroad.

Figure 9.3   Profile of EDC

Source: Berne Union Yearbook, 2012, Exporta Group

The option to mitigate risk through an export credit agency also allows a bank to support a transaction that may otherwise be outside acceptable parameters, as defined by bank credit and risk committees. ECAs, then, provide assistance to trade bankers, but also support end-clients by enabling banks to extend their offerings beyond what they could do independently.

Some ECAs, particularly those with a public sector element to their mandates, undergo periodic reviews of their mandates, and in the case of US Exim Bank, for example, engage in benchmarking and periodic reviews of market requirements and priorities.

Context

The most significant events that have shaped ECA activity in 2011 were: 1) the Eurozone sovereign debt crisis and 2) commercial bank efforts to prepare for compliance with the Basel III [capital reserve and adequacy] regulations. These influenced every aspect of international commercial bank lending, including the level of commercial bank net lending, capital flows into developing countries and even the role of commercial banks in ECA export finance.

Findings

The global financial crisis of 2008 steadily impacted commercial bank appetite for risk, thereby pushing spreads up and the cost of financing to the forefront as a key competitive factor among ECAs, reaching a dominant role in 2011. Moreover, anticipation of Basel III requirements combined with the European crisis reduced the final marketability of all long-term commercial bank financing. Against this backdrop, Exim Bank reported a third consecutive year of record-breaking activity in excess of US $32 billion in FY 2011. This surge in demand was led by the unprecedented activity in the aircraft, and the project and structured finance arenas, with the latter surge funded almost entirely by direct loans.

In that context, Exim Bank scored high marks in 2011 and its overall competitiveness grade stayed strong at "A-/B+." (Source: US Exim Bank Competitiveness Report, June 2012)

The mandate of US Exim is very clearly and consistently linked to the creation of jobs in the United States, and, consistent with the free market approach to business in the US, the agency is to provide support in areas where a private sector solution is not provided or available. Not only is US Exim mandated not to compete with private sector providers, the agency will exit a line of business if a new private sector provider enters such an area of activity. Additionally, the agency is very conscious of domestic and international perceptions around whether US Exim provides any sort of subsidy or unfair support to US businesses or to the transactions involving American interests.

The philosophy underlying the mandate of an ECA can be an important consideration for companies seeking support. In the same way that political perspectives shape the commercial nature of an international market, the same political context shapes the mandate and activities of a national ECA, and therefore, influences the nature of a commercial transaction between two businesses – or the dynamic across a global supply chain.

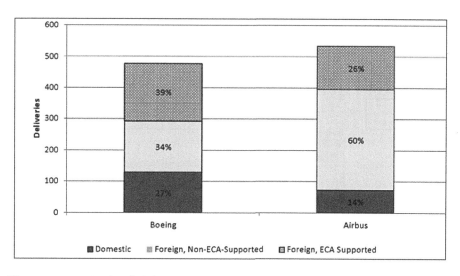

Figure 9.4   Boeing/Airbus ECA support comparison
Source: US Ex-im Bank Competitiveness Report, June 2012

US Exim supports a wide range of trade transactions and related supply chains – from aircraft export sales, to the trade aspirations and activities of small and medium-sized enterprises. As with many ECAs US Exim offers support specifically aimed at small businesses and entrepreneurial ventures, in addition to supporting the international activities of multinationals. Even global multinationals like Boeing and Airbus can benefit from ECA support, as illustrated in Figure 9.4.

Once again, from a corporate or small business perspective, knowledge of the sector-level areas of focus of a given ECA can be important, leading to additional/unexpected forms of support. Each ECA also differs on the requirements related to local (domestic) content, in determining whether a particular transaction or trading relationship qualifies for support under the terms of the ECA's mandate.

Whether ECA credit/cover is provided on the basis of a particular element of an agency's mandate, or a combination of various factors, the basis for approval can vary significantly between ECAs (see Figure 9.5).

Economic impact, content requirements or other drivers such as "market gaps" or "market windows" where an ECA is filling a need around trade or project finance, or where ECA support is part of an aid package that may have

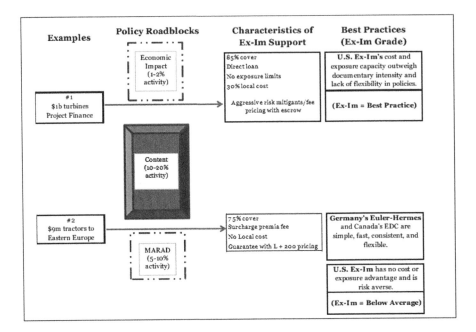

Figure 9.5   US Exim Bank transaction illustration

Source: US Exim Bank Competitiveness Report, 2012

certain conditions linked to its provision, the variety of drivers around ECA support can translate into a variety of commercial conditions under which a company, transaction or trading relationship may qualify for ECA support, as illustrated in Figure 9.6.

	Ex-Im Bank	EDC (Canada)	European ECAs	JBIC & NEXI (Japan)
Is there a requirement to ship foreign content from ECA's country?	Yes	No	No	No
Will the cover automatically be reduced if foreign content exceeds 15%?	Yes	No	No	No
Is there a minimum amount of domestic content required to qualify for cover?	No	No	Yes	Yes
Does domestic assembly of foreign inputs transform the foreign-originated input to domestic content?	No	Yes	Yes	Yes

Figure 9.6   Comparison of ECA support

Source: US Exim Bank Competitiveness Report, June 2012

In certain circumstances, ECAs collaborate, and it may be possible to work with ECAs that have complementary programs and value propositions, to gather the support needed to enable a transaction.

Export Development Canada, a federal Crown Corporation, is one of the most highly regarded ECAs in the world, combining its government status with a commercial orientation, and a comprehensive suite of trade and investment related solutions, including credit and risk mitigation.

EDC is a major contributor to trade and economic activity in Canada, as much in terms of financing and risk mitigation solutions, as in domain

---

EDC: Benefits to Canada

EDC carried out US $87.5 billion in international and domestic transactions on behalf of Canadian companies during 2012. The bulk of this business represents EDC's core international trade and investment activity, which accounted for US $85.2 billion or 97.4 percent of total volumes. An additional US $2.2 billion of domestic assistance (2.6 percent of total volumes) was provided...

During the late 1990s, EDC facilitated between 7 to 8 percent of Canada's total exports and direct investment outflows. During the past several years, this share had risen to more than 18 percent. The ratio pulled back to 15 percent in 2012 as the amount of business facilitated by EDC declined while Canadian exports increased an estimated 2 percent.

Canadian exports and CDIA to emerging markets grew by 0.5 percent in 2012 to reach US $72.5 billion. Exports and CDIA to emerging markets now represent 13 percent of total Canadian exports and CDIA, up from 6 percent a decade ago. EDC facilitated 37 percent of Canadian companies' exports and CDIA in emerging markets during 2012.

Contributing to the Canadian Economy

The exports, CDIA and domestic business facilitated by EDC in 2012 are estimated to have sustained US $57.2 billion in Canadian GDP, a drop of 14.1 percent from the previous year. The decline stems from lower EDC business volumes (down by 14.9 percent on the year). The contribution to the Canadian economy in 2012 remained significant, representing 4.0 percent of Canada's total GDP. In other words, for every dollar in income earned in Canada during 2012, 4.0 cents is attributable to EDC's trade and investment facilitation. The employment associated with the business EDC facilitated in 2012 is estimated at 573,773 full-time equivalent jobs, about 3.3 percent of national employment. (Source: EDC)

	2011	2012	% Change 2012/2011 (2)
1. Total EDC Volume (billions C$)	102.8	87.5	-14.9
– Core Business Volume (bn C$)	99.7	85.2	-14.5
– Domestic Business Volume (bn C$)	3.1	2.2	-29.0
– Volume in Emerging Markets (bn C$)	31.2	26.5	-15.1
– CDIA supported by EDC (bn C$)	5.9	6.6	11.7
2. Canadian GDP facilitated by Total EDC Volume (bn C$)	66.6	57.2	-14.1
– Share of Total Canadian GDP (%)	4.8	4.0	-16.8
3. Number of jobs facilitated by Total EDC Volume	665,805	573,773	-13.8
– Share of Total Canadian Employment (%)	3.8	3.3	-14.8
4. Number of Customers (Direct + Indirect)	7,787	7,427	-4.6
– Large	1,618	1,610	-0.5
– Medium	2,518	2,376	-5.6
– Small	3,651	3,441	-5.8
5. Number of Partnership Transactions	5,757	4,517	-21.5

Figure 9.7   EDC benefits to Canada scorecard, 2012
Source: EDC

expertise, transaction advisory and thought leadership. The impact of EDC's activities is illustrated in Figure 9.7.

Export credit agencies can sometimes be dismissed as bureaucratic government entities, and some of them are fully deserving of that characterization; however, the leading ECAs add significant value and capacity in support of international commerce, and should be part of an overall trade and supply chain financing strategy for businesses of all sizes, either directly, or as a complement to the services provided by bankers and boutique trade finance firms.

The importance and commercial impact of the differences in ECA mandates can be illustrated through an observation from Ernst & Young, relative to the role of the UK export credit agency, ECGD, the Export Credits Guarantee Department, now known as UK Export Finance. Prior to a recent re-organization, it was noted that:

"ECGD lacks an effective engagement strategy and an understanding of what it can deliver with its current resources. If this is to change, ECGD will need to take a more commercial approach. It needs to move its focus from the products and become more customer-orientated, focusing on what it can do to maximize delivery and how it can effectively, flexibly and innovatively leverage the resources of both existing and new delivery partners."

"The mass market rhetoric of the ECGD is not backed up in either resources or intention. A comparison with the German ECA, Hermes, illustrates the gulf between their capacities. In 2010, Hermes administered €32.5bn worth of business, 73% of which went to SMEs; by comparison, the ECGD administered a total of €3.3bn (£2.9bn), with almost no SME coverage and dominated by the aerospace sector." (Source: Winning Overseas: Boosting Business Export Performance, CBI/Ernst & Young, 2011)

UK Export Finance has since undergone a revision of focus, and both trade and supply chain finance have been identified as important priorities for the UK economy as enablers of international commerce, reaching into 10 Downing Street, with a senior-level discussion on the topic hosted by Prime Minister Cameron in late 2012. UK Export Finance has identified a very specific set of products and solutions offered in support of British exporters, as listed in Figure 9.8 below.

ECAs, Trade Finance and Corporate Social Responsibility

Historically, ECAs (and trade financiers) have been involved in supporting certain types of projects or transactions that were later found to have a variety of significant adverse effects, including on the environment, on indigenous peoples affected by large-scale development such as hydroelectric plants.

The activities of ECAs, especially those guided by a public sector mandate (and therefore ultimately answerable to a political constituency), have been subject for some years, to environmental impact assessments, standards around corporate social responsibility and related expectations of conduct and thresholds, that directly impact the types of transactions that such ECAs can support.

Product	How the product works
Buyer Credit Facility	We provide a guarantee to a bank that makes a loan to an overseas borrower to finance the purchase of capital goods and/or services worth at least £5 million from a supplier in the UK.
Supplier Credit Financing Facility - bills and notes	We provide a guarantee to a bank to cover payments due under bills of exchange or promissory notes purchased by the bank from a supplier in the UK, who has received them in payment for goods or services supplied to an overseas buyer.
Supplier Credit Financing Facility – loan (without bills and notes)	We provide a guarantee to a bank for a loan to an overseas borrower to finance a contract with a supplier in the UK.
Line of Credit	We provide a guarantee to a bank that makes a loan to an overseas borrower to finance several export contracts with different exporters.
Project Financing	We provide a guarantee to a bank that makes a loan of at least £20 million to an overseas borrower to finance a major project where the loan will be repaid out of the revenue generated by the project.
Export Insurance Policy	We provide insurance to an exporter in the UK against not receiving payment under an export contract and to cover costs which are wasted because of the contract being terminated for reasons not related to the performance of the exporter or because its performance is prevented by certain political events.
Bond Insurance Policy	We provide insurance to exporters against the unfair calling of bonds that they are required to provide under export contracts (for example, advance payment bonds or performance bonds).
Overseas Investment Insurance	We provide political risk insurance for a term of up to 15 years to investors in the UK who invest in overseas enterprises.
Letter of Credit Guarantee Scheme	We provide guarantees to UK banks to enable them to confirm letters of credit issued by overseas banks in favour of UK exporters. The guarantee covers part of the overseas issuing bank's obligation to reimburse the UK confirming bank for payments which it makes under the letter of credit
Bond Support Scheme	We help exporters raise tender and contract bonds by sharing with banks who issue those bonds (or who arrange for them to be issued by giving counter-indemnities to another bank) the risks of not being reimbursed by the exporter following a call on a bond.
Export Working Capital Scheme	We facilitate exporters' access to working capital finance for specific export contracts by sharing risks with banks on loans.
Foreign Exchange Credit Support Scheme	In connection with a specific export contact we increase UK Export Finance's guarantee under the Export Working Capital Scheme to provide additional credit capacity which will be used by banks to support forward foreign exchange hedging facilities in relation to that contract.

Figure 9.8   UK export finance product summary
Source: Quick Guide to UK Export Finance, 2012

A number of banks, ECAs and international institutions involved in trade and project finance have opted to demonstrate adherence to common standards in this area by adopting the Equator Principles – a set of guidelines for assessing and managing social and environmental risk related to trade and project finance activity, listed in Figure 9.9.

ECA Equator Principles
Principle 1: Review and Categorization
Principle 2: Social and Environmental Assessment
Principle 3: Applicable Social and Environmental Standards
Principle 4: Action Plan and Management System
Principle 5: Consultation and Disclosure
Principle 6: Grievance Mechanism
Principle 7: Independent Review
Principle 8: Covenants
Principle 9: Independent Monitoring and Reporting
Principle 10: EPFI Implementation Reporting

Figure 9.9   ECA Equator Principles
Source: Introduction to the Equator Principles, EP Association

The Equator Principles are currently undergoing a process of review and updating, however, it remains worth noting that certain transactions (the current minimum threshold is US $10 million) are subject to this assessment process for banks and other institutions that have adopted the framework.

International Financial Institutions

International Financial Institutions (IFIs), including various regional development banks and development finance institutions, also play an important part in facilitating and enabling access to trade finance, particularly when a transaction involves at least one party based in an emerging or developing economy.

Organizations such as the World Bank's International Finance Corporation, the Asian Development Bank, the European Bank for Reconstruction and Development, the Inter-American Development Bank and others have developed various forms of programs and products aimed at facilitating access to trade and supply chain finance, in support of international commerce.

While these programs have been in place for years, their contribution to facilitating international commerce was highlighted during the global economic crisis, and the scope of their activities and the comprehensiveness of programs have grown over the past several years. As Figure 9.10 below illustrates, the IFI trade finance programs have supported over US $35 billion in trade flows since their inception, notably with zero losses.

	EBRD	IFC	IDB	ADB
Program title	Trade Facilitation Program (TFP)	Global Trade Finance Program (GTFP)	Trade Finance Facilitation Program(TFFP)	Trade Finance Program (TFP)
Number of countries of operation	20	91	20	16
Program commencement	1999	2005	2005	2004
Number of transactions since commencement (year end 31 December 2011)	11,600	11,255	1,966	4,236
Value of transactions since commencement	EUR 7.2 billion equivalent to USD 9.5 billion	USD 15.8 billion	USD 1.96 billion	USD 8.8 billion (USD 3.5 billion of which in 2011)
Number of confirming banks	800	800	264	112
Claims to date	2 claims, zero losses	zero	zero	zero
Website	www.ebrd.com/tfp	www.ifc.org/gtfp	www.iadb.org/tradefinance	www.adb.org/tfp

Figure 9.10   IFI trade finance programs
Source: ICC Rethinking Trade & Trade Finance, 2012

While some of the processes related engaging with IFIs can be onerous and lengthy, it is worth highlighting that the trade finance programs offered by these institutions tend to focus on higher-risk developing markets, where access to financing can be difficult or prohibitively expensive. Under such circumstances, and given the fact that some of the support programs are aimed at the banks as providers of financing to importers and exporters, it is worth being aware of these programs and of the options they may offer which would otherwise not be available.

IFIs play a critical role in supporting international development and poverty reduction, as well as engagement of local private sector organizations in developing and emerging economies. This includes, in several cases, explicit efforts to encourage and enable emerging market banks to engage in the provision of export and trade finance. One way in which this is done, is by providing guarantees to foreign/international banks to mitigate certain types of risks involved in transacting with local financial institutions.

Figure 9.11 illustrates what could be a traditional documentary letter of credit transaction, with the notable difference that the Issuing Bank is located in a market served by the Asian Development Bank), and the Confirming Bank is likely to be an international bank approved for participation in the ADB Trade Finance Program. The Confirming Bank mitigates risk from the perspective of the transaction between buyer and seller, by agreeing to cover the risk of nonpayment by the Issuing Bank, as in any standard Confirmation transaction,

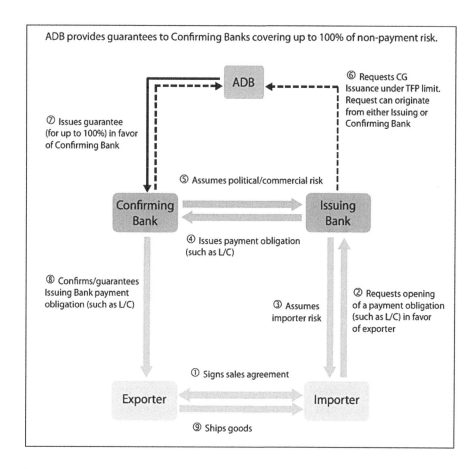

Figure 9.11   Asian Development Bank trade finance transaction
Source: Asian Development Bank Website

however the ADB facilitates this by providing a guarantee to the Confirming Bank, to cover against default by the Issuing Bank.

Such structures allow local financial institutions to engage in the financing of international trade, simultaneously encouraging international banks to participate in these transactions (which might otherwise be deemed too risky) on the basis of the guarantee provided by a trusted international institution such as the ADB.

Three of the IFIs shown in the preceding table report zero claims (and therefore zero losses), since the inception of their programs in 2004/2005.

The EBRD, which is the first institution to develop a trade finance facilitation program in 1999, reports two claims, and zero losses in that time.

The role of IFIs in facilitating access to liquidity and trade finance, in support of trade with developing and emerging markets, is important to the ability of these economies to engage in trade, reduce poverty and increase development, and assist their financial institutions in engaging successfully in the financing of international commerce.

Trade and supply chain finance is complex and esoteric.

Banks provide the vast majority of trade financing across the globe, however several boutique firms – led by senior trade finance specialists and ex-bankers – are offering alternatives.

These may be especially attractive to small businesses, or to industry sectors with unique financing requirements.

Entrepreneurs and company executives pursuing business and trade opportunities in developing markets should become aware of the support available through various IFIs. Even if that support is provided to certain participating banks, and not directly to the businesses engaged in the commercial relationship, the net result may well be to increase the options available to importers and exporters in accessing trade and supply chain finance in higher-risk, developing or emerging markets.

The engines of growth of the twenty-first century are expected to be developing and emerging market economies; engaging in these markets can be rewarding and challenging: international financial institutions, regional development banks and development finance institutions can be valuable partners in the pursuit of developing markets business, including access to trade and supply chain finance.

Alternative Sources of Trade and Supply Chain Finance

Trade and supply chain finance can be obtained from various sources, as indicated on several occasions.

While the banks, export credit agencies and international financial institutions provide and facilitate the vast majority of trade – and increasingly, supply chain – finance across the globe, it is worth noting that there are several other options, some aimed particularly at small businesses, others focused perhaps on a particular industry sector, and others yet focused primarily on the provision of trade finance in support of poverty reduction and international development through trade.

BOUTIQUE FIRMS

The specialized and technical nature of international trade and supply chain finance – and the potentially lucrative nature of the business – has given rise to the existence of several boutique firms in various parts of the world, providing trade finance solutions. The models can vary significantly, from long-established companies positioned as sources of alternative financing, to relatively new entities focused financing a subset of international commerce, such as commodity trade.

While some such firms leverage their own capital in providing financing, others act primarily as advisors in sourcing financing and in structuring transactions to meet the needs of their clients. Others still may offer financing solutions to a small group of clients, as was the case some years ago with a highly regarded trade promotion organization that sought to provide short-term facilities to its small business members.

Specialist firms of this type can support what is often a decidedly underserved segment of the trade finance market, and may serve as either a complementary source to bank-enabled trade finance, or as an alternative to such financing, which, in the current, crisis-affected financial environment, can be scarce, expensive or both.

Some boutique firms opt to conduct business as standalone entities, and have had success with such an approach. Other firms have deemed it best to take a partnership approach, with bank and/or export credit agency partners, to assist in extending both their international footprint and the financial capacity that can be leveraged to provide trade and supply chain finance.

FACTORS

Factoring houses, or factors, are companies that provide financing on the basis of receivables due to a prospective borrower. While some factors are affiliated to banks, others are independent service providers, and offer solutions linked to both domestic and international transactions. The basic transaction flow is illustrated in Figure 9.12.

Though there are variations, factoring involves the sale of an invoice approved for payment (or a portfolio, or series of invoices) by a business at an agreed discount, in order to expedite payment and thereby improve cashflow and working capital. The discount may be a combination of fees and charges, together with a percentage of the invoice retained by the factor as security.

The factor conducts appropriate credit analysis and purchases the receivable or the portfolio of receivables, providing immediate payment, typically a maximum of 80 percent of the invoice value.

In some models, particularly where business is cross-border, the factoring transaction is facilitated by two factors, much like a letter of credit transaction in its most basic form, typically involves two banks, one in each country.

In the event that the receivables are financed on a non-recourse basis, the factor loses the right to reclaim monies from the borrower, in the event of dispute, non-payment or other default of the company that was to pay the invoice(s) originally. Factoring with recourse provides the factor with the option to recover funds from the borrower, if deemed necessary. Financing on a non-recourse basis tends to be more expensive to the buyer, as the factor fully assumes the risk of non-payment, and may need to incur expensive collections costs or litigation, in the event of dispute or non-payment.

Ultimately, the factoring transaction results in payment of the face amount of the invoice(s) less agreed fees and charges. While factoring has traditionally been focused on domestic transactions, due to the lower risk, lower costs of recovery and generally lower complexity, there has been a marked increase in international factoring and cross-border receivables financing in recent years.

FCI, a leading industry association of factors, reports that its members held a 73 percent global market share of international factoring activity, covering over 240 million invoices and involving almost 4.2 million buyers across the globe in 2010. Cumulative transaction volumes are shown in Figure 9.13. While factoring volumes have historically been concentrated in Europe, about one third or nearly €8 billion of the cross-border factoring volumes reported by FCI for 2012 are linked to China. Year-over-year growth of 36 percent in

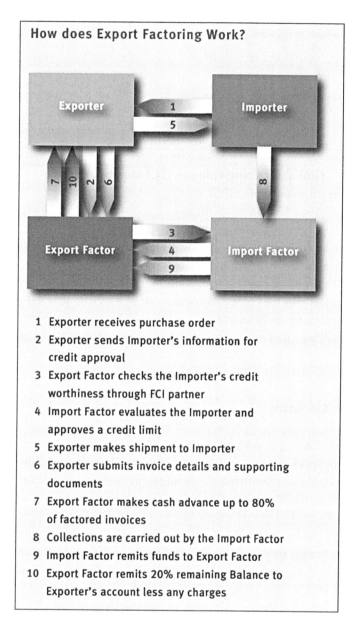

Figure 9.12 Export factoring
Source: Factors Chain International (FCI)

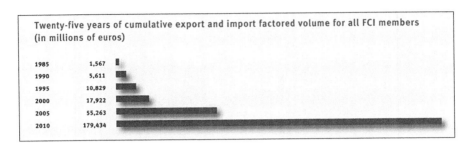

Figure 9.13   Global factoring volumes (FCI member firms)
Source: Factors Chain International (FCI)

cross-border factoring activity clearly demonstrates the emergence of this option as a viable means of trade finance.

Some factors offer a comprehensive suite of services that extend beyond invoice discounting, to insourced accounts payable management or to other forms of financing such as inventory and equipment finance and other related services.

Specialist Affiliates

The niche positioning of certain types of trade finance is well illustrated by the emergence of specialist trade finance units (or affiliated companies) linked to other well-established ventures, for example, in the transportation business or in the cards and payments business.

These entities have identified a niche opportunity linked to the servicing of a client base where they have established relationships, or where they have a particular knowledge of the transactional needs of their target clients.

Companies using the logistics and transportation services of an established global provider may have an opportunity to avail themselves of trade and supply chain finance solutions on the basis of the existing commercial relationship; likewise, small businesses seeking accelerated settlement (or financing) of low-value receivables may benefit from the services of a provider that is targeting this space based on its unique, global understanding of this space.

Hedge Funds

A small number of hedge funds, based in markets ranging from Saudi Arabia to the United Kingdom and the US, have shown interest in investing in portfolios of trade finance transactions as a means of generating returns while investing in what is now widely known to be a safe, low default asset class.

While these funds may not directly fund trade finance transactions, they are, in effect, providing additional capacity in the marketplace, most commonly by enabling banks to undertake additional trade financing activity, and by attracting capital to trade-based investment funds. While several such funds now exist, and are hedge funds in the traditional sense, a major global commodity trader has launched a large trade finance fund, with similar objectives.

Such vehicles are typically aimed at institutional investors such as pension funds and others; however, given the short tenor of trade finance transactions, the funds will require – and facilitate – a steady stream of trade finance deals to remain viable and sustainable.

While the banks welcome additional liquidity aimed at the trade finance market, they face a competitive challenge of sorts from hedge funds, and the fact that hedge funds do not face the same relatively stringent regulatory demands as banks do, poses a problem for financial institutions, but may allow certain transactions to benefit from hedge fund support. Initially, hedge funds in this space sought the higher returns associated with emerging markets trade finance, some focusing particularly on Africa, and on higher-volatility sectors associated with greater margins.

Network or Platform-Based Financiers

Efforts to modernize the transactional aspects of traditional trade finance have been underway since the late 1990s, with initial focus on improving process efficiency, reducing the level of manual intervention required in a transaction, and ultimately, the desire to dematerialize trade transactions, eliminating paper in favour of electronic documentation and communication.

Some early attempts are no longer in operation, while others have redefined their propositions several times, or shifted their focus geographically, by market segment or otherwise. Currently, there are credible and established platform and technology-based solutions around trade and supply chain finance. Such organizations may operate as closed, membership-based models, or may aspire to a more open structure, integrating with various providers including banks, logistics companies, export credit or risk insurance specialists and numerous others.

Numerous technology providers exist, whose objective it is to provide technology solutions to trade finance banks. These platform and network-based companies, while they may collaborate with banks, and may obtain capital and financial resources from banks in support of their trade business, can offer financing on the basis of their own independent capacity, risk appetite and credit adjudication processes.

They are, in that respect, a viable and credible alternative to traditional bank trade finance.

This category of alternate providers of financing can also be considered to include various solutions aimed primarily at accelerating payment and settlement processes. Several such solutions have articulated value propositions around enhanced cashflow and working capital, as a direct result of the acceleration of the settlement process. The unique element related to this group of solutions is that they do not necessarily offer financing, either in the conventional sense, or in terms of trade-related financing specifically.

Promoters of these solutions speak of:

- acceleration of settlement timelines;

- reduced impact on bank lines of credit or business operating lines;

- reductions in the overall cost of borrowing;

- enhancements around account tracking and reporting;

- improvements in processes.

Certain services enabling online payments and the maintenance of virtual accounts, likewise, promote the efficiency and financial advantages of their proposition – and its applicability across borders – as an important benefit, and a significant differentiator relative to traditional bank products and facilities.

NICHE PROVIDERS

Alternative sources of financing accessible in support of international trade include service providers that are perhaps affiliated to other businesses, or are providing trade finance in support of some existing client base.

The focus on working capital and liquidity is such under current market conditions, that several niche providers of trade and supply chain finance have emerged, aiming to service specific client segments with tailored solutions.

Whether such providers are associated to the logistics industry or the credit card business, or whether they are linked to specific industry sectors, the services of niche providers can be important and valuable complements to traditional sources of trade finance, given that they may possess unique insight into the clients and sectors they serve.

10

Flexibility of Financing: Small Business, Developing Markets

Trade and supply chain finance, though fairly esoteric and specialized, involves mechanisms, products and processes that are well established, highly flexible and adaptive, and solidly proven across a wide variety of contexts. The significant profile around international trade, and the financing of trade, may result in a greater, mainstream understanding of this category of financing over the medium term. This is particularly true of the traditional trade finance mechanisms, such as Documentary Collections and Documentary Credits.

Despite this flexibility and efficacy, however, a view persists almost universally that micro-enterprises and small businesses, and developing economies, suffer most acutely in terms of limited availability and high cost of trade finance.

The post-crisis environment may have the unintended consequence of reshaping this reality.

Political focus on the importance of the small business segment has increased sharply, and the demands on financial institutions to serve this segment have, likewise, been sharpened, particularly in the US and Europe, where bank bailouts have led directly to political leaders requiring their financial institutions to demonstrate greater support for SMEs. The reality in other jurisdictions can be significantly different, given that in many markets, the majority of businesses are small or medium-sized. In any event, the political context around SME financing is reinforced by a changing view among bankers, about the profitability of serving SME clients.

Some bankers have been referring to a "mid-market sweet spot," where financing is required, and where the profitability of client relationships is significantly more attractive than was commonly believed.

Additionally, in the context of supply chain management and supply chain finance, small businesses are no longer viewed in isolation, but rather, as part of a larger set of commercial relationships, typically anchored by a large corporate or multinational. Such a view further enhances the attractiveness of SMEs to bankers and trade finance bankers, and the nature of SCF, including the suitability of SCF structures to respond to the liquidity needs of small businesses.

The ability of businesses to mitigate foreign currency risk and to secure advisory support are equally well suited to smaller companies, and the re-focus on adequate risk mitigation in the context of trade and supply chain finance adds the final element that makes the value proposition compelling for developing and emerging markets. Figure 10.1 demonstrates how the World Bank's International Finance Corporation envisions supply chain finance – including specific provision for risk mitigation.

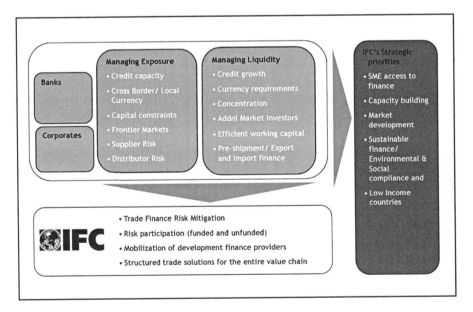

Figure 10.1   IFC trade and supply chain finance proposition
Source: IFC/World Bank Group, www.ifc.org/trade

Trade finance is often described as a countercyclical business: a business that performs well in times of crisis, as much because trade itself must continue even under the most difficult circumstances, and because the risk mitigation mechanisms of trade (and supply chain) finance are designed to work under the most challenging commercial conditions.

Financial obligations related to international trade are generally very carefully honoured by companies, banks and governments, due to the long-term and often severe consequences of failing to meet those obligations. Imports of food, critical raw materials, energy, strategically important commodities – all of these, and many more that comprise the flows of international commerce – must be paid for. This reality is one of the factors that contributes to the low default and loss rates experienced globally in trade finance; it is also another element that defines the countercyclical nature of trade finance, and makes this activity robust in times (and in contexts) of crisis.

Trade finance obligations have almost always been considered to be very high-priority obligations, by government as well as private sector entities, because they often involve trade in goods that cannot be sourced locally and may be strategically important (oil or resources), or fundamental to the well-being of a nation and its people (wheat or agri-food). This reality contributes to the favourable risk profile of trade finance transactions.

The outline of the IFC trade finance program and priorities illustrates the scope of activity and the breadth of support and solutions that can be provided through trade and supply chain finance, to developing economies and to small businesses in those economies.

Country-Level Support

The availability and maturity of trade financing programs and mechanisms has in the past been intimated to be directly correlated to the health and robustness of a national economy.

Trade and supply chain finance programs, and the instruments, financial structures business processes that enable their delivery, are of fundamental importance to developing economies, both in their efforts to combat poverty through trade, and in the activities required to create prosperity through international commerce.

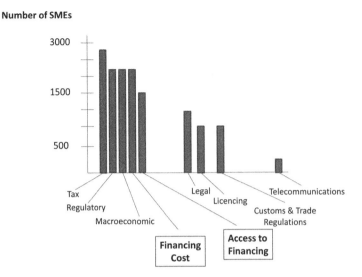

Figure 10.2   SME obstacles to growth

Source: Adapted from ITC Geneva: *How to Access Trade Finance, A Guide for Exporting SMEs*, 2009

Trade and supply chain finance have long included careful consideration of country risk in the context of international commerce, and while this discipline may seem somewhat defensive in nature – that is, designed to mitigate or manage risk – in the context of international development, the ability to asses country risk with some level of rigour and objectivity, arguably facilitates trade that may otherwise not take place.

Access to, and cost of, financing, have long been identified by small businesses and by developing economies, as significant obstacles to growth and success, as shown in Figure 10.2.

Risk that can be analyzed within some objective framework, can be quantified and priced – and therefore, mitigation options can be assessed for viability. Once the risk of a transaction or a series of transactions is determined, there is the possibility of determining whether the risk can be offset on commercially viable terms, or whether political decisions need to be made, to absorb such costs and enable the completion of a transaction.

Perhaps equally importantly, trade and supply chain finance include mechanisms and processes that allow financial institutions and others – including export credit agencies and international financial institutions (or development finance institutions) to engage in risk-sharing. Trade and supply chain finance can be provided on a collaborative basis among several institutions, with appropriate guarantees in place, such that a transaction that would be deemed too risky for a single institution or jurisdiction, can be completed because the relative risk is distributed – shared – to acceptable levels.

Trade, Finance and Development

The link between international development and cross border trade is almost axiomatic.

Development specialists have long argued – and devised programs based upon the view – that there is a direct and positive link between robust international trade, and efforts to combat poverty and to facilitate international development.

In that context, several development-oriented agencies and international institutions have extended the link to trade finance, and have worked to develop trade and supply chain financing solutions aimed specifically at supporting trade flows with companies in developing economies.

The tag line of the International Trade Centre in Geneva, "Export Impact for Good" is illustrative of the belief that international commerce can generate critically important economic value, growth and development, and the ITC includes among its enabling solutions, certain programs linked to the financing of international commerce.

The treatment of trade and supply chain finance as elements of a broader international development vision and strategy, and as a component of a trade-based development agenda, is a subject that merits specific attention in another text.

For purposes of this volume, it will be sufficient to focus on the commercial aspects of international trade, finance and international development.

Development and the Elements of Trade Finance

International development poses unique and enduring challenges, and the models followed by development specialists have evolved in several directions over a period of decades. Regardless of the dynamics in international development, however, the importance of trade as a driver of development has been consistently championed by practitioners, leading international institutions and others, even with the increasing acknowledgement of the imbalance in trade benefits, to the detriment of local producers in developing markets.

The link between trade and international development is well established, and more recently the connection between developing markets trade and trade finance has been highlighted.

Access to finance, including working capital and trade finance, are critical to the viability of micro and small businesses in developing economies.

It is often noted that developing economies and their small businesses suffer most from restricted access to capital in times of crisis.

Even with the increasing focus on fair trade as a means of shifting greater value (and a fairer share of value) to micro and small enterprises in developing economies, most stakeholders will acknowledge that trade and international development are directly and positively linked.

Focusing on the commercial dimensions of business in developing economies, it is widely recognized at this moment that the engines of global growth of the next generation will be the economies we currently classify as developing or emerging economies. Africa and emerging parts of Asia including Indonesia, Vietnam and other markets are currently seen to exhibit strong potential.

Trade finance is both critical and very well-suited to support and enable commerce with developing markets, for a variety of reasons, some of which relate to the characteristics of the markets themselves, and others that link to the nature and capabilities of trade and supply chain finance.

Characteristics of Developing Markets

Developing markets are unique and differentiated, as are most markets across the globe; however, there are several shared and relevant characteristics worth considering, in the context of international commerce and trade finance.

COMMERCIAL AND RELATED INFRASTRUCTURE

Developing economies can be challenging to engage in, owing to the limited infrastructure available to support business, including international commerce.

The absence of detailed commercial information such as credit reports and financial reporting, reliable market data and limitations on information and communication technology compose some of the issues that foreign companies can encounter in seeking to conduct business in certain jurisdictions.

Fundamentally important market characteristics, such as the nature of the legal system, protection of intellectual property, options for dispute settlement – even significant variance in what is considered to be appropriate/ethical business conduct – can prove difficult to navigate. Business and commercial practices can vary significantly, and the challenge can be amplified significantly when cross-border transactions are involved.

RISK: PERCEPTION AND REALITY

Developing economies are often seen as being high-risk, and while that is certainly true in certain cases, it is unfortunately the case that risk is often amplified beyond what can be objectively justified, largely because of optics and the reality that such assessments are often the product of secondary research, as opposed to informed, on-the-ground insight.

Risk is very much shaped by perception, and perception is shaped directly by relevant information, or indirectly when there is a vacuum or an absence of information that demands to be filled.

A senior diplomat prepared an after-posting report related to his most recent assignment in West Africa, noting high incidences of theft of a particular model of French automobile. An uninitiated reader interpreted this situation to present a risk for owners of such vehicles, when the intention was to communicate that this model should be the standard mode of transport for Embassy staff: the popularity of the model assuring an immediate and steady supply of spare parts and trained mechanics available to service these automobiles.

Risk, objective or perceived, is a reality of business, and an even more fundamental reality of international commerce. Companies and entrepreneurs in pursuit of opportunities in international markets – perhaps even more in developing markets, are able to make appropriate assessments of risk, identify that the risk level is acceptable, and take the measures necessary to optimize or mitigate that risk in relation to a target level of return.

COUNTRY-SPECIFIC AND ECONOMIC FACTORS

Developing economies typically involve a degree of country-level and sovereign risk that is higher than among established economies, for reasons ranging from political instability and the risk of revolution, to risks associated with political or economic conditions. These might include risks of expropriation or nationalization of foreign enterprises, or risks related to the inability to repatriate earnings or profits due to foreign currency restrictions.

Economic conditions may be such as to contribute to the risk of default or non-performance of trading partners, or to the inability of businesses to collect – or settle – foreign receivables. Local conditions in a foreign market may involve significant tax burdens, or may be such that business development and sales cycles are extended, creating adverse impact on working capital and cashflow for one or more of the trading partners involved.

CAPITAL MARKETS, FINANCING AND LIQUIDITY

Local financial and capital markets may be in early stages of development, in disarray or near non-existent, presenting challenges relative to access to financing and liquidity. Capital markets may be unreliable in their operation, and financing may be in such demand, as to be unavailable to support a particular transaction or trading relationship. In some markets, financing is certainly available, but at such a premium, that it threatens the commercial viability of transactions that would otherwise be very attractive.

The role of international institutions such as regional development banks and others is critical in enabling the development of banks and financial service firms, particularly as relates to their ability to engage effectively in the international financial system. Guarantee programs, aimed at reassuring international banks about the risk of conducting business with local institutions in developing economies, provide a critically important basis upon which banks in developing economies can support the trade aspirations of their local businesses.

Characteristics of Trade Finance

Trade finance is a form of finance, and an area of activity related to international commerce, that is uniquely suited to the needs, challenges and opportunities inherent in the pursuit of business with developing and emerging markets.

Several of the characteristics and features of trade and supply chain finance link directly to those of business in developing economies, and offer effective solutions to some of the most daunting commercial challenges involved.

RULES AND PRACTICES

The commercial and banking practices, and the various sets of rules published by the International Chamber of Commerce – and incorporated into legal traditions such as Common Law and others – provide a very effective, well-understood and globally adopted framework in support of trade finance.

Markets across the globe, irrespective of the maturity of their legal systems, adhere to rules such as the Uniform Customs and Practice for Documentary Credits, or the Uniform Rules for Demand Guarantees, among others, and most legal systems are capable of interpreting such rules and giving support to the intended commercial practices through their respective judicial systems.

National Banking Committees and the ICC's own Banking Commission provide guidance on the interpretation of the various sets of rules, and publish a variety of supporting resources, including opinions on articles, commercial scenarios and specific queries raised by individual financial institutions and other stakeholders.

EFFECTIVE RISK MITIGATION

Trade (and increasingly, supply chain) finance offers a wide range of proven and effective risk mitigation options, from specific instruments and their features (Confirmed Letters of Credit) to the ability to risk mitigate through export credit agencies, private insurers and by other means.

The range of risks covered is encompassing, from country and political risk to bank and commercial risk, and even transaction-specific risk such as foreign currency exposure and others.

Trade finance is designed to work well in the context of high-risk transactions, and has evolved its capabilities in a way that allows importers and exporters to do business in the most complex and challenging commercial environments on the globe. Whether the risk associated with a particular developing market is equitably assessed, or whether it is skewed by inaccurate perceptions, the mechanisms of trade finance are such that they support the successful conduct of trade under such circumstances.

The ability for importers and exporters to engage in international commerce, and yet, be able to transfer risk strategically between parties, bankers and countries, is a powerful advantage of the long-established and trusted practices of trade finance.

Trade finance facilitates the transfer of various forms of risk between parties, between banks and, ultimately, even from one country to another, and in so doing, can materially change the risk profile of a transaction and trading relationship, for the better. When an exporter can shift the payment obligation from a commercial counterparty in a high-risk market, to their own financial institution in their home market, which can and is routinely done through trade finance, the risk associated with that transaction and that trading relationship is reduced significantly.

Such changes in transactional risk profile can translate directly to a reduction in financing costs and a reduction or elimination of the cost of risk mitigation which might otherwise have been required, to make the transaction viable.

ACCESS TO LIQUIDITY

Emerging and developing markets are often characterized as having difficulty in accessing – and providing – adequate levels of liquidity in support of commercial activity, both domestic and international. To compound the situation, many local businesses are micro, small or medium enterprises (MSMEs), which makes borrowing and access to capital, in general, even more challenging.

Trade and supply chain finance provide effective means and mechanisms through which developing economies and their companies can access financing – and therefore, enable access to and from those markets for companies seeking to pursue commercial or investment opportunities involving counterparties located in developing markets.

Just as trade finance instruments and practices can facilitate the transfer of risk between parties, those same instruments and practices can enable access to financing and liquidity from various sources. These might include trading partners, foreign-based banks, international institutions and others, and the forms of financing available can cover the full lifecycle of a trade transaction, from pre-export to post-settlement.

The link between international trade and poverty reduction/international development enables and motivates international institutions to provide support in the form of trade finance, either directly or through various guarantee schemes, with the objective of enabling international commerce.

International institutions are ostensibly staffed with specialists who understand, intimately, the challenges and opportunities linked to developing economies, and that expertise, combined with the resources to support trade activity through trade finance programs, enables a direct connection between the needs of emerging economies and the features and capabilities of international trade finance.

In addition to the suitability of traditional instruments such as letters of credit, the needs of developing economies and their predominantly MSME businesses, are well met by new products, programs and solutions being developed under the umbrella of supply chain finance.

Programs where large global buyers work with their bankers to provide cost-effective financing to their suppliers (commonly in developing or emerging markets) are particularly effective, and are well suited to both developing export markets and to the MSME suppliers based in such markets.

International institutions have worked to devise programs aimed specifically at enabling access to trade finance. The ITC in Geneva extends its proposition in this respect beyond providing financing and liquidity, to providing coaching and support for small businesses, so that they are aware of suitable financing options and can pursue informed discussions with trade bankers and financiers. Certain priorities related to the ITC's program are listed in Figure 10.3.

ITC Trade Finance for SMEs Program: Allocation of Funds	
Adaptation of support materials by national consultants	25%
Development of local network of advisors with support institutions	15%
Training and coaching of MSMEs	15%
Adaptation of software to sector needs	9%
Training of bank staff in ITC methodology	2%
Pre-selection and assessment of SMEs	7%
Negotiating LoC/guarantees	5%
Information exchange	8%
Creating awareness	9%
Monitoring and evaluation	5%

Figure 10.3   Trade finance and development: ITC strategy and roadmap

Source: ITC Geneva: *Trade Finance for SMEs*

SECTOR-LEVEL SUITABILITY

Trade finance comprises a range of specialist subset forms of financing, often linked to specific industry groups or sectors of economic activity.

Commodity exports, including agriculture and agri-food, equipment, aircraft, oil and petro-chemicals and various other sectors, as shown in Figure 10.4, are trade-intensive, and core to the development of many emerging economies on the globe. Numerous leading financial institutions and boutique trade finance firms have cultivated sector-specific expertise, and developed products or solutions uniquely suited to the unique product characteristics – and liquidity needs – of particular sectors.

The major commodity groups (commonly natural resources) are often so critical to developing economies (and others such as Canada), that specialists speak of a resource poverty trap – with economies excessively dependent on natural resources to create economic value, while unable to create wealth, and unmotivated or unable to develop high value-added economic activity.

The realities of economic and political context, and the availability of support in the form of trade finance are important to note in assessing opportunities to engage in international commerce, including trade and investment. The active support of international institutions, coupled with the domain and sector-level expertise of trade finance specialists represents direct linkage between the finance of trade, and the needs and priorities of emerging and developing markets.

Major Commodities		
Agriculture	**Metals & Mining**	**Energy**
Biofuels	Aluminum	Crude Oil
Cocoa	Copper	Gas
Coffee	Steel	Electricity
Cotton	Gold	Petro-chemicals
Edible Oils		
Grain		
Soybean		
Sugar		

Figure 10.4   Commodity trade

Source: OPUS Advisory

Commodity finance specialists understand the intricacies of reserve-based lending in the crude oil sector, where financing is provided in line with estimated reserves of crude that can be economically extracted at a point in time. Likewise, the challenges of dealing with highly price-volatile commodities – some of them perishable – are understood by specialists.

Entrepreneurs and company executives seeking to do business in developing and emerging markets, in sectors as specialized as commodities, should become familiar with the specific features and capabilities of trade finance, that relate to such transactions.

Financing can be asset based, relying on the value of the commodity being traded and its impact on balance sheets, or it can be based on the cashflow to be generated by the eventual sale of the shipment or commodity being financed, for example.

Asset-based approaches to financing imply that the financing institution will need to maintain visibility – and often, legal control – of the shipment. Commodity finance can involve all of the familiar risks of engaging in international commerce, in addition to some that are perhaps more pronounced given the characteristics of global commodity markets, and the reality that producers and suppliers are often located in developing economies.

Risks related to commodity trade that can be effectively mitigated through trade finance mechanisms include:

- supplier performance risk;

- timing risk;

- price volatility;

- counterparty exposure risk;

- spread arbitrage;

- product-related risks (quality, perishability ...).

In the end, trade and supply chain finance are sufficiently advanced as dimensions of international finance, to enable and support commerce across the most challenging markets and market conditions in the world, whether the complexity relates an absence of reliable commercial data, to country and political risk, or to unique, sector-level or transaction risks that may be encountered by businesses of all sizes.

The ability to engage with export credit agencies, private insurers and various international and development finance institutions on the basis of well-established trade and supply chain financing practices, reflects the scope and value of trade finance to international commerce, including such activity involving MSMEs located in developing and emerging markets.

11

Financing, Risk and Cost: Realities of International Trade

Risk is a reality of business, and when business crosses borders, cultural contexts, legal systems and commercial practices, it is amplified both in the probability of encountering it, and in the impact it is likely to have on a transaction or trading relationship.

Risk increases significantly – some might suggest, exponentially – when commerce extends outside familiar domestic environments into foreign markets. At the same time, the existence of those risks can serve as a barrier to competitors, presenting (apparently) prohibitive risk levels and discouraging even exploratory initiatives around international activity.

The commercial, bank and country risk were introduced briefly earlier, however, the universe of risks facing companies (as well as banks and trade financiers) engaging in international business, trade and investment can be considered on a more granular level, as illustrated in Figure 11.1.

The various mitigation and risk management options that have been developed over decades can cover a wide spectrum of risk factors, and have been proven effective in a wide variety of commercial and economic conditions, including in the most volatile and high-risk markets on the planet.

A View of International Risk

The study of risk can be a complex combination of art and science, including rigorous actuarial models at one end of the spectrum, and reliance on "gut feel" honed through extensive experience in international markets.

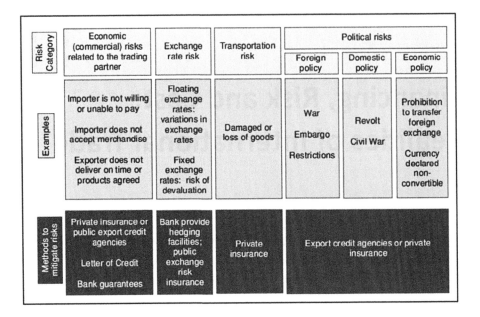

Figure 11.1   Risks in trade finance

Source: WTO Special Studies, Referenced in ITC Geneva "How to Access Trade Finance: A Guide for Exporting SMEs," 2009

For the purposes of consideration in the context of trade and supply chain finance, a discussion of risk can focus on practical factors with direct impact on decision makers and transactions involving entrepreneurial ventures or large multinationals.

Risk, at its core, comprises two components: objective risk and subjective risk.

It can be demonstrated objectively that a market in the midst of economic turmoil, or a region caught in the midst of civil unrest or outright war, will involve greater risk for businesses seeking to engage in those markets. At the same time, entrepreneurs and corporate executives charged with undertaking risk analysis may be (and often are) impacted by their own perceptions and expectations related to a market or a set of circumstances.

While some individuals (and companies) perceive opportunity and revenue potential in international activity – even in high-risk markets – others are averse to the pursuit of business in such markets, partly as a resulted of

Risk: Partly a Matter of Perception

A major financial institution sought to finance wheat exports to a then high-risk market in the Middle East.

The bank was asked to confirm letters of credit in support of numerous multi-million dollar shipments; however, the bank's central credit committee and the head of risk management – domestic bankers with little international experience – expressed serious reservations about supporting the transaction. Requests for country and bank-level credit lines were declined, despite the absence of competitors in the market and the attractiveness of margins on the potential transactions.

The head of trade finance, having visited the market with members of his team on numerous occasions, secured funding to invite the head of the risk management group to travel personally to the country, to meet local bankers and to see first hand, the state of the nation and the economy.

In the end, additional information coupled with a visit to the market reshaped perceptions about risk and opportunity, allowing the bank to finance several hundred million dollars' worth of wheat exports, earning significant revenue in the process, with appropriate risk mitigation measures in place.

unfounded perception, and partly because of a lack of awareness of effective mitigation options.

Risk can, theoretically, be addressed in several ways:

- ignored

- mitigated

- eliminated

A cavalier approach to risk, particularly in international business, can result in significant financial loss, even to the point of putting domestic business activities in jeopardy.

Ignoring the many risks inherent in international commercial activity is ill-advised. This includes underestimating such risk by assuming that domestic success will necessarily translate automatically to success in international markets. Entrepreneurs and company executives alike must take a proactive approach to identifying and understanding risks related to international trade, including risks that may be unique to a particular market, a foreign financial institution or a new international commercial relationship.

Risk can and should be effectively mitigated, and the mechanisms related to trade and supply chain finance are well suited to effective risk mitigation. Mitigation, however, is only a partial solution to the issue of risk.

In theory, many types of risk can be eliminated. The challenge is that elimination of risk – much like buying insurance for any possible eventuality, and seeking coverage that involves zero deductible, is generally not feasible, and if it were, would be a prohibitively expensive option.

Ultimately, the best approach is to optimize risk, as shown in Figure 11.2, with consideration for the risk appetite of an organization in a particular market (which will change over time and as circumstances shift), the options and cost related to mitigation, and the target return from a particular transaction or trading relationship.

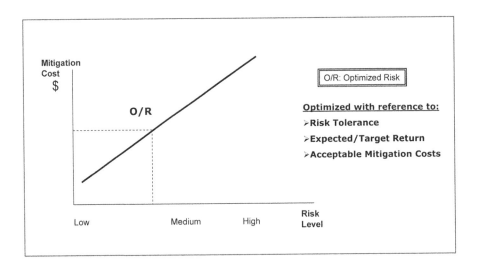

Figure 11.2   Risk and mitigation costs
Source: OPUS Advisory

Information Deficits

A significant amount of risk in international business links directly to a lack of information, insight and understanding about the conduct of business in international markets, or about the unique characteristics of a particular market.

The lack of information, or the lack of understanding, can relate to objective economic and commercial elements, such as a misunderstanding about the impact of foreign currency restrictions and exchange controls on a trading relationship, or to intangibles such as lack of understanding of the cultural context in which business takes place internationally and in a particular market.

Some sources of information readily available in certain markets such as credit data and credit reports can be unreliable, incomplete or simply nonexistent. This single element can complicate due diligence efforts executed across the globe. Certain markets and cultures are less likely to be open and transparent in facilitating information and data flow, while others depend significantly on the availability of such information, and on extensive analysis flowing from the availability of this data.

The credit manager of a major petrochemical company was attempting to provide credit facilities to major buyers, in a region where financial statements and credit reports are of questionable quality at best, and outright fabrications at worst. Meeting one buyer and requesting a copy of audited financial statements, the credit manager was presented with no less than five sets of financials and invited to choose the one best suited to his requirements.

Trade and supply chain finance has evolved from pure transaction focus, to include significant information flow between importers, exporters and their financial services providers and other business partners. Comprehensive, very timely reporting, transaction status and information-rich functionality have been designed into various technology platforms and are combining to enhance both transactional and financial visibility, and thereby reducing risk.

In addition to systemic issues such as the lack of credit bureaus, or the absence of credible financial reporting and commercial data, information deficits contributing to the higher risk in international business and trade can come from simple misinformation at the level of entrepreneurs or business executives leading international ventures or transactions.

> Risk can be seen as an attractive element of the conduct of international business and trade.
>
> Risk is partly subjective in nature and partly based on gaps in data, information and knowledge: that is, risk is often over-stated, especially by entrepreneurs and executives with limited international experience.
>
> Perceived risk is often directly reflective of the potential return of a transaction or trading relationship.

Even when all goes well in an international transaction, it is often the case that the timeframes involved in the conduct of business – and therefore the time involved in settling the financial aspect of a transaction – can be significantly longer than in a purely domestic transaction. This reality has very real implications for cash flow and working capital, with SMEs often running on limited cash and needing to collect payables as soon as feasible.

Entrepreneurs and executives who underestimate the impact of such delays due to incorrect information about the realities of international commerce introduce an element of financial risk that is avoidable, yet can create serious challenges for a business.

Transaction-Level Risk

There are risks at every stage of a transaction in international trade, from outright fraud to significant delays (in shipment or in payment), receipt of substandard goods, risks associated with exchange rate volatility, risk of non-performance, default or bankruptcy of a trading partner, as well as risk associated with the banks and with the stability, commercial practices or legal standards of the countries involved, among others.

Trade and supply chain finance practices, including related commercial practices such as the use of Incoterms in defining settlement terms, insurance requirements and the timing of transfer of ownership, combine to help businesses address a wide variety of risks.

The disciplines and practices involved in the financial dimensions of international commerce encourage and prompt the completion of adequate due diligence on the transaction, including the trading partner and the broader context of the financial transaction. Beyond that, settlement and financing options can, as indicated earlier, be matched to the maturity and trust associated with a particular trading relationship, and/or the risk profile of a market with which trade is to be conducted.

Traditionally, settlement options and mechanisms were selected to reflect the risk profile of a relationship or transaction, with Documentary Collections serving as a settlement and/or financing option for trusted relationships in stable markets, and Documentary Credits serving in the case where new relationships or higher-risk markets are involved.

In recent years, particularly pre-crisis, the risk (and risk mitigation) aspect of trade and trade finance was de-emphasized, at least in part due to the ease of access to liquidity and capital. Open account terms became the norm even in higher-risk markets, and supply chain finance models seemed, for a time, to disregard the risk mitigation proposition familiar in traditional trade finance.

The situation is normalizing, with risk very much in focus, and both businesses and financial institutions seeking to ensure adequate risk mitigation in the conduct of international commerce.

Trade financiers have noted for years that despite its cross-border nature and inherent connection to risk, the business of financing trade is a low-risk, and low loan-loss activity for the financial sector. Crisis-related regulatory pressure and reporting requirements have forced the banks to prove these assertions, and in seeking to do so, leading trade finance banks have contributed to a global Trade Finance Default Register, reporting defaults and losses across a variety of traditional trade finance products.

The portfolio-level data provided by 21 banks, and covering over 8.1 million transactions, demonstrates that, over the period 2008–2011, short-term trade finance transactions exhibited a default rate of 0.021 percent, of which actual loss rates were below 60 percent. Short-term trade finance recorded 1,746 defaults on a volume of over 8.1 million transactions, as summarized in Figure 11.3. This reference point can be informative to entrepreneurs and business executives, seeking to understand the risk profile of the trade finance business.

TOTAL 2008-11	TRANSACTION DEFAULT RATE	DEFAULTED TRANSACTION LOSS RATE	M (IMPLIED, DAYS)	SPECIFIC TXN-LEVEL LOSS RATE
Import L/Cs	0.020%	42%	80	0.008%
Export Confirmed L/Cs	0.016%	68%	70	0.011%
Loans for Import	0.016%	64%	110	0.010%
Loans for Export: Bank risk	0.029%	73%	140	0.021%
Loans for Export: Corporate risk	0.021%	57%	70	0.012%
Performance Guarantees	0.034%	85%	110	0.029%
Total	0.021%	57%	90	0.012%

Figure 11.3   Short-term trade finance default and loss summary

Source: International Chamber of Commerce, Paris

Risk Mitigation and Risk Transfer

Trade finance mechanisms and transactions enable proven and effective risk management options. Trade finance allows for significant and flexible transfer of risk between parties and service providers around a trade transaction and relationship.

The use of documentary letters of credit, for example, is fundamentally about two things: risk transfer and credit enhancement.

An exporter requests the issuance of a letter of credit, in order to avoid relying on the payment obligation of the buyer, preferring instead to trust a financial institution to make the required payment once the conditions agreed have been fully met. The involvement of a financial institution improves the credit quality of a transaction, lowers the cost of financing and reduces the overall risk, on the basis that the financial standing of the Issuing Bank will generally be stronger than that of the importing company.

Trade financing mechanisms and practices enable an important set of risk transfer options, shown in Figure 11.4, including shifts of risk from importer to Issuing Bank, Issuing or Advising Bank to Confirming Bank among others, as well as transfer of risk between exporter and importer, through the use of INCOTERMS.

The Incoterm selected by the trading partners in defining the parameters of their transaction, will determine the point to which the finished goods

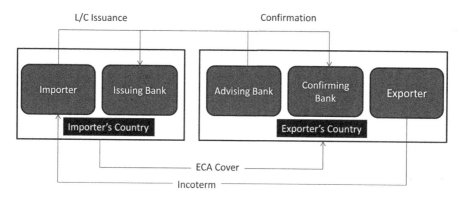

Figure 11.4   Risk transfer in trade finance
Source: OPUS Advisory

must be delivered by the exporter, the obligation to insure the shipment, the responsibility for the cost of shipment and, ultimately, the point at which ownership of the goods (and therefore risk) passes from exporter to importer. Figure 11.5 shows a version of an INCOTERMS Wall Chart, which can be obtained from the ICC.

An exporter faces very different risk if they are expected to deliver the goods to the door of their production facility, versus delivery of the shipment to the end destination, with all applicable import duties paid, for example.

Incoterms not only contribute to clarity around risk, but, in determining the transfer of ownership, can also impact financing options, in cases where the financing institution deems it appropriate to take the shipment as collateral against some form of financing.

There is a level of performance risk that, in most cases, remains with the exporter: only the exporter can produce and ship (or prepare) the goods as agreed, yet the practices of international trade and the mechanisms of trade finance can provide some protection even in this scenario, through a particular type of letter of credit, called a standby letter of credit, or variants such as guarantees, as well as various types of performance bonds. Such instruments protect the importer against the risk that the exporter will fail to deliver as promised, and provide for various forms of remedy, including outright financial compensation.

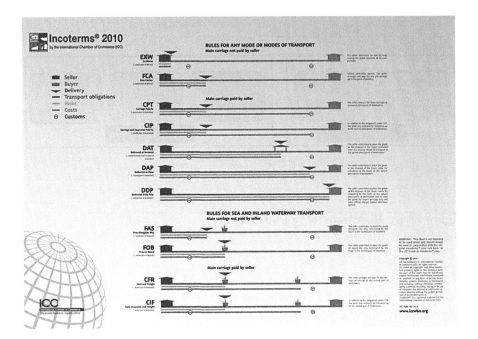

Figure 11.5   INCOTERMS chart

Source: International Chamber of Commerce (ICC)

Likewise, trade and supply chain finance, through the use of complementary export credit insurance cover, for example, facilitates the transfer of risk between banks and/or countries by enabling an exporter to do business in a high-risk market, while arranging insurance cover locally in the event of default or non-payment.

There are numerous varieties and options related to the shift of risk between parties in the context of a trade transaction. The specific options will vary based on the payment and financing mechanisms agreed between buyer and seller, and the terms of trade, including the timing of transfer of ownership of shipments, and the responsibility to insure shipments in transit.

While risk mitigation has long been a core element of the value proposition of traditional trade finance, it was, until recently, less significant in the context of open account transactions and elements of supply chain finance.

The ongoing challenges associated with the global financial and economic crisis, including the sovereign crisis in Europe, are motivating greater attention to risk mitigation and optimization in the context of supply chain finance. The risk mitigation component is becoming increasingly important in supply chain finance. One of the variations of supply chain finance products and programs available, referred to as buyer-centric supply chain finance, illustrates the importance of risk transfer in making such programs commercially viable, and acceptable to providers of trade and supply chain finance.

A large company, often a multinational buyer, can serve as a hub or anchor to a supply chain finance program, as illustrated in Figure 11.6. Such programs are developed with that company's trade finance bank with the objective of providing liquidity and financing, including trade finance and working capital facilities, to selected suppliers and other members of the company's global supply chain. A company may have hundreds of suppliers located in many parts of the world, delivering to a distributed manufacturing capability located, likewise, in several countries. Suppliers are often SMEslocated in emerging markets, where financial systems may be in a state of evolution, possibly facing significant constraints, and therefore providing only limited financing to small businesses, usually at exorbitant cost.

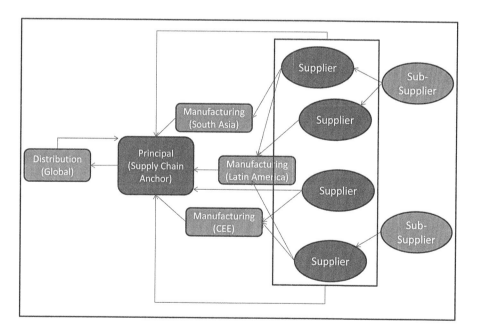

Figure 11.6   Buyer-centric supply chain finance
Source: OPUS Advisory

The buyer, seeking to ensure stable supply, particularly from strategic suppliers, may deem it worthwhile to allow selected suppliers to participate in a supply chain finance program, where the supplier is financed on the basis of the borrowing capacity and credit standing of the multinational buyer. Such programs operate when the buyer's bank agrees to finance a group of carefully vetted suppliers, on the basis of invoices accepted for payment by the buyer. In the event of non-payment, the financier pursues the buyer for reimbursement of funds – not the small supplier in the remote site in an emerging or developing market.

The entire structure is based upon risk transfer: the ability of a lender to provide financing to (potentially) dozens of small businesses on the basis of the standing and credit capacity of a large global buyer, as opposed to attempting to undertake expensive due diligence and risk mitigation on each remote borrower.

Variations of such programs can extend to providing financing to distributors and other members of an anchor or principal client's supply chain ecosystem.

Risk transfer also takes place in the context of a trade transaction – or a portfolio of transactions – in ways that are not necessarily visible to the importer and the exporter. Bankers and trade financiers may mitigate their own exposure and risk in a given transaction, for example, through participation or syndication of the transaction and of the related risk. Simply put, banks can arrange to share the financing with multiple other banks, reducing the overall exposure of a single financial institution, while still providing the end-client with the necessary financial facility. The fact that other banks have been invited to participate in a transaction may or may not be disclosed to a borrower.

A Banker's View of Risk

Trade bankers are almost universally caught in a challenge of balancing the desire to do additional business and to be at the forefront of trade flows – both objectives normally entailing some degree of risk appetite – and the imperative to demonstrate appropriate caution and sound judgment through careful adjudication of risk.

Companies in need of financing, particularly entrepreneurial ventures and small businesses seeking opportunities in international markets, perennially under-funded, will often characterize their international bankers as overly bureaucratic, plodding and conservative, whereas senior bank executives – most commonly career domestic bankers – view those engaging in cross-border activities as risk-takers.

Trade finance, like other areas of international banking, is poorly understood among conventional bankers, and in most financial institutions, bankers with largely domestic careers exercise immense influence and control over the activities and aspirations of trade financiers.

Relatively few financial institutions actively work to develop their trade finance businesses, much less their broader international activities, as a core element of their long term strategies.

Asked whether the trade finance unit had a mandate from the Bank's Board to grow its business, a General Manager responded by indicating that the Board would "leave him alone" as long as he was "not losing money"; some years later, a senior executive at a global financial institution described that his team, just implementing a new supply chain finance program, had direct access to one of the deputy chairs of the bank, who was prepared to meet clients or to exercise authority internally, to support the trade division in its growth strategy. Each approach has had demonstrable impact on client service and on the growth of the two trade finance units over time.

Trade financiers typically are allocated certain lines of credit for countries – and banks – with which their financial institution chooses to do business. When lines are allocated or delegated directly to the trade finance business, credit, risk and financing decisions can be made relatively promptly and generally on a very well-informed basis.

When credit lines are fully utilized, or when a client seeks support in conducting business in a new market, or with a foreign bank not yet known to the trade bankers, an internal risk assessment and credit request must be submitted, often subject to review and approval by bankers with limited understanding of international business, and less appreciation for the nature of trade and supply chain finance.

Awareness of the internal mechanics of trade financing (including credit approvals and risk assessment) within a particular bank can be very practical for business executives and entrepreneurs, in that a company can then seek to do business with a financial institution that understands trade finance, or perhaps has differentiated expertise in markets that are of interest to the company.

Similarly, an executive or entrepreneur can work with trade financiers to provide the information, transparency and understanding around a planned trading relationship or transaction, to maximize the likelihood of prompt approval of bank credit facilities, in the event this is necessary. It is under such circumstances also that a bank is likely to seek some form of risk mitigation – including at least partial risk transfer – to make the proposed transaction acceptable to internal credit and risk management specialists.

Fraud: A Different Type of Risk

Traditional trade finance has, as noted earlier, developed a range of very effective risk mitigation instruments, practices and features.

It is worth highlighting, however, that long-established practice in documentary letters of credit and documentary collections requires that trade financiers "deal only in documents" as they determine whether a payment is to be made to an exporter on the basis of compliance against L/C terms.

Banks must exercise judgment and be guided in their deliberations by the long-established practices and rules related to the use of traditional trade finance instruments, such as the UCP, currently version 600. They need not, and will not, seek to authenticate the veracity or accuracy of documents presented for payment under a letter of credit, if that document appears on its face to be legitimate.

If a document is genuine but incorrect relative to the terms and conditions included in a documentary letter of credit, a bank may identify a situation of non-compliance, and therefore refuse to make payment under the L/C.

Conversely, if a document is fraudulent, but appears genuine, and its content is accurate when compared against the terms of a letter of credit, a bank will approve, facilitate or effect payment as required under the terms of the letter of credit.

While traditional trade financing instruments are very effective in mitigating a wide variety of risks, and can be critically important in facilitating international commerce, such instruments exist and are widely utilized on the assumption that the trading parties are acting in good faith, and desire the successful and timely conclusion of a trade transaction, and perhaps the development of long-term trading relationships.

It is, of course, possible to define terms and conditions under a documentary credit, that can assist in avoiding certain types of fraud – like requiring the presentation of a third party certification from an international inspection company – to ensure that the correct goods have been shipped, at the agreed level of quality and with the agreed features. Once again however, even such a requirement, duly fulfilled by the exporter, will not completely eliminate the risk of fraud or loss.

Unless a bank has cause to suspect fraudulent conduct based on its examination of documents, or unless otherwise compelled through court injunction, the bank is required – and will make every effort – to make payment under a documentary credit or other trade finance instrument, if all terms and conditions are deemed to have been met. In some cases, this action will be counter to the interests of a particular client, but the bank will be compelled to honour its commitment.

A bank that has issued a documentary letters of credit, for example, will agree to honour its undertaking under a compliant drawing that is later found to have been fraudulent, though the importer – their client – may suffer a loss. The reason for this is that banks wishing to engage in international banking and trade finance activity must manage both their financial standing, and the trust of other financial institutions in the undertaking represented when such a bank issues a letter of credit.

Trade finance can be a powerful mitigator of risk in international markets, but there is a real risk of fraud, and other measures, starting from thorough due diligence to various forms of insurance, should be part of a broader approach to international commerce and trade finance.

Fraud: A Different Type of Risk

Perpetrators of fraud are criminals. The extent to which such criminals will go, to steal goods or monies linked to international transactions, or to use the instruments of international trade and trade finance to engage in money laundering, is striking.

A buyer requested an inspection certificate from a first-time supplier under a documentary letter of credit, with the intention of ensuring that the agreed quality and quantity of an item had been shipped, as a condition for payment under that L/C.

The inspection firm, globally known and respected, was to inspect the shipment at a mutually agreed port of transhipment, partway between the exporting country and the home of the buyer. The firm was to break the security seal on the container in which the goods were being shipped, effect the necessary inspection, issue the inspection certificate and re-seal the container prior to its onward voyage. The process seemed secure, and the certificate of inspection (together with the other necessary documents) fully met the terms of the letter of credit, with the result that the exporter was paid with the full agreement of the banks involved.

On arrival of the container at the port of destination, and upon completion of the necessary customs clearance formalities, the importer was dismayed to find that the container had been emptied, and his goods stolen. A subsequent investigation revealed that the inspector charged with verifying the shipment had been bribed to provide access to the container, to issue the required certificate of inspection and to re-seal the container at the port of transhipment.

It should be noted explicitly that trade finance instruments such as letters of credit and documentary collections have long been used, with varying degrees of success, to facilitate money laundering and terrorist financing. There are numerous techniques utilized in this respect, and competent trade finance specialists are aware of these activities, and are trained in the detection of suspicious transactions and activities.

This is one area where banks will look beyond the compliance of documents against L/C terms, seeking to identify signs of possible money-laundering activity, such as the presence of invoices that reflect an inflated value relative to the goods being shipped, with the result that a transaction would result in a transfer of excess funds under the guise of a legitimate trade transaction.

Risk and Trade Finance

The effective mitigation of risk is undoubtedly one of the core components of the overall value proposition around international trade finance. Portfolio-level industry data demonstrates the degree to which trade financiers have been effective – some argue, too effective – at mitigating risk, and the flexibility of certain instruments and financing structure in terms of risk management further reinforces the power of trade and supply chain finance in the mitigation of many forms of risk.

Trade finance has proven effective and robust in helping companies of all sizes to navigate the many risks that can be encountered in international commerce – even in the most challenging markets and commercial conditions on the globe.

International business and trade illustrate very clearly the positive correlation between risk and return: higher risk generally promises higher return, and in the pursuit of such higher returns in international markets, the practices, products and mechanisms of trade finance are extremely effective in mitigating risk and in facilitating access to those attractive commercial returns.

12

Trade and Supply Chain Finance: A Case Study

Trade finance is a highly specialized, but very practical and commercially oriented form of financing that links directly to real economy activities and supports a clearly identifiable flow of goods. One approach to illustrating certain practical considerations around trade and supply chain finance is to develop a detailed case study illustrating the various financing options and highlighting selected issues and opportunities inherent in the financing of international trade transactions (Figure 12.1).

Party	Home Country	Characteristics	Requirements
Les Aliments Caribou Inc. Importer/Exporter (Broker)	Canada	SME, No Experience	Finance/Risk
Heiligenberg, AG Supplier	Germany	SME, Expert	Payment
Langano Trading Importer	Ethiopia	SME, No Experience	Finance
Gondar National Bank Issuing Bank	Ethiopian Regional Bank	Limited Experience	Financing
Mount Royal Finance Advising Bank	Canadian International	Skilled	Risk
Ladenburg Global Trade Finance Advising Bank	German Global Bank	Expert	None
East Africa Development Bank IFI	Tanzania	Skilled	None
Canada Export Import ECA/Insurer	Canada	Expert	Canadian Content and Value Creation

Figure 12.1   Case study – parties to the transaction
Source: OPUS Advisory

The Scenario

Heiligenberg, AG is a family company, part of the highly regarded and economically powerful *mittelstand* segment of German business, and has a regional office and export management/buying unit based in a complex in Dossenheim, on the outskirts of Heidelberg, near the Fritz-Frey Strasse. The company has extensive international activity and commercial relationships in numerous international markets. Heiligenberg has been active in Canada for years, and has numerous trusted and established commercial relationships in the country, including prior successful business with Les Aliments Caribou, based in Montreal.

Caribou, a small private company launched by two partners, top-level chefs with extensive international training, enjoys an excellent reputation as a provider of high-end specialty foods.

The company has actively sought to identify sources of exotic and adventurous ingredients and foods, consistent with the belief of the partners that the most discerning palates seek more than a good meal – but rather, a culinary adventure. Caribou has spent several years establishing relationships in East Africa, with some focus on Ethiopia.

Trade can evolve from well-researched, objective commercial objectives, or from an unexpected and unsolicited offer to purchase, or from personal linkages or affinity to an international market: each path is legitimate, and trade finance can provide solutions related to most any scenario underpinning a trade opportunity.

One of the founding partners of Caribou had visited Addis Ababa, Ethiopia years ago, and retained the memory of a unique dining experience that included a sour-flavoured pancake-like bread called *injera*, a spice made of a rich combination of peppers, called *berberé*, served as a powder, or in oil, as *awazé*. The meal was accompanied with a traditional Ethiopian honey-wine called *tej*, and followed by a world-famous cup of Ethiopian coffee served in the traditional coffee ceremony, with the intoxicating aroma of local incense and roasting coffee beans.

Caribou has been sourcing various traditionally Ethiopian foods through Langano Trading, a small company based on Cunningham Street, past the Ghion and Sheraton hotels on the way in to Addis from the new Bolé International Airport.

Langano has asked Caribou to consider extending their commercial relationship, but with a reversal of roles: Langano has recently won a contract to supply the new Sheba Hotel Addis Ababa, a five-star hotel built by a wealthy local investor and one of two or three hotels typically serving as home to expatriates and visitors from international institutions.

Langano wishes to assist the Sheba in providing a menu that combines local and international flavors, and is looking to Caribou to assist in procuring top-quality German foods and ingredients, as well as uniquely Canadian products such as maple syrup, ice wine and Pacific salmon.

Risk Considerations

Canada and Germany are both solid economies, having managed effectively through the global economic crisis, on the basis of export activities, relative strength of their banks and financial sectors and lack of exposure to toxic mortgage assets, among other factors. Ladenburg and Mount Royal Finance are both considered excellent risks in international banking circles.

Both countries are members of the OECD, and enjoy a favourable risk profile as trading nations. First and second-tier financial institutions in Germany and Canada, likewise, have earned solid reputations and credit ratings, with the effect that their undertakings are trusted and well received, internationally.

Commercially, Heiligenberg is an established and well-rated company, with relatively a strong balance sheet reflecting good equity and limited debt. Although Les Aliments Caribou is a small business, they have been in operation for several years and enjoy a good credit standing. As with many small businesses, however, they do face challenges in assuring adequate levels of cashflow, and their founders are culinary specialists with limited finance backgrounds.

Ethiopia has had a long and checkered history. The only African country never to be colonized, and once referred to as the "bread basket of Africa," the country has long suffered from drought, poverty and extreme famine. The revolution of the early 1970s, which resulted in the overthrow of the Emperor Haile Selassie in 1974, brought decades of oppressive and damaging dictatorship. More recently, Ethiopia has shown some sign of revival, partly due to investment inflows from China, Saudi Arabia and elsewhere, and partly due to contributions from the Ethiopian diaspora.

The economy is still relatively closed, and the country is not particularly well known or understood. The country's war with its former province of Eritrea has left it landlocked, and proximity to politically and commercially unstable markets, coupled with internal tensions is not helpful.

Gondar National Bank is one of the stronger domestic institutions, but is not well known in international banking circles, as it maintains only a limited number of correspondent relationships. Financial information on the bank is incomplete at best, and not deemed to be objectively verifiable by rating agencies.

Langano Trading is an established business, with excellent local and regional potential, and good prospects in the context of COMESA, the Common Market for Eastern and Southern Africa; however, financial constraints and restrictions on flows of foreign currency have proven to be an issue for Langano.

The East Africa Development Bank (EADB) is a long-established regional development institution funded by 20 countries, and Canada Export Import is a quasi-public sector trade credit and insurance entity, with an excellent international profile and reputation.

While the trade transaction could be looked at as one deal, with the Canadians acting as brokers, and could be structured on the basis of transferable or back-to-back letters of credit, there may be some advantage to viewing these as two separate transactions, one between Ethiopia and Canada, and one between Canada and Germany.

Given the scenario described above, the parties involved will wish to consider several issues and requirements:

1.   Arrangement of secure and timely payment;

2.   Appropriate mitigation of various forms of risk;

3.   Access to liquidity, coupled with options related to the provision of favourable trade terms for business partners;

4.   Ability to secure steady and trusted sources of supply;

5.   Adequate transactional and market-related advisory support.

Heiligenberg and Les Aliments Caribou could, with relative comfort, agree to trade on open account terms, with Caribou potentially inviting Heiligenberg to participate in its existing supply chain finance program, put in place and managed by Mount Royal Finance. If necessary, Heiligenberg could supplement the financing support offered through Caribou, by securing foreign receivables insurance from a local provider.

An adequate understanding of the nature of a trading relationship, including the various risks and interests at play, will assist businesses of all sizes to identify and structure optimal trade and supply chain financing solutions.

Les Aliments Caribou could face some challenges in exporting Canadian and German foods and ingredients to Ethiopia, primarily because of the combination of actual and perceived political, bank and commercial risks associated with this market. In addition to such risks, transactions with certain markets require a higher degree of compliance and regulatory scrutiny due to the risk of money laundering.

Caribou will wish to ensure maximum security of its financial interest: even if the commercial relationship between Caribou and Langano Trading were strong and trusted, there are macro-level factors that could prevent shipment to Langano – not least the ongoing piracy off the coast of East Africa – or payment to Caribou for any number of complicating reasons. Caribou will want to avail itself of the risk transfer feature available through trade finance.

Caribou has wisely sought counsel from an experienced trade finance banker at Mount Royal Finance, outlining the nature of the transaction contemplated, candidly describing its own capabilities and limitations, and being transparent about the risks of conducting business in Africa, and in Ethiopia specifically. At the same time, the company has asked Mount Royal's advice about the degree to which German businesses and banks are insulated from the periodic issues of sovereign risk in the European Union.

Mount Royal has assessed the country and political risk in Ethiopia, noting the periodic flare-ups of tension with Eritrea, the past engagement of Ethiopian troops in incursions into Somalia, and the general economic conditions of the country. Country limits are not currently available for Ethiopia at Mount Royal, and while Gondar appears to be a solid financial institution with acceptable risk profile, there is no existing bank-to-bank relationship.

TRADE FINANCE: ONE SOLUTION

Trade finance specialists at Mount Royal, together with the partners at Caribou, review the commercial details of the two transactions contemplated: an import transaction from Germany to Canada (or directly to Addis), together with an export transaction from Canada to Ethiopia, both viewed from the perspective of Les Aliments Caribou.

Caribou and Mount Royal map the various relationships, including the roles and potential positions of banks in each country, outlining a transaction structure as shown in Figure 12.2.

The transactions contemplated – that is, the export of German goods to Ethiopia, plus the export of Canadian products to Addis, could be facilitated through the use of two separate Documentary Letters of Credit. One flow might look like the transaction reflected in Figure 12.3.

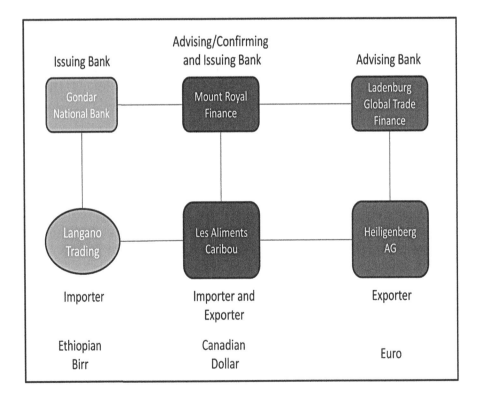

Figure 12.2   Case study transaction outline
Source: OPUS Advisory

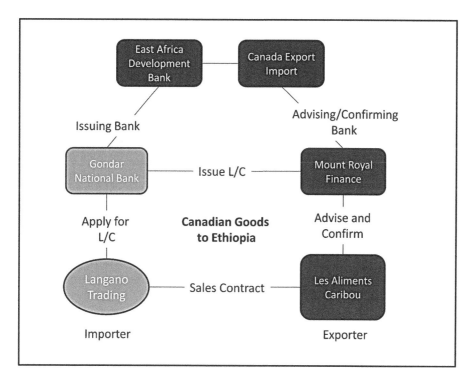

Figure 12.3   Case study – export to Ethiopia
Source: OPUS Advisory

One L/C issued by Gondar National Bank in favour of Les Aliments Caribou through Mount Royal Finance, to cover the shipment of Canadian product to Addis, and a second credit, also issued by Gondar on behalf of Langano Trading in favour of Caribou, but this time, with the option to transfer the credit (or a portion thereof) to a third-party supplier (Heiligenberg).

Mount Royal's trade finance specialists attempted to secure approval from the bank's credit and risk specialists to undertake a transaction with Gondar, but are not successful, given the risk profile of the transaction. Mount Royal approaches Canada Export Import, and learns that there may be an opportunity to collaborate with the agency, on a risk-shared basis only. An account director at Canada Export Import, with previous experience in Africa, recommends a discussion with the East Africa Development Bank.

- What measures can Les Aliments Caribou take to assist Langano Trading in obtaining adequate liquidity over the life of the transaction?

- How can Caribou protect its own interests and ensure payment against compliant documentation?

- How can Caribou enhance its own working capital position?

In the end, Gondar National Bank applies to participate in a trade finance guarantee program overseen by East Africa Development Bank, and qualifies to join the program as a local Issuing Bank.

EADB offers to provide a guarantee against non-payment by Gondar, in support of the transaction between Langano Trading and Les Aliments Caribou, providing the option that the guarantee can be provided directly to Mount Royal Finance, or, if preferred, it can be provided to Canada Export Import.

Mount Royal's credit specialists are ill at ease with the risk associated to this transaction, and despite the recommendations of their trade finance specialists (a situation that is very common in banking), insist on securing cover from Canada Export Import, with the effect that the guarantee from EADB is provided to Canada Ex-im.

In the interim, Gondar National Bank has issued a documentary letter of credit in favour of Caribou, denominated in euros as agreed between the trading parties. Issuance of the letter of credit, once demonstrated to the Ethiopian Central Bank, triggers approval for the reserving of €220,000 to cover settlement of the L/C.

Caribou is aware of the local challenges in Addis, in securing financing and liquidity, and has agreed to be paid 120 days after shipment of the goods to Langano Trading, to allow ample time for the sale of the shipment to the Hotel Sheba. Thereafter, Langano can keep the profit due, and settle the amount due under the letter of credit.

In parallel to the primary transaction, it is learned by Mount Royal through EADB that financing costs in Ethiopia are extremely high. Mount Royal envisions additional, lucrative business from Caribou and, to support this eventuality while earning additional revenue from the transaction, offers to finance Gondar National, by lending their new correspondent the funds to extend their access to €220,000 to 360 days, covering the initial financing period of 120 days to Langano, and extending by an additional 240 days.

Caribou has taken measures to ensure a successful and viable transaction for their trading partner, but at the same time, is aware, thanks to good advice from Mount Royal and from Canada Exim, that the best intentions of Langano could become irrelevant, if the political or bank risk scenario in Addis were to deteriorate to the point of interfering with the transaction.

Caribou has arranged for the L/C from Gondar to be Confirmed by Mount Royal Finance, and for Mount Royal to discount the Accepted Bill of Exchange (a legal document evidencing the existence of a financial obligation), and to provide Caribou with immediate payment of an agreed discounted amount.

Caribou will pay significant amounts of fees and interest for the risk mitigation and financing envisioned in the trade financing options described above; with good advice and adequate preparation however, these expensive measures will have been adequately estimated, and built in to the price charged to Langano for the goods shipped.

The protection of Caribou's interests under a letter of credit – even one confirmed by their own bankers – relies entirely on the requirement that documents presented by Caribou for payment under the L/C are fully compliant with the terms and conditions of the documentary letter of credit. In the event that documents are deemed non-compliant by Mount Royal (as the Confirming Bank), all the protection for Caribou evaporates, and Langano can accept the shipment (in effect, waiving discrepancies under the credit), or refuse the shipment outright. Langano may also take advantage of the situation and demand a substantial discount from Caribou.

In order to maximize the likelihood of success, and to ensure full and timely payment, Caribou must:

- Review the terms and conditions of the proposed letter of credit with great care, to ensure that Caribou will be able to fully meet those terms and conditions – and that compliance will be clearly demonstrable through the documents required for presentation under the L/C. Caribou is aware that banks deal in documents alone, and will examine documents as presented, against the terms of the letter of credit.

- Request an amendment to the term(s) of the letter of credit that could be problematic, prior to effecting shipment, in order to ensure that revised terms will be fully met and complied with;

- Pay particular attention to documentary requirements that cannot be corrected by Caribou directly, ensuring that there is full clarity on the requirements and sufficient time for the necessary documentation to be produced;

- Carefully verify that the expiry date of the letter of credit allows for enough time for Caribou to prepare the shipment, collect and present the documents, and collect payment (or assure a payment at an agreed future date) prior to the expiry of the L/C. Also verify that the Latest Shipment Date is attainable, and that the number of days for presentation of documents after shipment allows enough time for Caribou to complete a drawing under the letter of credit.

- Given that the L/C is denominated in euros, Caribou may need to hedge against unfavourable volatility in the exchange rate between the euro and the Canadian dollar, and should arrange such a mechanism with Mount Royal Finance.

- Langano, as the buyer, seeking to satisfy a five-star hotel such as the Sheba Hotel Addis, will have several concerns as well.

- Ensure that the goods provided are as promised, and of the quality expected. The company must ensure that any requirements related to the goods purchased from Caribou can be reflected or demonstrated by some form of documentation – a transport document showing routing and shipment date, any necessary quality and inspection certificates, any health certifications required to enable entry of the goods to Ethiopia.

- Given that the L/C is denominated in euros, and that Gondar National will seek payment from Langano at maturity, 120 days after shipment date, Langano may also need to take measures to hedge against unfavourable currency volatility between the euro and the Ethiopian Birr.

The transaction covering shipment from Canada to Ethiopia is largely addressed by the foregoing approach: the interests of parties to the transaction are fully met, the numerous risks associated to the transaction are adequately covered, and the trading relationship between Langano and Caribou is strengthened by the eventual conclusion of another transaction, to mutual benefit. Langano gains credibility with the Sheba Hotel Addis as an effective supplier of desirable product into Ethiopia, and Caribou turns an existing supplier into a client and buyer.

Having devised an effective financing structure for what might have been a fairly challenging transaction, the trading partners and their bankers and service providers turn to the transaction where Caribou will source from Heiligenberg, and arrange for delivery to Langano Trading, shown in Figure 12.4.

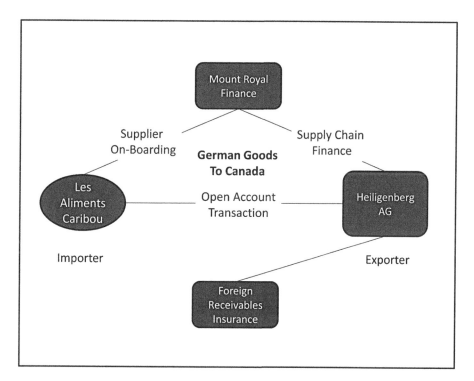

Figure 12.4   Export to Canada
Source: OPUS Advisory

Given the (low) risk profile around the Germany-to-Canada transaction, the strength of the two banks involved, and the established nature of the trading relationship between Heiligenberg and Caribou, it would appear that a straightforward and inexpensive open account transaction will meet the requirements of all parties involved.

This issue that arises is a question of whether the most efficient approach is to ship the German products to Canada for eventual re-export to Ethiopia, or whether a more direct approach is available.

In light of the recent experience with Langano and with Caribou, it is decided between Caribou, Mount Royal Finance Canada Exim that a transferable, confirmed documentary credit, along the lines shown in Figure 12.5, is perhaps a more appropriate solution.

The approach adopted builds upon the structure devised for trade between Langano and Caribou, given that credit and risk analysis has already been completed, appropriate risk-sharing and mitigation options have been identified, and the use of a transferable credit achieves several objectives:

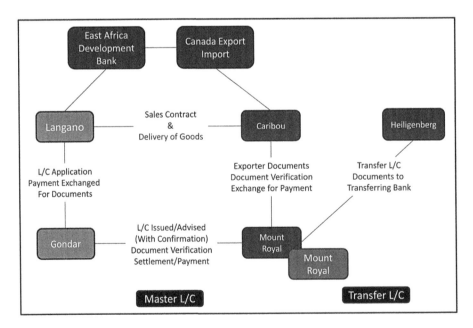

Figure 12.5   Transferable L/C option
Source: OPUS Advisory

- Caribou can effectively position as a broker between Langano and Heiligenberg, without necessarily divulging the identities of importer and supplier to each other, which allows Caribou to generate revenue ad remain engaged in the trade flows.

- Enables shipment from Germany to Ethiopia, and allows for substitution of documents, with the documents prepared by Heiligenberg serving to assure payment to the German company under the Transfer, and documents prepared and submitted by Caribou under the Confirmed Master L/C, assuring Caribou of timely payment by Mount Royal, as the Confirming and Transferring bank.

The risk in using a transferable L/C is that any certain discrepancies occurring in the transfer, such as an error in the transport document, that is cannot be corrected or substituted, will potentially carry over as a discrepancy under the Master L/C between Langano and Caribou. Such a situation effectively becomes a domino effect, with the discrepancy potentially causing protection under both the Transfer and the Master to evaporate, placing Heiligenberg and Caribou at significant risk.

The structuring of the Master L/C must account for this risk, and Caribou, together with Mount Royal Finance, must work together to ensure that the terms and conditions of the credit can be fully met by Caribou, and that the related terms in the Transfer can be fully complied with by Langano Trading.

Ideally, Mount Royal and Gondar National are relatively aligned in their document verification processes and practices, and will examine documents to the same standard – again ideally, the standard of substantial compliance – with the effect that the likelihood of disagreement between the banks is minimized. In any event, given that the credit is confirmed, Caribou and Heiligenberg are insulated from the decisions of Gondar National, and will depend only on Mount Royal Finance.

The Confirmation of the L/C is critical to the process of protecting Caribou and Heiligenberg; without this Confirmation, the transaction – and related settlement and flow of funds – could depend entirely on the decision of Gondar National, and/or on the situation in Ethiopia at the time that payment is due.

—

There is rarely just one right way to structure a trade or supply chain finance solution. Close collaboration between the parties involved, and appropriate leverage of the expertise of domain specialists is critical to the success of trade finance transactions, particularly when a certain degree of complexity is introduced.

Trade and supply chain finance are truly flexible and effective at facilitating a wide range of international commercial activity, in the most complex and challenging markets, and market conditions, across the globe.

Looking Ahead: Trade and Supply Chain Finance Tomorrow

The global financial and economic crisis that began in late 2007 has had significant and lasting adverse impact on trade and supply chain finance, and by extension, on the conduct of international commerce.

In addition to the relatively short-term evaporation of export finance at the peak of the crisis, and the somewhat more persistent rise in the cost of trade finance, at peak, more than 500 percent of normal, the crisis has engendered consequences, the full impact of which is unclear to this day.

A series of high-level issues impacting trade finance – adversely and favourably – merit focus and attention over the coming medium term, as illustrated in Figure 13.1.

Context and Selected Observations

Numerous banks, particularly in Europe and in the United States, were forced to refocus their activities and priorities following the need for substantial public sector investment and in some cases, effective nationalization, because of their exposure to toxic mortgage assets. The refocus of activity comprised a back-to-basics strategy, shifting resources and activity from high-risk, high-return investment banking, and complex financial engineering to core deposit taking and traditional lending.

The result has been significant new focus on transaction banking activity, which for some banks, has included trade finance, cash management, foreign exchange and working capital and liquidity management.

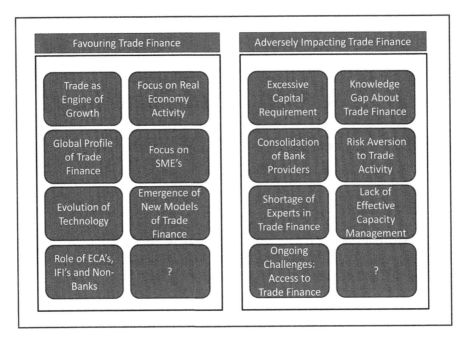

Figure 13.1   Issues impacting trade finance
Source: OPUS Advisory

At the same time, the "back-to-basics" argument has meant, for some, a retrenching to domestic activity or a significant narrowing of focus to local or regional markets, at the expense of international and trade banking activity. With trade finance already at a significant disadvantage in terms of profile and understanding in numerous financial institutions, the impact was, for a time, a demonstrable reduction in global capacity around bank-assisted trade finance.

The crisis also added, quite understandably, great urgency and political pressure around the regulation of the activities of banks, and in some circles, serious discussion around a redesign of the global financial system.

There has been significant focus on tightening and increasing requirements related to capital adequacy and the strength of bank balance sheets. Where trade finance had historically enjoyed appropriately advantageous regulatory treatment due to its low default and loan loss history, this advantage was largely squandered as a result of lack of engagement by trade finance specialists in championing the industry to political leaders and regulators.

Traditional trade finance was for many years treated as fundamentally less risky than, for example, straight lending, with significantly less capital required to be held in reserve against trade transactions than other types of banking transactions – commonly, perhaps 20 percent of the capital required in support of trade, compared to other businesses, making trade finance at least five times more efficient (or one fifth as expensive) from a capital perspective, as other banking activity. This advantage allowed trade finance to compete favourably with other lines of business, for access to bank resources and capital.

In light of the relatively modest returns earned from traditional trade finance as a line of business, the capital efficiency advantage would have been highly valuable during the peak of the global financial crisis, in ever-increasing competition for scarce bank capital. That advantage disappeared for several years, however, and the industry is just gaining some degree of traction in redressing this unfortunate outcome, based on the portfolio-level loan default and loss data provide to regulators and political leaders by leading trade finance banks.

Capital adequacy and reserve requirements imposed by regulators are necessary and prudent, and they must be adjusted periodically to ensure the viability of the global financial system as well as the safety of deposits and investments entrusted to financial institutions. At the same time, capital requirements should be defined on the basis of an informed understanding of lines of business such as trade finance, and on equitable treatment of such businesses on the basis of default and loss rates.

The capital adequacy discussion has very direct implications for the availability and cost of trade finance. Regulatory requirements, incorrectly defined, risk reducing the availability and raising the cost of trade finance, with adverse impact on the ability of businesses of all sizes, to successfully conduct international trade.

Longer-term, the incorrect treatment of and adverse impact upon traditional trade finance could, if it remains uncorrected, extend to supply chain finance and other emerging forms of trade financing, to further reduce trade financing options for businesses across the globe.

The capital requirements imposed on trade finance combine with a significant retrenching of banks away from international activity to contribute to the risk of reducing access to trade finance. At the same time, banks are taking a back-to-basics approach, focusing on real economy activity and an underlying flow of goods, reducing focus on financial engineering activities.

Political leaders in many jurisdictions are placing significant emphasis on the imperative of serving SMEsand entrepreneurial ventures, which, like international trade, are seen as important drivers of economic activity and growth.

Industry estimates have suggested that capital adequacy requirements could result in an increase in financing cost of 20 percent or more, a reduction of global trade flows of US $250 billion or more per year, and a commensurate reduction in global GDP of 0.5 percent or more.

Trade finance, particularly with current emphasis on global supply chains, sourcing patterns and supply chain finance, is well placed to respond to the requirements to serve the SME client segment, and likewise, well positioned to facilitate real economy commercial activity.

Trade growth is projected to accelerate over the coming years, and financing will remain a fundamentally important enabler of international commerce, no matter what form it may take – whether it continues to combine traditional trade finance mechanisms with variations on supply chain finance, or whether the inexorable evolution of technology will enable a fundamental transformation of the business of financing trade.

One challenge that will impact the ability of banks, certainly, to provide adequate levels of trade finance, links back to the regulatory requirements, but relates equally to the banks' ability to manage their portfolios of trade finance assets and risk, in order to allow adequate flow of business through the financial system, in support of international trade.

Supply chain finance programs are growing and gaining momentum and popularity in the market, as buyers and suppliers become increasingly aware of the business benefits of well-designed programs. Such solutions can involve facilities in the hundreds of millions of dollar or more, and in the last three years or so, the levels of utilization of these facilities have reportedly grown from 10 percent to well above 85 percent for the most successful programs.

Growing demand, coupled with still disproportionate capital reserve requirements will make it challenging for banks to respond to the needs of the market, and increasingly difficult for banks to compete with other providers that are not regulated, and not subject to requirements to maintain capital reserves against their trade finance portfolios.

While there are numerous factors at play in shaping the future of trade and supply chain finance, on balance, the value proposition around this form of financing is both robust and difficult to replicate. The future of trade finance, and its central role in supporting the successful conduct of international commerce, appears promising.

The central role of trade and trade finance to economic prosperity and growth has been well demonstrated and brought sharply into focus over the past several years.

One notable illustration of the profile of trade and supply chain finance was the invitation extended by UK Prime Minister Cameron to a subset of the FTSE 100 to attend a meeting at Number 10 Downing Street to discuss supply chain finance.

Following the profile at the several G-20 and WTO meetings, and coupled with the continued global focus on trade, the core role of trade finance in contributing to global growth is all but assured.

The business of financing international commerce has a long and robust history of adapting to the needs of businesses; even the current challenges related to regulatory requirements – the need to demonstrate adequate knowledge of trading parties, the imperative to counter efforts to launder money through trade mechanisms and the drive to assure adequate capital reserves – will be appropriately addressed. The long-term impact of these realities will be to assure an unprecedented level of profile for trade finance and a new level of engagement among senior trade executives. Trade finance will adapt its proposition to meet the evolving requirements of companies involved in international trade, business and investment.

Supply chain finance programs are being applied by leading providers to support both cross-border and domestic ecosystems of commercial relationships, and are, likewise, well suited to support increasingly important regional trade flows in Asia, the Middle East, Africa and the EU among others.

The Bank Payment Obligation: Innovation in Trade Finance

Traditional trade finance mechanisms, and arguably, elements of supply chain finance have been in existence and in use for many decades, even several hundred years.

While several attempts at innovation in this area have shown some level of market uptake and acceptance, no single proposition to date has reached a level of market dominance comparable to the traditional trade finance products at their peak of global usage.

A BPO is an irrevocable undertaking given by one bank to another bank that payment will be made on a specified date after a successful electronic matching of data according to an industry-wide set of rules.

The industry may be on the verge of such a transformational change, with the recent momentum exhibited by a relatively new instrument of trade finance called the Bank Payment Obligation, or BPO.

The BPO was first developed as a technology and messaging based solution to the needs of trade finance banks, by Belgium-based SWIFT – the same organization that transmits the majority of letters of credit, documentary collections and bank-to-bank payments in the world today.

While SWIFT prefers to maintain a distinction between the traditional documentary letter of credit, and the BPO, in practical terms, there are parallels in the product and in the transaction flow. A BPO is a payment undertaking that is triggered by a process of matching data/electronic documents, akin to the way a payment under a letter of credit is triggered when documents presented by an exporter match the requirements stipulated under the L/C.

The BPO achieves the long sought-after automation of the transaction process and dematerialization of the related document flow, reducing the manual intervention required, and allowing for automated triggering of settlement when the data elements are deemed to match.

The BPO provides a viable solution to the needs of importers, exporters and trade banks, and does so through a globally trusted network already in use by banks – and increasingly by corporates – in the conduct of business.

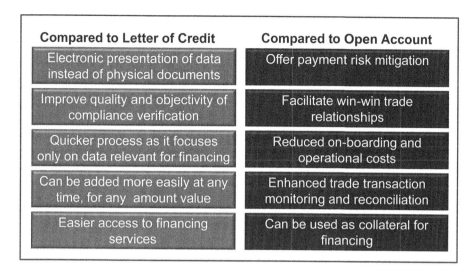

Compared to Letter of Credit	Compared to Open Account
Electronic presentation of data instead of physical documents	Offer payment risk mitigation
Improve quality and objectivity of compliance verification	Facilitate win-win trade relationships
Quicker process as it focuses only on data relevant for financing	Reduced on-boarding and operational costs
Can be added more easily at any time, for any amount value	Enhanced trade transaction monitoring and reconciliation
Easier access to financing services	Can be used as collateral for financing

Figure 13.2   Bank payment obligation, comparison to L/C and open account
Source: SWIFT/ICC BPO Education Committee

The BPO is positioned somewhere between straightforward open account transactions and documentary credits, as shown in Figure 13.2, providing greater security than the former, and enhanced flexibility and efficiency compared to the latter.

One of the important characteristics of a BPO relates to the standardization and objectivity of the data matching (and therefore, payment) process. Unlike documentary credits, where paper documents or their scanned images are physically verified by trade banking specialists, and a judgment call is often required about whether documents are compliant or not, the BPO process is clear and objective. This eliminates the scenario under L/Cs, where one bank deems documents compliant and another determines that they are discrepant when assessed against the terms of the L/C.

The objectivity of the BPO process, and the opportunity afforded, to correct the data elements or to waive the mismatch of data, further allows for objective, successful conclusion of a trade transaction.

The technology upon which the BPO is based allows for cost-effective use of this service by companies of all sizes, and the ability to introduce a BPO at various stages in a trade transaction can have significant favourable impact in terms of reducing the duration of a financial exposure, and the time during which a financial facility is utilized in support of a particular transaction.

A letter of credit, to be effective, must be issued prior to the shipment of the goods, and commonly, even before production of the goods has been initiated. This ties up lines of credit and extends the exposure period under the L/C beyond the timeframe required under a BPO, which can, by mutual agreement, be opened significantly later in a transaction, and still retain its effectiveness.

The BPO combines the security of a letter of credit with the relative transactional simplicity of open account, largely as a result of the data-driven and automated nature of this new instrument of trade finance. Transaction flows are contrasted in Figure 13.3.

The first commercial BPO transaction was announced publicly at a leading industry event in 2010, involving a transaction between the Bank of Montreal and the Bank of China, and their respective trade customers.

While volumes are still low, banking industry adoption of the BPO is progressing, and leading financial institutions, as well as several large corporations are promoting the BPO model as a desirable approach to the conduct of trade and the provision of trade and supply chain finance.

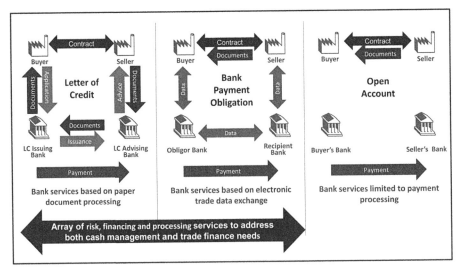

Figure 13.3   BPO transaction flow
Source: SWIFT/ICC BPO Education Committee

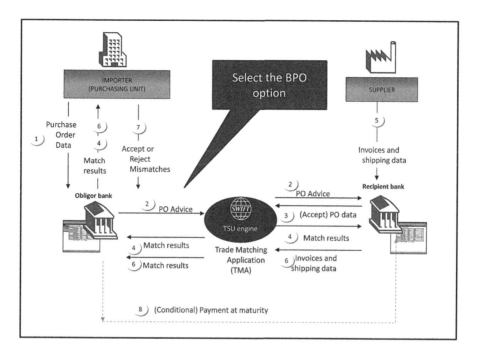

Figure 13.4   BPO detailed transaction flow
Source: SWIFT/ICC BPO Education Committee

As illustrated in Figure 13.4, the BPO involves a contract between buyer and seller, as is the usual case, however, the documentation related to the shipment (typically representing title to the goods, and the ability to claim them at destination) is sent by the exporter directly to the importer. The payment and/or financing decision under a BPO is triggered by transmissions of data from the buyer and seller to the obligor bank (the issuer of the BPO) and the recipient bank, respectively. Those banks then undertake a matching of the two data sets through technology.

One data set is extracted from the contract signed between the buyer and seller (or the relative Purchase Order), and the other data set originates from the invoice and transport document prepared by the exporter. A match in data elements – those elements having been selected by the importer and exporter – indicates that the exporter has fulfilled requirements outlined in the contract.

In addition to the automated extraction and transmission of data, the BPO, through an approved, underlying decision engine, compares the two data sets and determines, automatically and objectively, whether or not they match, in which case payment is triggered. In the event that the importer and exporter have agreed to settlement at a future date, the obligation is rendered effective once a data match is confirmed.

In the event of a mismatch of data, there is an opportunity to correct the mismatch and retransmit the data for comparison, or to simply waive the mismatch and authorize the payment. The Transaction Matching Application (TMA), shown in this case to be the Trade Services Utility (TSU), but potentially another compatible matching and decision engine, is critical to the functioning of the BPO.

The TMA drastically reduces the time, inconvenience and cost associated with managing and correcting the high rates of discrepant documents presented under documentary letters of credit described earlier.

The BPO enables banks to offer a variety of services to their client, ranging from financing options to cash management solutions, as shown in Figure 13.5. Pricing of the BPO will be determined by individual financial institutions, as is the case with existing trade finance mechanisms.

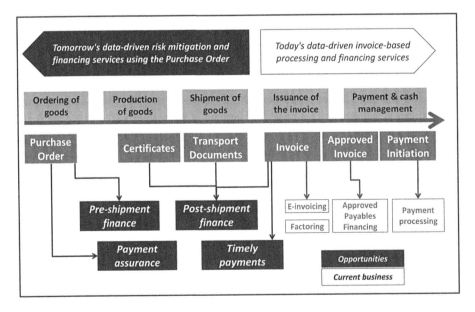

Figure 13.5   BPO financing options
Source: SWIFT/ICC BPO Education Committee

At this stage, no industry benchmark exists, and it is not fully clear whether the BPO will be positioned as a cost-effective alternative to an L/C, or a premium product among existing trade and supply chain financing options.

The value proposition around the BPO, and SWIFT's underlying decision engine, the TSU is significant, in terms of efficiency, security and flexibility. The BPO offers opportunities for payment, financing and cashflow management solutions over the lifecycle of a trade transaction, while at the same time, the risk mitigation dimension of the BPO is significantly more robust than under an open account transaction. The BPO is positioned favourably in terms of both risk mitigation and process efficiency, as shown in Figure 13.6.

The BPO compares favourably against various forms of letters of credit (including standbys and guarantees), as well as open account terms, when viewed in terms of process efficiency and risk mitigation. Depending on the pricing models developed for the BPO, it has the potential to be well-positioned in the market on pricing, as well.

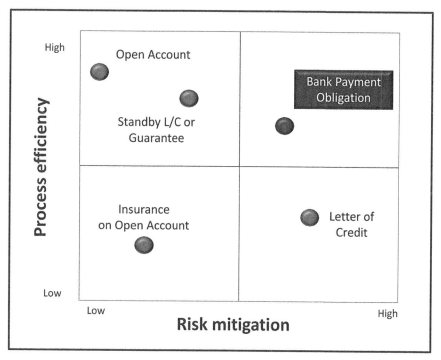

Figure 13.6   BPO efficiency and risk positioning
Source: SWIFT/ICC BPO Education Committee

In addition to an effective business model and robust, trusted technology, the BPO has been appropriately positioned to become an industry-wide, global solution. SWIFT and its members banks, having initially developed the TSU and the complementary BPO, have opted to partner with the International Chamber of Commerce in Paris, to replicate the success of letters of credit, by ensuring that a global set of regulations and practices are developed to govern the use of the BPO, just as is the case with documentary letters of credit, with documentary collections and numerous others related instruments.

Industry adoption, coupled with interest from importers and exporters, will be critical to the success and long-term viability of the BPO. The adoption of a universal set of rules and practices that apply across legal jurisdictions, and that are supported and promulgated by the ICC, is a critical component of the proposition around the BPO.

The Uniform Rules for Bank Payment Obligations have been drafted, have undergone extensive international review and were adopted in mid-2013. The adoption of the rules will be important to the level and rate of adoption of the BPO.

The importance of ICC rules linked to the use of the BPO cannot be overstated: it is one of the great successes of the letter of credit, that this instrument operates under a set of rules in effect since 1933, revised very collaboratively roughly every 10 years, and of such impact, that the rules are cited in legal cases and have becoming integrated in legal precedent in certain jurisdictions.

The development and application of global, industry-wide rules related to the use of the BPO is one element that distinguishes this solution in trade and supply chain finance as a milestone in the evolution of the industry. Another is the delivery of this model through the globally trusted SWIFT network, though the BPO can be coupled with any compatible, non-SWIFT data matching and decision engine in lieu of the TSU.

The regulatory treatment of the BPO is one factor that will impact its adoption rate among banks, and may, in the extreme, determine the viability of the product. If regulators recognize the nature of the transaction – and its associated risk – as being similar to traditional letters of credit, and grant an equitable but relatively favourable status from a reserve and capital adequacy perspective, the BPO will be favourably looked upon by the banks.

In the event that regulators deem this to be a new product lacking objective, portfolio-level historical data related to defaults and losses, and therefore subject to high levels of capital reserve, the BPO may be a promising but short-lived new solution to the needs of importers and exporters.

Mobile Payments and Supply Chain Ecosystems

The financing of international trade was, for years, a static business in terms of innovation. Existing instruments and processes, though far from optimal, were deemed adequate for the purposes of importers and exporters, and in any event, there were few viable options.

The situation has changed significantly, with technology finally able to fulfill its promise in advancing the processes and business models around trade and trade finance, and with niche providers, technology-driven, innovative companies, hedge fund managers and others showing an interest in the potential around trade finance.

Bankers accustomed to effective dominance of the trade finance market were, for a time, threatened by the global shift to open account terms, and are now facing pressure to innovate, if not outright competitive threat, by developments in the market and by the higher expectations of importers, exporters, entrepreneurs and treasury/finance executives across the globe.

Technology vendors have succeeded in developing and marketing so-called multi-bank solutions that serve as portals for clients to conduct and access their trade business from one access point into multiple financial institutions. Likewise, the advent of various online and e-invoicing solutions, together with significant momentum around mobile banking and financial services, will shape the evolution of trade and supply chain finance in the short to medium term.

Increasingly strategic focus on global sourcing, supply chains and supply chain finance, likewise, will impact developments in this area. Corporates, banks and others will look at global supply chains as more than a collection of buyer/seller relationships, but rather, a complex ecosystem of commercial partnerships with a commensurately rich financing, working capital, cash management and risk mitigation requirements.

Partnerships are increasingly seen as an important element of activities in international commerce, including in the provision of global and regional services related to trade finance. Banks of all sizes, including top-tier financial institutions with extensive international presence are looking to creative partnerships to extend both their capabilities and their delivery channels around trade finance, with some already looking actively at collaborations across traditional industry boundaries.

Partnership models have been articulated using a variety of approaches. In 2010, the Bank of New York Mellon and OPUS Advisory Services authored a white paper entitled "Global Transaction Banking: Evolution through Collaboration," in which consideration was given to the state of financial institution collaboration in selected markets across the globe. The notion of a collaborative ecosystem of partners was discussed in the context of trade and transaction banking, as shown in Figure 13.7, and the characteristics of the model remain relevant under current – and medium-term – market conditions.

The role of mobile banking and the potential for offering integrated solutions related to trade finance, cash management, payments and foreign exchange, were envisioned as components of a potential collaboration model.

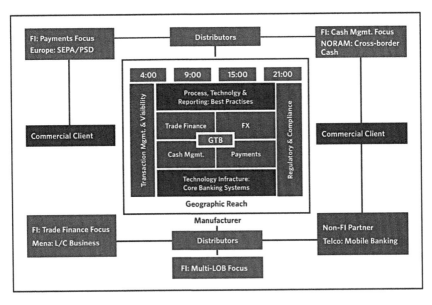

Figure 13.7   Trade and supply chain finance in transaction banking
Source: BNY Mellon/OPUS Advisory Thought Leadership White Paper, 2010

Trade and supply chain finance and its evolution over the next several years, will be influenced by ecosystem-based views of global supply chains, and by the increasingly urgent need for service providers to develop differentiated, high-value partnerships in support of their clients, and in support of the strategic business partners of those clients.

The imperative to compete, to innovate and to respond to the direction of political leaders as a result of the global economic crisis provides a unique opportunity for trade financiers to be creative in defining the future of their industry. Those same dynamics offer a unique opportunity for importers and exporters of all sizes to articulate their requirements and expectations, and to shape the development of effective solutions in trade and supply chain finance.

Payment Technologies and Solutions

It was observed some years ago that trade finance, in its shift to open account terms, was becoming increasingly similar to international cash management, and that international cash management, with its increasingly sophisticated infrastructure and cross-border capabilities, was taking on features comparable to certain aspects of trade finance.

This convergence continues to some degree, though it may be more accurate at this moment to suggest that the cash/trade propositions are increasingly complementary, and that treasury and finance executives, as well as entrepreneurs, are looking at trade, cash and payment needs in a more integrated manner than had been the case historically.

The increasing importance of non-cash payment and settlement options, including electronic payments and mobile payments, will inevitably have direct implications for the way in which international commerce transactions are settled – and by extension, on the ways in which such transactions are financed and risk mitigated.

Markets are evolving at different rates, and some emerging markets have been successful in accelerating their payment and (trade and other) financing evolution by leapfrogging the legacy technologies that have constrained advancement in other jurisdictions. The cost of decommissioning such legacy technologies is so high as to be prohibitive, with the effect that banks and other major technology users have been building new capabilities on top of existing technologies, while emerging economies have been able to design and develop new models on the basis of the most current technology.

An assessment of the level of non-cash transactions in a country can be a useful proxy to reflect the level of advancement and technological capability – as well as the adoption rates – prevalent in various jurisdictions.

Some bankers and other practitioners will argue that a core aspect of trade finance is the payment or settlement dimension, and that trends observable in the payments space merit tracking, relative to international trade transactions and trade finance.

While certain leading online payment solutions were initially viewed as niche solutions aimed primarily at retail customers, adoption rates have increased materially, and have extended to commercial clients and transactions. The growth of online settlement options is likewise evident in cross-border transactions, and it is worth monitoring leading providers, as they may devise solutions aimed at the settlement of international trade transactions. Figure 13.8 provides a view of the state of non-cash transactions in selected countries.

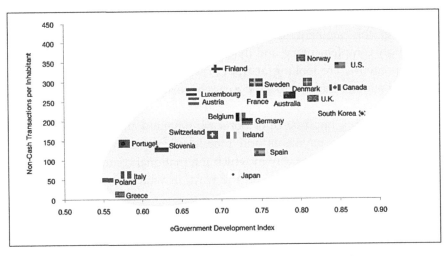

Figure 13.8   Level of non-cash transactions in leading markets

Source: *World Payments Report 2011*, Capgemini Financial Services and RBS

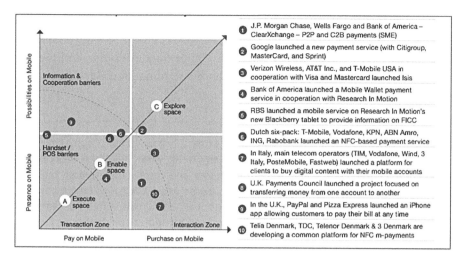

Figure 13.9   Mobile payments

Source: *World Payments Report 2011*, Capgemini Financial Services and RBS

Just as there are well-established models of partnership between trade finance banks, export credit agencies and others, there are emerging models in the payment and settlement space that involve organizations across industry sectors.

Developments in the payments space and in the electronic invoicing and settlement space offer a variety of options – arguably, change the landscape, around needs and expectations related to international settlement and the financing of cross-border transactions. Figure 13.9 illustrates the variety of mobile payment models available in various markets.

The combination of developments – and the acceleration of market acceptance and adoption – in online settlement together with mobile access, has the potential to significantly reshape the world of international commerce and the realities around international trade finance.

Trade financiers that respond quickly enough, and anticipate the changing needs and expectations of importers and exporters, will thrive, while those that revert to complacency will again find the need to reach defensively to the emergence of another competitive threat, much as was the case when companies shifted decisively to open account trade.

Business executives and entrepreneurs are in a position of leverage relative to their bankers and finance providers in a way that perhaps has never been the case, and there is an opportunity to actively shape the development of the next generation of trade and supply chain finance solutions, in collaboration with leaders in the industry.

The trade finance industry has always been extremely good at adapting to change and circumstance, and while the sector may be in what has been described as a 'golden age', there are numerous factors and trends that remain highly challenging for banks and corporates alike. Some tough decisions lie ahead for institutions that want to remain in the business with viable and value added offerings for their clients, while at the same time being truly profitable. [...]

While major corporates have easy access to trade funds at the present time, the access to funds for small and medium-sized enterprises (SMEs), in developed and developing economies, is still not easy or straightforward – despite the sector being highly liquid. This surely must relate to the attitude of many of the commercial banks and their shift to service core relationship corporate borrowers – predominantly large multinational companies. In the context of this, one has to look at the astonishingly complex range of regulatory pressure that commercial banks are being placed under. [...] The actual funding situation has left SMEs crying out for funding in many markets and many regions. [...] It has also meant the increased involvement of export credit agencies (ECAs) in providing short-term loan and guarantee programmes. It can be expected that the agencies will become even more instrumental in supporting global recovery and economic development in future years. (Source: "Hard Decisions Required as Trade Finance Enters a Bold New Era," Jonathan Bell, editor-in-chief, *Trade & Export Finance* 2013, www.txfnews.com)

Trade and Supply Chain Finance Tomorrow

Trade finance is a well-established and proven discipline within international banking and finance, with instruments, solutions and financing structures that have effectively supported the conduct of trade over many decades, even several hundred years.

The robustness of traditional trade financing mechanisms is both a positive characteristic, and a disadvantage to an industry not particularly known for its innovation and creativity; however, changing circumstances, advances in technology and the shifting priorities and requirements of businesses of all sizes, have combined to drive trade finance providers to innovate.

Financing and liquidity are less easily accessible today than was the case prior to the global financial and economic crisis – a situation likely to remain for some years to come – and thus, the ability to access and package trade and export finance is again a competitive advantage to businesses pursuing opportunities in international markets. Similarly, the need to optimize working capital and liquidity, and an increasingly strategic role for treasury and finance executives in companies of all sizes, contributes to the increased profile of effective financial management across the globe.

This includes an unprecedented focus on trade and supply chain finance, by business and political leaders across the globe, as economies continue to rely on robust trade as a driver of recovery and growth.

Trade and supply chain finance can be perceived to be highly complex – and this is sometimes the case, however, the fundamentals related to the financing of trade can be illustrated, and grasped in straightforward manner, without undue complexity, and the proven tools, techniques and solutions of trade and supply chain finance can prove effective and valuable to any party in a trade transaction, or in the most complex of global supply chains.

The advent of highly portable, functionality-rich technology solutions, coupled with the increased focus on international markets and the efforts of industry leaders and visionaries to devise innovative, twenty-first century solutions in trade and supply chain finance, combine to suggest that the next five to ten years will see a fundamental reshaping of the industry, and an imperative to ensure a broader and wider-ranging understanding of trade finance than exists today.

Appendix A:
Selected Sources of Trade and Supply Chain Finance

Banks

Major regional and international banks offer at least some level of support in traditional trade finance, and a growing number of banks are developing propositions around supply chain finance. Some banks have excellent material available online, that explains various financing options and mechanisms related to international trade.

Most of the following material is taken verbatim from the websites of the various organizations listed, without revision, validation or commentary. Companies seeking to do business with the entities profiled below are strongly advised to undertake appropriate research and due diligence to ensure a match between company needs and the services and expertise of each of the following organizations.

ECAs and IFI's

Leading export credit agencies, including some of the public/private partnerships in this area, offer excellent and comprehensive programs related to trade and supply chain finance. Details are best obtained through each ECA website or through industry bodies such as the Berne Union (http://www.berneunion.org)

Likewise, several international institutions and development agencies have developed and deployed very effective programs aimed at supporting and facilitating access to trade and supply chain finance.

EUROPEAN BANK FOR RECONSTRUCTION AND DEVELOPMENT

The Trade Facilitation Programme has been running successfully since 1999.

The programme aims to promote foreign trade to, from and amongst the EBRD countries of operations and offers a range of products to facilitate this trade.

Through the programme the EBRD provides guarantees to international confirming banks, taking the political and commercial payment risk of international trade transactions undertaken by banks in the countries of operations (the issuing banks).

We also provide short-term loans to selected banks and factoring companies for on-lending to local exporters, importers and distributors.

The programme can guarantee any genuine trade transaction to, from and among the countries of operations.

The programme strengthens the ability of local banks to provide trade financing and through these banks gives entrepreneurs throughout our countries of operations the support they need to increase their access to their import and export trade.

Source: http://www.ebrd.com/pages/workingwithus/trade.shtml

ASIAN DEVELOPMENT BANK

ADB's Trade Finance Program (TFP) fills market gaps for trade finance by providing guarantees and loans to banks to support trade.

Backed by its AAA credit rating, ADB's TFP works with over 200 partner banks to provide companies with the financial support they need to engage in import and export activities in Asia's most challenging markets. With dedicated trade finance specialists and a response time of 24 hours, the TFP has established itself as a key player in the international trade community, providing fast, reliable, and responsive trade finance support to fill market gaps.

A substantial portion of TFP's portfolio supports small and medium-sized enterprises (SMEs), and many transactions occur either intra-regionally or between ADB's developing member countries. The program supports a wide range of transactions, from commodities and capital goods to medical supplies and consumer goods.

The TFP continues to grow, supporting billions of dollars of trade throughout the region, which in turn helps create sustainable jobs and economic growth in Asia's developing countries.

Source: http://www.adb.org/site/private-sector-financing/trade-finance-program

ISLAMIC DEVELOPMENT BANK/IITFC

The International Islamic Trade Finance Corporation (ITFC) is advancing trade to improve the economic situation and livelihoods of people across the Islamic world. As an autonomous entity within the Islamic Development Bank Group, the ITFC was formed to consolidate the trade finance business that was formerly undertaken by various windows within the IDB Group. The consolidation of the bank's trade finance activities under a single umbrella increases the efficiency of service delivery by enabling rapid response to customer needs in a market-driven business environment.

As a leader in Shari'ah-compliant trade finance, we deploy our expertise and funds to businesses and governments in member countries of the OIC. Our primary focus is encouraging intra-trade among member countries, and we are active in developing and diversifying Islamic finance solutions to further trade. As an international financial service organization, we have a rigorous commitment to work with our clients in proactive, accountable and efficient ways.

As a member of the Islamic Development Bank Group, we have unique access to governments and work as a facilitator to mobilize private and public resources to achieve a measurable impact on trade and development. The ITFC helps businesses in Islamic countries gain better access to trade finance and provides them with the necessary education and training to compete successfully in the global marketplace. Our efforts are geared to building stronger trade relations between member countries and giving individuals opportunities to grow and prosper.

Respect for our Islamic heritage is at the heart of everything we do. We have a clear vision: to share and apply our intra trade skills – linking together people, partnerships and possibilities to make strong connections that empower, expand and enrich economies, communities and individuals. We are robust and responsible at our core but balance this with an energy and drive – seeking out new opportunities that enable the Islamic world to prosper.

The four cornerstones of our business – our customers, business partners, member countries and our products and services – provide a solid foundation on which we are building a promising and exciting future. Operating to world-class standards, the ITFC promotes the IDB Groups developmental objectives through its two main pillars, Trade Finance and Trade Promotion, to fulfill its brand promise of "Advancing Trade & Improving Lives."

Source: http://www.itfc-idb.org/content/what-itfc

WORLD BANK/INTERNATIONAL FINANCE CORPORATION

The US $5 billion Global Trade Finance Program (GTFP) extends and complements the capacity of banks to deliver trade financing by providing risk mitigation in new or challenging markets where trade lines may be constrained.

GTFP offers confirming banks partial or full guarantees covering payment risk on banks in the emerging markets for trade related transactions. These guarantees are transaction-specific and may be evidenced by a variety of underlying instruments such as: letters of credit, trade-related promissory notes, accepted drafts, bills of exchange, guarantees, bid and performance bonds and advance payment guarantees. The guarantees are available for all private sector trade transactions that meet IFC's eligibility criteria. A price incentive or longer tenors may be available for equipment and projects that have clearly defined climate change benefits as part of our Climate Smart Trade initiative.

Through the GTFP bank network, local financial institutions can establish working partnerships with a vast number of major international banks in the Program that can broaden access to finance and reduce cash collateral requirements. This enables the continued flow of trade credit into the market at a time when imports may be critical and the country's exports can generate much-needed foreign exchange.

How Does IFC Support Trade Transactions?

The program offers confirming banks partial or full guarantees to cover payment risk on banks in the emerging markets. These guarantees are transaction-specific and apply to:

- letters of credit;

- trade-related promissory notes and bills of exchange;

- bid and performance bonds;

- advance payment guarantees;

- suppliers credits for the import of capital goods.

In addition, IFC provides funding to banks for short-term pre-export financing.

What Does the Global Trade Finance Program Do for Business?

The program combines global reach and maximum flexibility to assist trade finance deals by:

- delivering trade solutions through a global network of participating banks;

- covering large and small transactions in challenging countries;

- using master agreements, which facilitate 24–48 hour response time via SWIFT for individual transactions;

- having in place a dedicated trade unit to serve business needs;

- offering commercial pricing with no commitment fees;

- supporting all valid private sector trade transactions meeting IFC criteria;

- covering up to 100 percent of transaction value;

- providing tenors of up to three years to support capital goods imports.

Trade Development through Trade Finance Training

Technical training for issuing banks represents an integral part of the Global Trade Finance Program. Technical assistance modules comprise basic and intermediate courses on trade finance. On a selective basis, IFC places experienced trade finance bankers with issuing banks to help them develop trade finance and other banking skills. In addition, IFC assists in arranging training at major international trade banks for trade officers of issuing banks.

Source: http://www1.ifc.org [Global Trade Finance Program]

Boutique Firms

NORTHSTAR TRADE FINANCE

Northstar Trade Finance is an internationally recognized specialist in providing financing solutions to small and medium-sized enterprises involved in, or pursuing opportunities in international markets.

At Northstar Trade Finance, we have been supporting clients in their international activities since we were first established in Canada in 1994.

Our success and our ability to meet financing commitments even in the most difficult economic circumstances, or in some of the more challenging markets across the world, has earned Northstar an enviable reputation in the business of financing international trade. Northstar has developed a unique, partnership-based approach in providing financing solutions to our clients – and their buyers – across the world.

Northstar's partners include several of the top financial institutions in North America who are shareholders of the Company (please see our Shareholders & Partners pages for further detail), as well as leading government agencies and export credit insurers in Canada, the United States, Europe and Australia among others.

Northstar's approach to financing international trade includes a strategic approach to developing effective public-partnerships with key government agencies and departments, particularly successful in the provision of trade-related financing and insurance/guarantee solutions.

Source: http://www.nstfglobal.com

MAPLE TRADE FINANCE

When opportunity knocks, we make sure you can answer the door.

Growing a business is hard and when the right opportunity comes along you can't afford to miss it. That's where we come in.

We're not a bank or a factor. Instead, we combine the flexibility of a factor with the depth and stability of traditional banking.

Perhaps you've just negotiated a large one-time deal. Or maybe you've been awarded multiple smaller contracts. Quick access to working capital can give you an advantage over your competition. We evaluate your financing needs based on the strength of the transaction, not just your balance sheet – whether you're a growing one-office business, a medium sized firm with rapid growth, or a well-established leader in your industry with complex financing challenges. That way you get the backing you need, when you need it. No more missed opportunities.

Here are some of the financing options we provide:

- Increase your cash flow with Receivable Financing.

- Leverage your greatest asset with Accounts Receivable Operating Facility.

- Secure cash for purchasing materials with Contract Financing and Supply Chain Financing.

Source: http://www.mapletradefinance.ca

FALCON TRADE FINANCE

Falcon Group has provided financial solutions and advice to our clients since 1996.

We are recognised as a key alternative source of corporate finance – acting as a partner to our clients with respect to their global, regional and local requirements. Falcon Group operates throughout the Middle East, Asia-Pacific, North and Latin America.

Bank lending in nearly all regions of the world has become constrained, leaving many companies facing liquidity issues. Falcon Group is able to fill this void, offering bespoke supply chain and working capital finance solutions to companies despite the continued challenging market conditions.

Source: http://www.falcontradecorp.com

A-TRADE FINANCE

A-TRADE is the collective name for a group of companies, headquartered in Hong Kong and operating around the world in order to provide:

- extended payment terms and increased cash flow for buyers;

- advanced development and working capital for producers and suppliers;

- improved balance sheet management, risk mitigation, and other value-added services.

Our broad industry and wide geographical presence is the result of a co-joining, in 2012, of two independently successful businesses: A-Trade Finance Limited and the Tower Bridge Group.

A-Trade Finance Limited was founded by Lawrence Webb, former Global Head of Trade & Supply Chain at HSBC Bank, and Robert Barnes, founder and former CEO of PrimeRevenue Inc. Lawrence and Robert had previously worked together developing a fully integrated commercial bank supply chain finance proposition. In so doing, they identified an opportunity to complement traditional banking services by leveraging an innovative structuring approach to providing infrastructure, development and working capital funding for commodity producers, offtakers, and other large value project developers.

Tower Bridge Group, managed by Charles Reynolds and Henry Biddulph, was established to provide a comprehensive range of trade related financial solutions for exporters and importers of a wide variety of goods and industries. Since its founding in 2002, Tower Bridge grew rapidly to become a widely respected international trade finance entity with a sound market reputation and presence over three continents.

A-TRADE today is a highly experienced trading and financial structuring business servicing a multi-industry client base ranging from SMEs to large corporates and multi-national companies.

Details of our client and industry focus, product offerings and other value added services are highlighted on our website. For additional information or enquiries, please contact us directly.

Source: http://www.atradefinance.com

SYNCADA FROM VISA (GLOBAL TRADE)

These days, cross-border trade is no longer exclusively the domain of multinational organizations. Most businesses can sell goods or access suppliers around the world easily. This means your institution needs to be able to handle these transactions and support your customers' global expansion. With Syncada Global Trade, you can be a partner in your clients' global business strategy, whether you're a regional financial institution or a global bank.

As part of the Syncada network, you can offer clients access to a payment network built for cross-border transaction processing, financing, and payment. Clients choose the service offerings they need based on their global trade flows, business partners, or cash flow needs. And you gain access to an international network of banks that allows you to compete on a global scale.

The Syncada Global Trade solution includes an end-to-end offering, from invoice and trade document processing and matching to many types of financing, depending on your level of risk. Syncada also provides different payment methods allowing best-in-class service to your customers. They'll benefit from transparent cash flow performance, improved supplier relationships, lowered risk with visibility into transactions, and reduced administrative and training costs. So no matter where you or your clients are located, you can help them do business, better.

Source: http://www.syncada.com [Global Trade]

DEMICA

Demica's innovative and award winning working capital management technology is used around the globe by the world's leading banks, private equity sponsors and global corporations to implement innovative trade receivables securitization, supply chain finance and invoice discounting solutions.

Demica specialises in providing bespoke solutions and works with a diverse range of multi-national clients on trade receivables securitization, supply chain finance, invoice discounting and all forms of asset based lending, enhancing working capital management. Read our case studies to find out more about the ways in which Demica has helped clients.

Demica delivers its receivables financing, supply chain finance and asset based lending technology worldwide, with global transactions processed on Demica's Citadel platform. Demica's factoring or invoice discounting solution offers our clients a flexible method of providing business through asset backed lending and receivables financing by offering a real-time, detailed view of their invoice portfolio.

Source: http://www.demica.com

Platform Providers

TRADECARD

Since 1999, TradeCard, Inc. has transformed global supply chain collaboration by boosting visibility, cash flow and margins for over 10,000 brands, retailers, suppliers and service providers operating in 78 countries. TradeCard delivers a cloud-based network that enables complex, multi-enterprise sourcing transactions across multiple layers of the supply chain. More than 45,000 individual users leverage the TradeCard Platform to streamline transaction flows, from purchase order through production tracking, shipment and payment. Embedded financial services throughout the supply network reduce capital costs and minimize risk. Multi-enterprise collaboration on the platform delivers visibility into the movement of goods, from raw materials to the store shelf. TradeCard's on-the-ground trade experts around the world allow entire supply networks to rapidly join and drive value through the platform.

The world's leading retailers and brands, including Levi Strauss & Co., Columbia Sportswear, Guess and Rite Aid, leverage the TradeCard Platform and its member network for sourcing and global trade. TradeCard, Inc. is headquartered in New York City, with offices in San Francisco, Amsterdam, Hong Kong, Shenzhen, Shanghai, Taipei, Seoul, Ho Chi Minh City and Colombo.

Source: http://www.tradecard.com

[Merger in progress with GT Nexus, http://www.gtnexus.com]

BOLERO

Founded in 1998, with significant backing from the bank community and from the global logistics industry, Bolero was created as a neutral, trusted third party to develop an open and legally certain platform to deliver paperless trading between buyers, sellers, financial institutions and logistics service providers anywhere in the world, delivering transaction visibility, predictability, speed, accuracy and security.

Today Bolero brings Corporates, Commodity Traders and their Banks together to share the benefits of collaborative Trade Finance, providing an open, neutral and secure multi-party channel designed specifically for the fully electronic communication of trade and trade finance documents and related messages. In addition Bolero delivers powerful collaborative Trade Finance solutions delivered as a global hosted service reducing the cost of deployment and substantially reducing the time to benefit.

Corporates, Commodity Traders and their partner Banks are rapidly deploying Bolero solutions delivering significant reductions in cost and working capital, increased visibility and improvements in operating efficiency.

Source: http://www.bolero.net

PRIME REVENUE

Founded in 2004, PrimeRevenue has become an acknowledged leader and innovative award-winning provider in multi-bank Supply Chain Finance. Our PrimeRevenue OpenSCi™ vision is to become the standard global platform for processing Supply Chain Finance transactions to the world's largest Buyers and Suppliers.

Our leadership brings industry experience from multiple disciplines, including supply chain solutions, financial advisory services, information technology delivery, and trading partner enablement.

Our board of directors brings perspective unrivalled by like providers in our space, and helps to guide the company's direction with the experience that has benefited some of the world's most successful financial, software, investment and manufacturing companies.

PrimeRevenue has several opportunities for Careers, and is an equal opportunity employer. We continuously seek new teammates who are intellectually eager and highly motivated to excel.

PrimeRevenue has a solid History of success in defining the burgeoning Supply chain Finance market on a global basis. We are so innovative and successful that Google web tracking indicates that competition follows us, copies our content and registers for our webinars to learn about the future of SCF!

PrimeRevenue has been recognized with multiple Awards for being the innovation leader in Supply Chain Finance. With the introduction of OpenSCi™ in 2011, we expect to continue being the innovation leader for years to come!

We work with multiple Clients & Partners all over the world, in 18 separate nations, in multiple currencies, and with 38 banks funding. See a short subset of our Who's Who.

Why PrimeRevenue?

- Running the World's largest Supply Chain Finance programs;

- The only true multi-bank (38) SCF system, for your financial freedom;

- Global, with SCF trades in multiple nations, languages & currencies;

- A complete, end-to-end solution with 100 percent proprietary technology and services.

PrimeRevenue OpenSCi™ begins with the understanding that your supply chain is really a supply web. Each single strand of this integral system must relate to all the other parts of your supply chain, or else your results will be limited and inflexible.

Taking a holistic view is therefore the critical path to long term success in improving financing for your supply chain. PrimeRevenue OpenSCi is a unified approach to successful Supply Chain Finance, accessible over the Cloud yet integrated with your existing ERP system, and supported by coordinated services and support to deliver broad benefits across your supply chain.

With financing from multiple banks and financial institutions around the world, PrimeRevenue OpenSCi gives you the tools to continue achieving and improving your results, and to make changes as your supply chain finance strategy develops and becomes more nuanced. Don't be trapped by any one bank and its policies, fly OpenSCi!

Source: http://www.primerevenue.com

ORBIAN

Orbian is the world's leading supply chain finance company. For more than a decade, we have been providing large, global corporations with collaborative supply chain finance solutions and services. Our innovative, trust-enabled approach to SCF delivers significant benefits to our clients that cannot be found with any other SCF offering.

Orbian was conceived and developed in the late 1990s as a joint venture between global leaders in financial services and enterprise software. Orbian became an independent, private company when its current owners purchased the company in 2003.

In 2004, Orbian launched its trust-enabled funding structure that, combined with the company's state of the art SCF technology platform, allows Orbian to offer comprehensive SCF solutions and services to its large corporate clients globally. The universal funding structure allows Orbian to offer programs with virtually unlimited funding capacity while mitigating the operational risks inherent in other SCF offerings.

The Orbian solution helps buyers and suppliers enhance business performance – optimize working capital, mitigate supply chain risk, and reduce operational costs – by delivering the most efficient form of receivables financing and streamlining and automating the payment and settlement process.

Orbian is comprised of top talent from the world's leaders in finance, technology and customer service. The company is headquartered in Norwalk, Connecticut with global operations located in London in the UK. In addition to its direct sales force, Orbian distributes its solution through several strategic partners that include many of the world's leading financial institutions and technology companies.

Source: http://www.orbian.com

Appendix B:
Traditional Trade Finance: Industry Product Definitions – Global Trade Industry Council, BAFT-IFSA, February 2012

Traditional Trade Finance products have existed in some form for hundreds of years. Generally speaking, banks have served as intermediaries to facilitate the flow of documents (information) and payments related to the flow of goods in international trade or to provide assurance relating to the performance or financial obligations of a person or company to another. Different products provide importers and exporters with varying levels of risk mitigation and/or financing.

1. Collections

Collection refers to the handling by banks of documents, in accordance with instructions received, in order to obtain payment and/or acceptance or deliver documents against payment and/or against acceptance or deliver documents on other terms and conditions (Source URC 522).

Specifically,

(i) A Collection that is payable at Sight is known as **Documents against Payment (D/P).** The documents are sent to the presenting/drawee bank and delivered to the drawee against payment. (ii) A Usance Collection is known as **Documents against Acceptance (D/A).** The documents are sent by the principal/drawer to the presenting bank and delivered to the drawee against the buyer's commitment to pay at a future date. Such commitment is usually evidenced by a bill of exchange, issuance of a promissory note, or an undertaking to pay at a future date, which, when accepted by the drawee/buyer for payment at a future date, is known as a trade acceptance.

Unlike a letter of credit there is no explicit undertaking by a bank to make finance available, however, the Remitting bank may choose to finance the exporter at the bank's own risk with or without recourse, by purchasing the bill or by discounting the unaccepted bill before despatch to the presenting or collecting bank. The remitting bank may also discount the advice of the drawees acceptance without cognisance of the presenting or collecting banks co-acceptance. If the presenting/collecting bank is requested to co-accept or avalize the accepted bill it may do so. In some circumstances the presenting/collecting bank may also offer finance to the remitting bank by discounting its own acceptance, or in response to the request of the drawer through the presenting bank, provide a discounted advance payment.

2. Letters of Credit (L/Cs)

A letter of credit is an arrangement, however named or described, that is irrevocable and thereby constitutes a definite undertaking of the issuing bank to honor a complying presentation. There are two main types – a Commercial (or Documentary) Letter of Credit and a Standby Letter of Credit. Commercial Letters of Credit typically are used to assure payment for a transaction involving the movement of goods and involve the presentation of commercial documents that usually transfer title of the underlying goods, while Standby Letters of Credit are typically used as performance or financial assurances and are payable against a simple demand or a demand and a statement. These are defined in greater detail below.

A. COMMERCIAL (DOCUMENTARY) LETTERS OF CREDIT

A Commercial (Documentary) Letter of Credit is a written undertaking given by a bank (Issuing Bank), at the request of a buyer (Applicant), to pay the seller (Beneficiary) of goods or services provided that the seller strictly fulfills a defined set of documentary terms and conditions specified in the letter of credit. Any amendment of the L/C requires the consent of all participants. Such credits are normally governed by the International Chamber of Commerce (ICC)'s Uniform Customs and Practice (UCP). UCP 600 came into effect in July 2007.

(i) Commercial (Documentary) Letters of Credit – Availability

The Commercial L/C will specify how and when the payment/proceeds will be made available:

a. **Sight** indicates the Letter of Credit is payable upon presentation of documents in compliance with the terms and conditions of the L/C and may or may not include a Draft/Bill of Exchange.

b. **Usance** indicates the Letter of Credit is payable on some future date after presentation of documents in compliance with terms and conditions of the L/C.

i. **Deferred Payment** is a promise of the Issuing Bank to pay a certain sum of money on a future fixed date. No Draft/Bill of Exchange or other negotiable instrument is required.

ii. **Acceptance** of Draft(s) drawn on the Issuing Bank (or Nominated Bank) represents a promise of the accepting bank to pay a certain sum of money on a fixed date. Such future date may be a pre-determined fixed date or based on a period of time after shipment date or presentation date

c. **Negotiation** indicates that the L/C may be negotiated either by any bank of the beneficiary's choosing (freely negotiable), or, by a specifically nominated bank.

(ii) Commercial (Documentary) Letters of Credit – Risk Mitigation

a. **Unconfirmed Letter of Credit** – The Issuing Bank is obligated to pay upon presentation of conforming documents and at the designated time specified within the letter of credit. There is no obligation on the part of the Advising Bank should the Issuing Bank not pay. The Advising Bank is solely responsible for the authenticity of the letter of credit.

b. **Confirmed Letter of Credit** – A Commercial Letter of Credit in which the Issuing Bank requests and nominates a second bank (often the Advising Bank) to add its payment undertaking to the letter of credit in addition to that of the Issuing Bank. The confirming bank becomes a participant of the L/C and their consent to any amendment or cancellation is also required. Such commitment from this second bank provides additional comfort to the seller who wishes to mitigate the country and bank risk of an Issuing Bank.

3. **"Silently" Confirmed Letter of Credit** – A Silent Confirmation is typically undertaken at the request of the Beneficiary instead of the Issuing Bank, and without the knowledge of the Issuing Bank. A bank that adds this type of confirmation undertakes to honor or negotiate compliant documents by direct arrangement with the beneficiary. The "'Silent'" Confirming Bank's obligation is evidenced by a separate undertaking document which is outside the terms of the letter of credit and this distinct bilateral arrangement is not covered by the ICC rules. By contrast to an "open" confirmation, the silently confirming bank is not a participant in the L/C according to UCP.

4. **Reimbursement Undertaking** – Irrevocable guarantee by the reimbursing bank to a nominated bank/claiming bank (to whom documents under a letter of credit would be presented for payment) to honor their reimbursement claim. An IRU can be based upon the request of an issuing bank or can be silent to the issuing bank.

(iii) Commercial (Documentary) Letters of Credit – Special characteristics

a. **Revolving Credit** – A commitment on the part of the issuing bank to automatically restore the credit value to the original (or other) amount after it has been drawn upon. This is typically used for instalment or multiple delivery contracts and may revolve around time or value.

b. **Transferable Credit** – The original letter of credit allows the beneficiary to transfer all or part of the originally issued letter of credit (Master L/C) to another party (one or more second beneficiary) and specifically states that the L/C is transferrable.

c. **Back-to-Back Credit** – A separate letter of credit is issued at the request of the beneficiary of an original letter of credit using the original letter of credit as a model and/or collateral for the bank issuing the second letter of credit.

d. **Front-to-Back or "To Arrive" Credit** – The second letter of credit is issued without the benefit of the original Master credit being available. In some markets this is also known as an "Export will Buy" credit where the master credit leg is replaced with a commitment to discount or purchase an export collection to pay out the import credit.

e. **Red Clause** – A clause authorizing the nominated bank to make advances to the beneficiary (usually by simple receipt) prior to the shipment of goods or presentation of documents.

f. **Green Clause** – A green clause credit is the same as a "Red Clause" credit except that pre-shipment advance is made against beneficiary's presentation of title document to the goods made to the order of the bank or its nominated agent, evidencing storage of the goods in a warehouse in the exporter's country.

g. **Assignment of Proceeds** – A beneficiary may assign all or part of the proceeds of a letter of credit to another party (assignee). The original beneficiary maintains sole rights to the letter of credit and the payment to the assignee is contingent upon payment under the original letter of credit.

B. STANDBY LETTERS OF CREDIT

A Standby Letter of Credit is a written undertaking given by a bank (Issuing Bank), at the request of an Applicant, which can be a bank, to provide assurance to a Beneficiary regarding the Applicant's (or a third party's) performance or financial obligations, that promises to pay the Beneficiary against presentation of a documentary demand conforming with the terms and conditions specified in the letter of credit. Unlike a commercial letter of credit, which is expected to be the means of payment in the underlying transaction, a standby letter of credit is typically not drawn unless there is some manner of default in the underlying transaction. Such credits are normally governed by the ICC rules (UCP or ISP 98).

(i) Standby Letters of Credit – Risk Mitigation

a. **Confirmed Standby Letter of Credit** – A Standby Letter of Credit in which the Issuing Bank requests and nominates a second bank (often the Advising Bank) to add its undertaking to the Standby Letter of Credit, in addition to that of the Issuing Bank, to honor a compliant claim without recourse to the Beneficiary. Generally governed by ICC rules, such confirmation provides additional comfort to the Beneficiary who wishes to mitigate the bank risk of the Issuing Bank, or to credit enhance the undertaking of the Issuing Bank.

b. **"Silently" Confirmed Standby Letter of Credit** – A Silent Confirmation is typically undertaken at the request of the Beneficiary instead of the Issuing Bank. A silently confirming bank undertakes to honor a compliant claim made under a Standby Letter of Credit. The Silent Confirming Bank's obligation is evidenced by a separate undertaking document, which is outside the terms of the Standby Letter of Credit and this distinct bilateral arrangement is not covered by the ICC rules.

(ii) Standby Letters of Credit – Categories

a. **Performance Standby Letters of Credit (or Performance Bond)** – is issued to guarantee performance of the Applicant (or a third party) under a contract. It is considered a show of "good faith" and is not normally expected to be drawn upon. Advance Payment and Bid Bonds are also generally considered to be similar in nature to Performance Bonds. Performance standby L/Cs are related to underlying commercial trade transactions.

b. **Financial Standby Letter of Credit** – is issued to guarantee future payment obligation(s). The Financial Standby L/C will only be drawn upon should the Applicant (or a third party) not make the payment(s) as expected. This instrument may also be used in lieu of cash collateral. Financial standby L/Cs are NOT related to underlying commercial trade transactions.

* Financial standby L/Cs may NOT be considered trade products where there is no underlying trade transaction.

(iii) Standby Letters of Credit – Special Characteristics

a. **Evergreen Clause** – Allows the letter of credit to be automatically extended until the issuing bank informs the beneficiary of its final expiration date.

3. Letters of Guarantee

A bank guarantee is an irrevocable promise of a bank to compensate the beneficiary under clearly prescribed conditions fully, immediately, and without failure for damages suffered. To be utilized in the event of default by the applicant of the Letter of Guarantee (L/G). Guarantees are usually governed by local law and different ICC rules (URDG 758 and others).

a. Letter of Guarantee issued on behalf of another bank – Issuing Bank issues a Letter of Guarantee at the request of another bank, which issues a counter guarantee in favour of the Issuing Bank.

b. "Silently" confirmed Letter of Guarantee issued by another bank – Issuing Bank adds at the request of its customer a silent guarantee to a L/G issued by another bank in favour of said customer.

SECTION 3: TRADE FINANCE DEFINITIONS – TRADITIONAL FINANCING PRODUCTS

Trade Finance lending also uses traditional products that have existed in practice for a long period of time, but are not necessarily governed by the same structured ICC rules that traditional documentary products use. Nevertheless, industry practice and standards have demonstrated these instruments to be fairly widely used, fairly consistent in structure and application, and consistently low risk. These are funded assets that in some cases originated as contingents. The key differentiating component of these financing methods are that they all support identifiable trade transactions.

1. Trade Loans

Trade loans occur when a lender grants a loan to a corporate or bank client to finance clearly defined trade transactions. The proof of the underlying trade transaction comes either from local regulatory practice (e.g., currency control), documentary evidence, or from the way the transaction is structured. Such evidence may include shipping documents or other documents that demonstrate the financing to be consistent with the goods or services imported/ exported (e.g., tenor of loan is consistent with goods being financed). Loans typically come from a flexible short-term borrowing facility and may facilitate a pool of trade transactions (e.g., bank loans) or be linked to single transactions. Loans may be made against either corporate risk or bank risk.

A. **Import Loans** – provide financing for the importation of goods or services. These loans are often a bridge to enable importers to pay suppliers on a timely basis, while providing additional time to convert imported goods into cash receipts. Import loans are often made against evidence of shipment and/or supplier invoices.

B. **Export Loans** – provide financing for the exportation of goods or services. Export loans are typically needed to fund activities required prior to shipment. Loans may be made to banks to enable them to fund pre-export activity on behalf of their customers. Some banks may consider L/C discounting a form of export loans, while others measure L/C discounting separately.

2. L/C Financing

Letters of credit are contingent instruments, that are payable only at such time as the terms of the letter of credit have been complied with. Nevertheless, there are instances when banks choose to advance funds during the course of the lifecycle of the letter of credit, and certain events trigger the contingent liability to become on-balance sheet.

A. **Negotiation** – the purchase by the nominated bank of drafts (drawn on a bank other than the nominated bank) and/or documents under a complying presentation, by advancing or agreeing to advance funds to the beneficiary on or before the banking day on which reimbursement is due to the nominated bank. Banks often deduct the cost of advancing funds from the proceeds based on the expected time between the negotiation and reimbursement from the Issuing Bank.

B. **Acceptance** – the accepted draft under the L/C becomes a negotiable instrument. The holder in due course can hold until maturity, or receive discounted funds in advance.

C. **Bills of Exchange/Promissory Notes** – a bill of exchange is a written order from the drawer to the drawee to pay the payee on demand or at a fixed date. A promissory note is a written unconditional promise to pay the payee (or bearer) on demand or at a date in the future. In negotiable form, these instruments also function similar to acceptances in that the holder in due course can hold until maturity or receive discounted funds. The difference being when the maker of a note pays the payee directly, rather than ordering a 3rd party to do so.

D. **L/C Refinancing/Post-Shipment Financing** – through the wording of the L/C, the issuing bank requests the presenting bank to pay the exporter through a loan granted to the issuing bank. At final maturity, the issuing bank repays the presenting bank the principal plus interest.

E. **L/C Financing by Reimbursement Bank** – The Issuing Bank opens a commercial L/C and nominates a Reimbursement Bank which agrees to pay the reimbursement claim of an entitled claiming bank and grant a pre-agreed loan to the Issuing Bank. The Issuing Bank repays principal plus interest to the reimbursing bank at maturity.

3. Trust Receipts

When issuing a Trust Receipt, the bank enables the importer to obtain goods and/or shipping documents while retaining title/ownership. The importer that obtains the goods (or proceeds from sale of the goods) is obligated to identify and maintain them separate from other assets.

Payment is made by the importer by the Trust Receipt due date. Trust receipts may be set up as specific facilities, or may be treated as import loans.

4. Shipping Guarantees

A Shipping Guarantee is an indemnity that the bank executes jointly and severally with its customer in favour of a shipping company, enabling the importer to obtain goods without the actual title documents (e.g., bills of lading). This is used when the goods arrive prior to the actual title documents, and the buyer wishes to obtain the goods so as to avoid demurrage charges or losses due to deterioration of goods (esp. perishables). Settlement occurs upon receipt and processing of the documents. Release of the Guarantee occurs after the surrender of the original bills of lading to the Steamship Company.

5. Forfaiting

Forfaiting is the sale of an export receivables transaction to a 3rd party for immediate payment at a discount. It includes a number of different underlying instruments including:

- Bills of exchange/promissory notes – negotiable instruments which provide for payment of a fixed sum on a fixed future date and which can be transferred to third parties through endorsement, assignment or novation. These instruments can also be used in other Traditional Trade Finance solutions.

- Deferred payment letters of credit;

- Loans and payment undertakings/receivables including open account receivables;

- Any other trade finance instrument that has a fixed value and maturity date;

- Forfaiting differs from factoring in that it is transaction-based as opposed to pool-based, and typically has relatively large transaction sizes. Forfaiting instruments may also carry the guarantee of a bank or foreign government. Transactions normally have a tenor of 6 months to medium-term (3–5 years), but may range from less than 6 months to upwards of 10 years. Forfaiters may hold the assets to maturity or trade them in a well-established secondary market.

Appendix C:
Product Definitions for Open Account Trade Finance BAFT-IFSA, December, 2010

Section 1: Introduction

Banks have provided trade finance services such as processing purchase orders and managing shipping information and associated documentation and have provided financing through traditional trade finance products (namely letters of credit) for centuries. With the advent of the internet and new technologies, the way buyers and sellers interact has evolved. More and more, trade transactions are handled on Open Account terms yet the need for Open Account transaction processing, servicing and financing (that build on the core trade services that banks have long provided) remains.

Open Account is a common trade term generally used by buyers to pay their suppliers for the purchase of goods without necessarily requiring 3rd party payment guarantees. New technologies facilitate collaboration among supply chain partners and provide more precise information, and thus allow banks to provide processing and financing services at various points throughout the life cycle of a trade transaction. These products and services are beneficial to buyers and sellers who have been developing deeper and more collaborative relationships to strengthen their supply chains to gain competitive advantage.

Given the rapid growth of Open Account trade there is a need for common understanding of the terminology used in these transactions. BAFT-IFSA, as part of its mandate to evaluate and guide standardization, improve risk management and enhance the role and relevance of financial institutions, has established the following definitions to provide clarity on Open Account-related products and services. They describe Open Account life cycles and identify related trade service processing and financing services a bank may provide. Additionally, these definitions provide the necessary flexibility to encourage service customization and differentiation, factors critical to ongoing trade services and trade finance evolution and development.

On the basis of market feedback, BAFT-IFSA will build upon these definitions and will further international standards and documentation to govern Open Account transactions among financial institutions.

Section 2: Processing/Servicing Definitions

Open Account Processing leverages the existing trade services processing capabilities of financial institutions. It can include purchase order upload to create transactions, document examination and/or data matching, tracing and follow up for payment and payment services. An important activity in Open Account transaction Processing is the exchange and sharing of documents and document data which can be sent to a bank via a number of methods, including paper documents and electronic records hereafter referred to collectively as documents.

These processing activities which are further defined below can trigger Supply Chain Finance opportunities. A bank may engage in some or all of these activities and/or financing opportunities.

1. PURCHASE ORDER ADVICE

A purchase order specifying the goods and terms is created by the buyer. The seller is then notified of the purchase order and other shipping instructions through a collaboration platform, fax, email, portal or other method. Once notified, the buyer may require the seller's acknowledgement.

2. DOCUMENT CHECKING AND/OR DATA MATCHING

Documents are created and presented by the seller. Matching criteria under Open Account are defined by the buyer. They may consist of simple checking for the presence of all the required documents or detailed checking of specific data values within or among documents in an automated, semiautomated, or manual fashion.

3. DISCREPANCY HANDLING/DISPUTE RESOLUTION

If the matching results include discrepancies between the buyer's matching criteria and the presented document data, the buyer is typically notified to determine if the documents will be rejected or approved. For efficiency purposes, the buyer can preauthorize the bank to pay documents where there are no discrepancies. Dispute resolution enables buyers and sellers to resolve disputes related to Open Account activity on-line or via other methods of communication.

4. MANAGEMENT OF APPROVED INVOICES/DRAFTS

The bank manages the approved documents process with respect to potential financing and the scheduling of transaction settlement.

5. DOCUMENT PAYMENT

The buyer pays at maturity (usually the document due date) and the seller is paid or seller's financing (if any) is repaid with any remaining proceeds going to the seller.

6. DOCUMENTS/PAYMENT RECONCILIATION

When payment is received, the bank may, on behalf of the buyer and the seller, reconcile payment to the documents' value (usually the invoice/draft value) and keep track of PO balances.

Section 3: Trade Finance Definitions

SUPPLY CHAIN FINANCE

As applies to Open Account transactions, Supply Chain Finance (SCF) solutions encompass a combination of technology and services that link buyers, sellers, and finance providers to facilitate financing during the life cycle of the Open Account trade transaction and repayment. The below financing opportunities fall within the overall definition of Supply Chain Finance.

1. Purchase Order Commitment to Pay

The buyer's bank issues its commitment to pay the seller (at sight or at maturity) once the seller ships and makes available the required documents that match the purchase order and other stipulated conditions. This service allows the seller to take the risk of the bank issuing its commitment to pay instead of that of the buyer.

2. Pre-Shipment Finance

Pre-Shipment Finance, also known as Purchase order financing, is made available to a seller based on a purchase order received from a buyer. This financing can cover all the related working capital needs of the seller including raw materials, wages, packing costs and other pre-shipment expenses. Once the goods are ready, refinancing or repayment can occur.

3. Warehouse Finance

Warehouse financing is a form of trade finance in which goods are held in a warehouse for the buyer, usually by the seller, until needed. At a minimum, warehouse receipts are commonly required as evidence for the financing.

4. Post-Shipment Finance

Post-shipment financing is provided to a seller using the receivable as collateral. The seller presents shipping documents as evidence of a receivable and the bank may also require a bill drawn on the buyer for the goods exported. The bank may prefer to purchase and discount a bill drawn on the buyer for the goods exported.

5. Approved Payables Finance

Approved Payables Financing allows sellers to sell their receivables and/or drafts relating to a particular buyer to a bank at a discount as soon as they are approved by the buyer. This allows the buyer to pay at normal invoice/draft due date and the seller to receive early payment. The bank relies on the creditworthiness of the buyer.

6. Receivables Purchase

Receivables Purchase allows sellers to sell their receivables/drafts relating to one or many buyers to their bank to receive early payment. The bank may require insurance and/or limited or full recourse to the seller to mitigate the risk of the pool of receivables.

Index

For Product Safety Concerns and Information please contact our EU
representative GPSR@taylorandfrancis.com Taylor & Francis Verlag GmbH,
Kaufingerstraße 24, 80331 München, Germany

Printed and bound by CPI Group (UK) Ltd, Croydon, CR0 4YY
01/05/2025
01858418-0003